ALL THE WORLD'S ANIMALS
FLIGHTLESS BIRDS & BIRDS OF PREY

ALL THE WORLD'S ANIMALS
FLIGHTLESS BIRDS & BIRDS OF PREY

TORSTAR BOOKS
New York · Toronto

CONTRIBUTORS

PJB Philip J. Bacon DPhil
Institute of Terrestrial
Ecology
Grange-over-Sands, Cumbria
England

JB Jack Barr PhD
Guelph, Ontario
Canada

JFB J. F. Bendell PhD
University of Toronto
Ontario
Canada

BCRB Brian C. R. Bertram PhD
Zoological Society of London
England

MEB Michael E. Birkhead DPhil
Edward Grey Institute of Field
Ornithology
University of Oxford
England

DFB Donald F. Bruning PhD
New York Zoological Society
Bronx Park, New York
USA

RWB Robert W. Burton MIBiol
Great Gransden, Bedfordshire
England

NJC Nigel J. Collar PhD
International Council for Bird
Preservation
Cambridge
England

PRC P. R. Colston
British Museum (Natural
History)
Sub-department of
Ornithology
Tring, Hertfordshire
England

FHJC Frank H. J. Crome BSc
CSIRO, Wildlife and
Rangelands Research
Atherton, Queensland
Australia

TMC T. M. Crowe PhD
Department of Zoology
University of Cape Town
South Africa

JPC John P. Croxall PhD
British Antarctic Survey
Cambridge
England

SJJFD Stephen J. J. F. Davies PhD
Mount Helena,
Western Australia
Australia

AWD A. W. Diamond PhD
Canadian Wildlife Service
Ottawa, Ontario
Canada

JH James Hancock
Winchester, Hampshire
England

MPH Michael P. Harris PhD
Institute of Terrestrial
Ecology
Banchory, Kincardineshire
Scotland

JAH John A. Horsfall BA DPhil
Edward Grey Institute of Field
Ornithology
University of Oxford
England

RH Robert Hudson
British Trust for Ornithology
Tring, Hertfordshire
England

JNJ James N. Jolly MSc
Wildlife Service
Department of Internal
Affairs
Wellington
New Zealand

JK Janet Kear PhD
Wildfowl Trust
Ormskirk
England

JAK James A. Kushlan PhD
University of Miami
Coral Gables, Florida
USA

JBN J. Bryan Nelson DPhil
University of Aberdeen
Scotland

IN Ian Newton PhD
Institute for Terrestrial
Ecology
Abbot's Ripton
Cambridgeshire
England

MAO Malcolm A. Ogilvie PhD
Wildfowl Trust
Slimbridge, Gloucestershire
England

TWP T. W. Parmenter
British Museum (Natural
History)
London
England

PAP Peter A. Prince MIBiol
British Antarctic Survey
Cambridge
England

MWR M. W. Ridley DPhil
Edward Grey Institute of Field
Ornithology
University of Oxford
England

EAS Elizabeth Anne Schreiber BA
Los Angeles County Museum
of Natural History
Los Angeles, California
USA

RWS Ralph W. Schreiber PhD
Los Angeles County Meseum
of Natural History
Los Angeles, California
USA

DS-C Douglas Siegel-Causey PhD
Museum of Natural History
University of Kansas
Lawrence, Kansas
USA

GFvT G. F. van Tets PhD
CSIRO
Lyneham, A.C.T.
Australia

CAW C. A. Walker
British Museum (Natural
History)
London
England

**ALL THE WORLD'S ANIMALS
FLIGHTLESS BIRDS & BIRDS OF PREY**

TORSTAR BOOKS INC.
41 Madison Avenue, Suite 2900, New York, NY 10010

Project Editor: Graham Bateman
Editors: Peter Forbes, Bill MacKeith, Robert Peberdy
Art Editor: Jerry Burman
Art Assistant: Carol Wells   *Production:* Clive Sparling
Picture Research: Alison Renney   *Design:* Chris Munday

Originally planned and produced by:
Equinox (Oxford) Ltd, Littlegate House, St Ebbe's Street,
Oxford OX1 1SQ

Editors
Dr Christopher M. Perrins   Dr Alex L. A. Middleton
Edward Grey Institute of Field   University of Guelph
Ornithology   Ontario
University of Oxford   Canada
England

Library of Congress Cataloging in Publication Data

Flightless birds & birds of prey.

(All the world's animals)
Bibliography: p.
Includes index.
1. Birds. I. Title: Flightless birds and
birds of prey. II. Series.
QL673.F68   1986   598   86-4354
ISBN 0-920269-83-4

ISBN 0-920269-72-9 (Series: All the World's Animals)
ISBN 0-920269-83-4 (Flightless Birds & Birds of Prey)

On the cover: Bald eagle   *Pages 4–5:* Goshawk
Page 1: Turkey vultures   *Pages 6–7:* Ostriches
Pages 2–3: Adelie penguins   *Pages 8–9:* Goshawk

9 8 7 6 5 4 3 2 1

Printed in Belgium

In conjuction with *All The World's Animals*
Torstar Books offers a 12-inch raised relief
world globe.
  For more information write to:
**Torstar Books Inc., 41 Madison Avenue
Suite 2900, New York, NY 10010**

CONTENTS

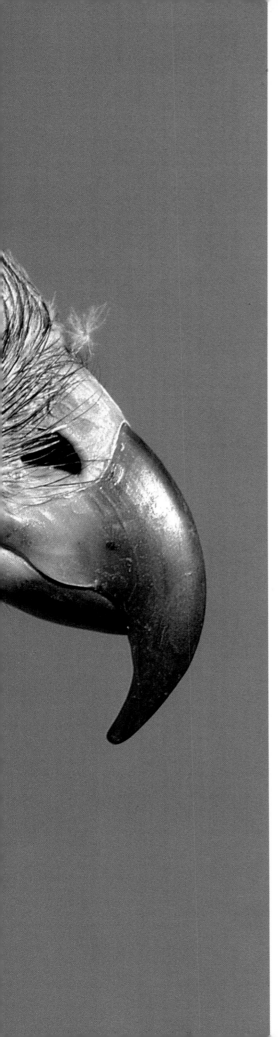

FOREWORD

Flightless Birds & Birds of Prey introduces the reader to the extremes of aviation evolution. These range from the world's largest bird, the ostrich, which is resolutely earthbound but can reach an impressive running speed of up to 30 miles an hour, to the spectacular peregrine falcon which dive-bombs its prey at speeds up to 250 miles an hour, and the tallest of all flying birds, the crane, which scales the Himalayas at heights of 30 thousand feet.

It is unlikely that many of the birds discussed here will arrive to roost or feed in your yard, but many of them will nonetheless be familiar if only for their legendary, symbolic or folkloric associations. The proud and flamboyant peacock, the ill-omened albatross, the greedy gannet, along with the equally evocative ostrich, pelican, stork, crane, falcon, kiwi and, of course, the king of the birds, the eagle, all find a place here.

This volume is not simply devoted to an exploration of the skills of the grounded or the effortlessly airborne: many other large or fairly large birds are also considered. From pelicans to petrels, all are brought alive in the highly readable and authoritative text and the excellent artwork. Superb color photographs taken on location show the brilliance of plumage and markings, while dynamic line drawings amplify the text. This impressive volume will refresh the professional as much as it will enthrall the amateur.

How this book is organized

Bird classification, even for professional ornithologists, can be a thorny problem. Here we have used a widely accepted classification, based, with only a few exceptions, on the so-called Wetmore order employed in *Checklist of Birds of the World* by J. L. Peters. Other taxonomic works referred to are listed in the Bibliography.

The layout of the book follows a fairly simple structure. Each article deals with a single family or with several related families or subfamilies. The text gives details, where relevant, of physical features, distribution, evolutionary history, classification, breeding, diet and feeding behavior typical of that family. Social dynamics and spatial organization, conservation and relationships with man are also covered. Color artwork shows representative species engaged in typical activities.

Preceding the discussion of each family or group of families is a panel of text that provides basic data about size, habitat, plumage, voice, nests, eggs and diet. Where a number of families are considered, a supplementary table gives this detailed information for each family (or in some cases subfamilies). For each family, there is a map of natural distribution (not introductions to other areas by man). Unless otherwise stated, this is the global distribution of the family and includes breeding and wintering grounds for migratory birds. For each family, there is a scale drawing comparing the size of a representative species with that of a six-foot man or a 12-inch human foot. Where there are two silhouettes, they are of the largest and smallest representatives of the family. Generally, dimensions given are for both males and females. Where sexes differ in size, the scale drawings show the larger.

Every so often a really remarkable study of a species or behavior pattern emerges. Some of these studies are so distinctive that they have been allocated two whole pages, enabling the authors to develop their stories. The topics of these special features give insight into evolutionary processes at work and span social organization, foraging behavior, breeding biology and conservation. Similar themes are developed in smaller "box features" alongside the main text.

As you read these pages, you will marvel as each story unfolds. But as well as relishing the beauty of these birds you should also be fearful for them. Again and again authors return to the need to conserve species threatened with extinction. The following symbols are used to show the status accorded to species at risk as listed by the International Council for Bird Preservation (ICBP) at the time of going to press. Ⓔ = Endangered—in danger of extinction unless causal factors (such as habitat destruction) are modified. Ⓥ = Vulnerable—likely to become endangered in the near future. Ⓡ = Rare, but neither endangered nor vulnerable at present. Ⓘ = Indeterminate—insufficient information available, but known to be in one of the above categories. (Some species that have become extinct within the past 100 years are indicated by the symbol Ⓔx.)

However, not all the species listed as threatened by the ICBP are discussed in this book, and information about the total number of threatened species in each family is included as follows: where all such species are included in the summary panel or table of species devoted to a particular family, no further comment is added. Otherwise, a figure for the "total threatened species" is given, either at the end of the list of representative species or, where the list is divided into subfamilies or other groups, at the head of the tabulated information on the family.

OSTRICHES AND THEIR RELATIVES – THE RATITES

Orders: Struthioniformes, Rheiformes, Casuariiformes, Apterygiformes
Families: Struthionidae, Rheiidae, Dromaiidae, Casuariidae, Apterygidae.
Ten species in 6 genera.
Distribution: see maps and table.

Emus

Rheas

Kiwis

Ostrich

Cassowaries

▶ **Representatives of the five families of ratites.** (1) A male South Island brown kiwi (*Apteryx australis australis*) settling on an egg. (2) A One-wattled cassowary (*Casuarius unappendiculatus*) resting. (3) A One-wattled cassowary feeding on fallen fruits, showing a different color variant to (2). (4) A male Masai ostrich (*Struthio camelus massaicus*) chasing two displaying females. (5) Head of a Gray rhea (*Rhea americana*). (6) A male Darwin's rhea (*Pterocnemia pennata*) in an aggressive posture. (7) A male emu (*Dromaius novaehollandiae*) guarding eggs and a chick.

S EVERAL groups of flightless birds are often grouped together as the ratites. Their most striking common characteristic is the lack of a large keel on the sternum (hence ratites from the latin *rata*, a raft, as opposed to the birds with a keeled sternum, the carinates from *carina*, a keel). However, with the evolution of flightlessness, the need for the large flight muscles and their attachment areas becomes unnecessary. Hence this loss of the keel would be what one would expect with the development of flightlessness and it is not clear whether all these groups are really closely related or not; further fossil finds may help to elucidate this problem.

The **ostrich** is famous for being the largest living bird and for being flightless. Despite the allegation of legend and unflattering popular sayings, no ostrich has yet been observed to bury its head in the sand.

Ostriches are widely distributed on the flatter open low-rainfall areas of Africa, in four clearly recognizable subspecies. The North African ostrich with pink neck inhabits the southern Sahara; the blue-necked Somali ostrich occupies the Horn of Africa; adjacent is the pink-necked Masai ostrich which lives in East Africa; and south of the Zambesi is the blue-necked South African ostrich.

The ostrich is enormous. Its feathers are soft and without barbs. The jet-black plumage of the male makes him highly conspicuous at long distances by day, and his long white outer "flight" feathers (primaries) contrast strikingly. The brownish color of females and juveniles renders them well camouflaged (newly hatched chicks are fawn with dark brown spots and a concealing hedgehog-like cape of bristly down on the back). The neck is long and highly mobile, the head small, the gape of the unspecialized beak wide, the eyes enormous.

Vision is acute. The thighs are bare, the legs are long and powerful, and there are only two toes on each foot. The bird can kick forwards powerfully and can run at about 31mph (50km/h). Ostriches are tireless walkers.

Thanks to their large stride, long neck and precise peck ostriches are highly efficient selective gatherers of the sparsely dispersed high-quality food items in their habitat. They take a very wide variety of nutritious shoots, leaves, flowers and seeds. The takings of many pecks are amassed in the gullet and then pass slowly down the neck as a large ball (bolus) which stretches the neck skin as it descends. Ostriches feeding with their beaks down among vegetation are vulnerable to predators (lions, and occasionally leopards and cheetahs); they periodically raise their heads to scan the landscape for danger.

Breeding seasons vary with locality, but in East Africa ostriches mainly nest in the dry season. A male makes a number of shallow scrapes in his territory. A female (the "major" hen), with whom he has a loose pair bond, selects one of these scrapes. She lays, on alternate days, up to a dozen eggs. Up to six or more other females ("minor" hens) also lay in the nest, but play no other role there. The major hen and the cock share equally, for increasing periods, in first guarding and later incubating the clutch — the female by day, the male by night. Unguarded nests are conspicuous from

above, and vulnerable to predation by Egyptian vultures which throw stones at the huge eggs to break through their shells (0.008in thick). Even guarded nests are at risk from hyenas and possibly jackals. Fewer than 10 percent of the nests started survive the roughly three-week laying period and six-week incubation period.

Ostrich chicks are well developed (precocial). They are accompanied by both male and female who try to protect them from the many threatening raptors and ground predators. Chicks from several different nests usually combine into single large groups, escorted by one or two adults. Only about 15 percent of chicks hatched survive to be one year old, when they will be full height. Females can breed at two. Males start to acquire adult plumage when two, and can breed at three or four. They can probably live to over 40.

Males defend their territories in the breeding season by patrolling and by displaying to and chasing out intruders, and by booming. Their call is surprisingly loud and deep, and is accompanied by inflation of the brightly colored neck skin. Aggressive displays consist of repeated flicking of wings and postures with both wings raised. Breeding males display dramatically yet absurdly to females by squatting and waving their huge spread wings alternately. Females solicit by lowering the head and both wings and quivering the latter. Groups of birds are usually small and not cohesive. Adult ostriches spend much of their time alone.

In few other bird species do some individuals willingly look after the eggs of other individuals, since natural selection usually disfavors such apparently altruistic behavior. The large size of ostriches and the vulnerability of their nests to predation are

The 4 Orders and 5 Families of Ratites

Ostrich

Order: Struthioniformes
Family: Struthionidae
Sole species *Struthio camelus*.

Africa (found also until recently in Arabia). Semidesert and savanna. Size: about 98in (250cm) high, weight about 253lb (115kg); males slightly larger than females. Plumage: males black with white primary feathers on wings and white tail; female earthy brown; neck and thighs bare with skin in males blue or pink, according to subspecies, in females pale pinkish gray. Voice: loud hiss and booming roar. Eggs: 10–40, shiny creamy white; 39–67oz (1,100–1,900g); incubation 42 days. Diet: grasses, seeds, leaves, flowers.

Subspecies: **Masai ostrich** (*Struthio camelus massaicus*), **North African ostrich** (*S. c. camelus*), **Somali ostrich** (*S. c. molybdophanes*), **South African ostrich** (*S. c. australis*). The **Arabian ostrich** (*S. c. syriacus*) became extinct early in the 20th century.

Rheas

Order: Rheiformes
Family: Rheidae
Two species in 2 genera.
Darwin's or **Lesser rhea** (*Pterocnemia pennata*): S America in Patagonia and Andes Scrublands. Size: height 35in (90cm); weight 22lb (10kg); females slightly shorter. Plumage: brown with white flecking throughout. Voice: female voiceless; male has booming call. Incubation: 35–40 days. Longevity: less than 20 years in wild; up to 40 in captivity.

Gray or **Common rhea** (*Rhea americana*): S America from R Amazon S to N Patagonia. Grasslands (both wet and dry). Size: height 4.8ft (1.45m), weight 55lb (25kg); females slightly shorter. Plumage: gray with white under wings and on rump; in breeding season males have a black bib and collar at the base of the neck. Voice: female voiceless; male has booming call. Incubation: 35–40 days. Longevity: less than 20 years in wild; up to 40 in captivity.

Emu

Order: Casuariiformes
Family: Dromaiidae
Sole species *Dromaius novaehollandiae*
Australia, in all areas except rain forest and cleared land; rare in deserts and extreme north. Size: height 5.7ft (1.75m), weight 110lb (50kg); females weigh about 11lb (5kg) more than males. Plumage: dark after molting fading to brown. Voice: grunts and hisses; females make resonant, booming sounds. Incubation: 56 days. Longevity: 5–10 years; longer periods known in captivity.

Cassowaries

Order: Casuariiformes
Family: Casuariidae
Three species of the genus *Casuarius*.
Australia, New Guinea and adjacent islands. Forest (rain forest, swamp forest, montane forest). Plumage: brown in chicks and young birds; black in adults. Voice: croaks, squeaks, howls, grunts and snorts. Incubation: 50 days. Longevity: at least 10 years in captivity. Species: **Bennett's cassowary** or **moruk** (*Casuarius bennetti*), New Guinea, New Britain, Yapen Island, height 3.8ft (1.1m); **One-wattled cassowary** (*C. unappendiculatus*), New Guinea and Yapen Island, height 5.3ft (1.6m); **Southern cassowary** (*C. casuarius*), Australia (Cape York Peninsula), New Guinea, Ceram, Aru Island, height 5.8ft (1.8m).

Kiwis

Order: Apterygiformes
Family: Apterygidae
Three species of the genus *Apteryx*.
New Zealand. Forest and scrub. Eggs: one or two, white, 10.5–15.9oz (300–450g). Incubation: 65–85 days. Diet: invertebrates, including worms, spiders, beetles, insect larvae; plant material, especially seeds and fleshy fruits. Voice: loud, repetitive call, high pitched in all kiwis except female Brown kiwi which has a rasping call. Species: **Brown kiwi*** (*Apteryx australis*), height 13.8in (35cm), weight 4.8lb (2.2kg); **Great spotted kiwi** (*A. haastii*), height 13.8in (35cm), weight 5lb (2.3kg); **Little spotted kiwi** (*A. owenii*), height 9.8in (25cm), weight 2.2lb (1.2kg). Females larger and up to 20 percent heavier than males in all species. Feathers: streaked light and dark brown in Brown kiwi; banded light and dark gray in the other two species. Downy type only on both adults and chicks.

*Three subspecies: **North Island brown kiwi** (*A. a. mantelli*), **South Island brown kiwi** (*A. a. australis*), **Stewart Island brown kiwi** (*A. a. lawryi*).

---

probably the factors allowing it in this species. An ostrich egg is not only the largest bird's egg, but also the smallest in relation to the size of the bird. As a result an ostrich can cover a great many of them, either more than a female can lay or more than is worthwhile her laying herself (with the delays and risks involved in doing so). The skewed sex ratio among breeding adults, with about 1.4 females per male, and the high rate of nest destruction by predators both mean that there are many hens without their own nests to lay in. It obviously benefits them to lay somewhere. The major hen benefits from the presence of extra eggs in her nest, because her own are protected by a dilution effect against small-scale predators (ie her own eggs, probably a dozen among about 20, are less likely to be damaged). If, as frequently happens, more eggs are laid in her nest than she can cover, at the start of incubation she rolls away the surplus into an outer ring outside the nest, where they are not incubated and are doomed. As she is able to discriminate among the many eggs in the nest, she ensures that the eggs she rolls out are not hers. It is an astonishing feat of recognition, for ostrich eggs do not vary much in appearance.

High levels of predator density or of

▲ **New life in the desert.** Many chicks of two species of ostrich (North and South African ostriches) hatch in the desert, in this case the Namib Desert in Southwest Africa. Being well developed on hatching, the chicks can survive in the harsh conditions and soon be led away in search of water holes and food.

◄ **Brilliant displays.** Huge wings, long neck and legs and great flexibility enable the ostrich to have a great range of highly developed displays. Here a hen attacks with wings full-spread (1), a hen solicits (2), a hen feigns injury (3), and a cock struts about in a threatening posture (4).

human activity make nests unlikely to survive. Delinquent hunting drove the once abundant Arabian ostrich to extinction earlier this century. Ostrich populations today are decreasing with human intrusion into their habitat, but the species is not severely threatened.

Ostrich feathers have long been used by African peoples for adornment, and by Europeans since Roman times. An ostrich feather, being symmetrical, was the symbol of justice in ancient Egypt, where also ostrich brains were a delicacy. Pieces of egg shell are used in necklaces and waistbands, and in some places whole eggshells are believed to have magical properties that protect houses and churches against lightning. More mundanely, the Hottentots used

empty eggshells as water containers.   BCRB

Rheas are large flightless birds frequently called the South American ostrich. Anatomically and taxonomically rheas are quite distinct from the ostrich. Rheas may stand up to 5ft (1.5m) tall, but most never weigh more than 88lb (40kg). Ostriches may reach over 6.5ft (2m) in height and may weigh up to 440lb (200kg). Apart from size the most obvious difference occurs in the feet: ostriches have only two enlarged toes, while rheas possess three toes, as do most other birds.

The Gray or Common rhea was once a common inhabitant of the grassland regions from central and coastal Brazil down to the pampas of Argentina. This species contains three distinguishable subspecies. The smallest, from Brazil, weighs only 44lb (20kg) while the larger Argentinian subspecies may weigh up to 88lb (40kg). The Darwin's or Lesser rhea is also divided into three subspecies. The Darwin's rhea is found on the semidesert grass and scrublands of Patagonia and on the high-altitude grasslands of the Andes from Argentina and Chile, north through Bolivia into Peru. Charles Darwin was the first to recognize and describe the difference between the Gray rhea and the Darwin's rhea. One evening in the 1830s as H.M.S. *Beagle* was making its way south along the Patagonian coast Darwin noted a difference in bone structure while eating rhea leg.

Both rhea species tend to congregate in flocks for the winter months and divide into smaller flocks for the breeding season, when males may become solitary for incubating (see box). Rhea chicks are raised by the males. They feed largely on insects for their first few days, but gradually follow the example of their fathers and begin feeding on vegetation. Male rheas defend their chicks from all intruders, including other rheas—males with chicks are often seen driving females away from the chicks. Male rheas with chicks have been known to attack small planes and regularly charge gauchos (South American cowboys) on horseback. The threat of a rhea charge, which could cause a horse to shy and bolt, is one reason why most gauchos are accompanied by dogs, so they can if necessary scare off or divert the attack of a male rhea. By the end of the summer males, chicks and females gather into large flocks for the winter. In spring, when males

◄ **Food all around,** a solitary male Gray rhea in his habitat. Abundant vegetation in the range of the Gray and Darwin's rheas in South America allows them to remain sedentary, unlike some of their ostrich relatives in Africa and emus in Australia, and exempts them from loss of habitat which threatens the future of many bird species. The main threats to rheas come from the hunting of adults by man and the killing of chicks by predators.

► **Male mothers.** The two species of rhea both exhibit reversed sexual roles in rearing young. (1) Each male attempts to gather a harem of 2–12 females with his elaborate courtship displays. The male approaches females with his wings spread. Eventually the females begin to follow the dominant courting male. He then drives off all other males and displays vigorously. Once mating occurs the male proceeds to build a nest consisting of a scrape in the ground surrounded by a rim of twigs and vegetation.

(2) The females now proceed to lay eggs in the nest, each female laying one egg every second day for a week to ten days. On the second or third day the male remains at the nest and starts incubating the eggs. The females return at midday each day to lay their eggs beside the male who carefully rolls each new egg into the nest with his bill. The females move on from one male to another throughout the three-month breeding season. Males regularly incubate 10–60 eggs.

Each male must incubate the eggs and hatch the chicks alone. The chicks synchronize hatching and most hatch within a 36-hour period. (3) The male must now lead the chicks to food, while protecting and brooding them.

◄ **At home in his nest,** a male Darwin's rhea with a newly laid egg.

become solitary and females form small groups, the yearlings usually remain as a flock, which lasts until they are nearly two years old and ready to breed.

Adult rheas are largely vegetarian, feeding on a great variety of plants. The Gray rhea eats some grass but strongly prefers broad-leaved plants and frequently eats even obnoxious weeds, such as thistles. Clover seems to be a favorite. The Darwin's rhea, found generally in a drier or harsher environment, will eat almost anything green, but prefers broad-leaved plants. All rheas eat insects and small animals, such as reptiles, when they have the opportunity.

When rheas have come into contact with humans they have usually been persecuted. They have been hunted for years and are one of the main animals caught with the famous *bolas*. Rhea feathers are used to make feather dusters throughout South America. Rheas and their eggs are regularly eaten by local people or are killed and used for dog food. Rheas can coexist with cattle and sheep ranching even though many ranchers accuse the rhea of competing with cattle or sheep. In actuality competition is probably minimal because rheas eat a lot of unwanted plant species as well as vast numbers of insects. However, once land is put to agricultural use the rheas are eliminated because they will eat almost any agricultural crop. They now thrive only in remote areas, away from man or where they are protected.

The decline of rhea populations has prompted the Convention for International Trade in Endangered Species to list both of the rhea species and all subspecies as either endangered or threatened, thereby requiring permits for their export or import.

In recent times adult rheas have had few natural enemies other than man. The Gray rhea on the pampas of Argentina and in the savanna and riverine grasslands has a virtually limitless food supply. The large predatory cats like the jaguar and Mountain lion do not regularly frequent the vast pampas grasslands and smaller predators cannot readily kill an adult rhea. However, rhea chicks are quite vulnerable to a number of predators, including an array of mammals and birds of prey like the caracara. While protected by the male small chicks are safe; however, small chicks separated from the male, particularly after a sudden thunderstorm, are easily taken by predators. Even the small kestrel-sized chimango can be a successful predator when chicks have become separated from their parent.   DFB

In Australia there is a saying "As stupid as an emu." **Emus**, however, have been resident in Australia for at least 80 million years, ever since it broke away from the great prehistoric antarctic continent, Gondwanaland, and began drifting north. In fact the nomadic emu is well adapted to survive in the harsh Australian environment. Studies show that the way of life of the bird nicely matches the conditions with which it has to come to terms.

Until the late 18th century there were several species and subspecies of emu. The Dwarf emus of King Island (Bass Strait) and Kangaroo Island (South Australia) as well as the Tasmanian subspecies were exterminated soon after Europeans settled in Australia. On mainland Australia the emu remains widespread, taking its place as one of Australia's large native herbivores. It lives in eucalypt forest, woodland, mallee, heathland and desert shrublands and sandplains. In desert areas it is rare, being found there only after heavy rains have induced the growth of an array of herbs and grasses and caused shrubs to fruit heavily. The emu also lives close to Australia's big cities, but is no longer found where native vegetation has been cleared to provide agricultural land. Whatever the habitat, however, the emu must have access to fresh water, usually every day.

Emus are large shaggy birds; their loose double feathers, in which the aftershaft (the secondary feather that branches from the base of the main feather) is the same length as the main feather, hang limply from their bodies. Their necks and legs are long but their wings are tiny, reduced to less than 8in (20cm). After molting the birds are dark,

◄ **Emu wings** are not totally useless. Although hidden by the bird's bushy feathers, the wings can be held out, in hot conditions, to expose the bare "under arm" and its dense superficial blood vessels and thus enable the bird to discharge some heat with ease.

▼ **Protection for survivors.** Until a barrier was erected to keep emus out of wool- and cereal-growing areas of Western Australia the state government encouraged the killing of emus, thus threatening the future of the only emu species to have survived earlier onslaughts.

but as sunlight fades the pigments (melanins) that gave the feathers their brown color, so the birds become paler. Their long legs enable them to walk long distances at a steady 4mph (7km/h) or to flee from danger at 30mph (48km/h). Emus have three toes (differing in this from the ostrich which has only two). Emu chicks are striped longitudinally with black, brown and cream, so they blend easily into long grass and dense shrubbery.

The emu prefers and seeks a very nutritious diet. It takes the parts of plants in which nutrients are concentrated: seeds, fruits, flowers, young shoots. It will also eat insects and small vertebrates when they are easily available, but in the wild it will not eat dry grass or mature leaves even if they are all that is available. It ingests large pebbles, up to 1.6oz (46g), to help its gizzard

grind up its food; it also often eats charcoal. Its rich diet enables it to grow fast and reproduce rapidly, but at a price. Because such rich foods are not always available in the same place throughout the year emus must move to remain in contact with their foods. In arid Australia the exhaustion of a food supply in one place often means moving hundreds of miles to find another source of food. The emu shows two adaptations to this way of life. Firstly, when food is abundant it lays down large stores of fat; it is able to use these while looking for more food, so that birds normally weighing 105lb (45kg) can keep moving at bodyweights as low as 44lb (20kg). Secondly, emus are only forced to stay in one place when the male is sitting on eggs. At other times they can move without limitation, admittedly at a slow pace when with small chicks. During incubation the male does not eat, drink or defecate, so he is then independent of the state of the local food supply.

Emus pair in December and January, two birds defending a territory of about 11.7sq mi (30sq km) while the female lays her clutch of 9–20 eggs in April, May and June. Once the male starts sitting many females move away, sometimes pairing with other males and laying further clutches. A few stay to defend the male on the nest, using their characteristic loud booming call. Males are very aggressive when the chicks hatch, after 56 days; they drive the female away and attack approaching humans. The male stays with the chicks, though they lead him rather than the reverse. After 5–7 months the parent–young bond breaks down and the male may then remate for the next season's nesting.

Emus have probably benefited from man's activities in inland Australia, because the establishment of watering points for cattle and sheep has provided permanent water where there was none before, and so much of Australia is unoccupied or used as open rangeland that the emu is in no danger of extinction.   SJJFD

Nomads of the Australian Mainland

The emu's biology centers around its need to keep in touch with its food. In Australia the seeds, fruits, flowers, insects and young foliage that the emu eats become available after rainfall. Emus therefore orient their movements towards places where rain has recently fallen. The orientation seems to depend mainly on the sight of clouds associated with rainbearing depressions, but sound cues from thunder and the smell of wet ground may also be involved. In Western Australia summer rain regularly comes from depressions moving west and south from the north coast, whereas winter rain comes from antarctic depressions moving up from the southwest. Emu movements therefore take on a regular pattern in the western half of Australia. The number of birds involved in a movement may exceed 70,000 —a ravaging hoard as far as farmers are concerned. To protect the cereal-growing areas of the

southwest from invasion by movements of emus from the inland a 600mi (1,000km) long fence has been built.

Emu migrations may be a phenomenon generated by man's own actions. The establishment of large numbers of artificial but permanent watering points in the inland, where cattle and sheep are grazed, has enabled emus to expand into places from which they were previously excluded by lack of water.

The total emu population of Western Australia (between 100,000 and 200,000) is therefore larger than before, so that when food runs low many more emus are ready to move. With the regular alteration of weather systems, from the north in summer and the south in winter, very large numbers are sometimes drawn south in winter. By spring, as the crops ripen, they would reach the farms were it not for the barrier fence.   SJJFD

There is some of the mystery of the jungle about the **cassowaries.** Many people have seen their footprints, their feces or even heard them call, but glimpses of the birds are rare. For the largest land animals in New Guinea they have kept their secrets well; we still have only the barest outline of their life history.

The three species of cassowaries live in New Guinea. The largest, the Southern cassowary, also inhabits Cape York, Ceram and Aru Island. The One-wattled cassowary,

only slightly smaller than the Southern, is confined to New Guinea. The moruk or Bennett's cassowary, little more than 40in (1m) tall lives in New Guinea, New Britain and Yapen Island.

All three species have sleek, drooping, brown or black plumage. Their wing quills are enlarged, spike-like structures, used in fighting and defense. The three toes on their feet are also effective weapons: the kick of a cassowary has disemboweled many adversaries. In all species the legs and neck are long, and the head is adorned with a horny casque (higher in the female than the male). The neck is ornamented with colorful bare skin and small fleshy flaps (wattles). The sexes are alike. When chicks the plumage is striped brown, black and white, changing to a uniform brown for the first year of life. The glossy black adult plumage begins to grow during the second year and is fully developed at four years. The casque on the head is often thought to be used by the birds to push through the thick jungle. Recently a captive bird was seen using it to turn over soil as it sought food. Perhaps wild cassowaries use the casque to turn over the litter, seeking small animals, fallen fruit and fungi.

Cassowaries feed mainly on the fruit of forest trees, which they eat whole. As the fruit of these trees grows high in the canopy and the cassowaries cannot fly they are dependent on finding fallen fruit. Furthermore they need a supply of fruit throughout the year, so only forests with a good diversity of tree species will sustain a population of cassowaries. Many forests used for timber production no longer retain their primitive diversity, so that in a slow and subtle way they are becoming less capable of supporting cassowaries. The moruk, unlike the other two species which live only in jungle, also has sparse populations in many mountainous parts of New Guinea. In these places it seems to feed on the fruits of those shrubs and heathy plants from which it can take direct. All species will also feed on insects, invertebrates, small vertebrates and some fungi.

Cassowaries are solitary animals, forming pairs in the breeding season but at other times found alone. The male incubates the 4–8 eggs in a nest on the forest floor. He accompanies the chicks for about a year before returning to his solitary life. The bird's most commonly heard call is a deep "chug chug," but during courtship in the Southern cassowary the male approaches the female giving a low "boo-boo-boo" call, circling her and causing his throat to swell

and tremble. Most contacts between wild cassowaries observed outside the breeding season led to fights. It is assumed from their distribution that individuals, at least of the Southern cassowary, are territorial.

Cassowaries need large areas of forest in which to live. Studies of the Southern cassowary on Cape York showed that it ate the fruits of 75 species as well as fungi and land snails. Breeding (in winter) coincided with the period when the maximum amount of fruit was available in the forest. The survival of the cassowaries may therefore depend upon the survival of diverse forests where it is possible for them to obtain food throughout the year.

Individuals of all three species are kept in captivity by the peoples of New Guinea. The birds' plumes are plucked and used for the decoration of headdresses, the quills are

Conserving Kiwis

In New Zealand kiwis have suffered considerably since European settlement began 150 years ago. Large areas were cleared for farming and, in addition, the European settlers introduced mammal predators such as cats and stoats.

The Great spotted kiwi and the Brown kiwi in the South Island and the Brown kiwi on Stewart Island are still widespread and appear to be able to hold their own. In the North Island, however, the Brown kiwi is under threat from land clearance over much of its range. Dedicated catching teams attempt to remove the kiwis before land is cleared but cannot cope with the large areas involved. Fortunately the kiwi has adapted to some man-modified habitats and also lives on in the few large forest reserves within its range.

The Little spotted kiwi has fared the worst and is endangered. The species would be all

▲ **Bird of the night,** a Great spotted kiwi. Though numerous and widely distributed, kiwis prefer bushy habitat in which they can scavenge and are adapted for nocturnal activity. They are famous among birds, but have been seen by few. Much remains to be discovered about their behavior and biology.

◀ **Peculiar and mysterious,** a Southern cassowary. Casque, wattles and "feathers" all provoke questions about origin and function, but few answers are yet available. The wing feathers consist solely of quills and may protect the bird's flanks as it moves through foliage; the casque may provide protection for the head or serve as a tool for digging. But how does one account for the extraordinary combination of colors?

but extinct but for the foresight shown in the transfer of this species to Kapiti Island, a 4,900 acre (2,000ha) island in Cook Strait. It is believed that the island's population, now numbering over 1,000 birds, was established from as few as five liberated birds. The success of the liberation is all the more remarkable because at the time the habitat on the island was in a poor state.

Although Kapiti Island is a reserve, the Little spotted kiwi remains in a critical situation, with only one substantial population on one island. Attempts are being made to breed the species in captivity, both to learn more about its breeding biology and to make birds available for liberation on suitable islands. On Kapiti Island the species' habitat requirements, foods and breeding are being investigated, so that islands can be selected for establishing more populations. This work has led to two further transfers of Little spotted kiwis.   JNJ

used as nose ornaments and the whole animal is finally butchered for a feast. Cassowaries have been traded throughout southeastern Asia for at least 500 years. The populations of the Southern cassowary on Ceram and of the moruk on New Britain probably arose from the breeding of escaped captives, brought from the main island of New Guinea.   SJJFD

Kiwis have taken flightlessness to the extreme. Their tiny vestigial wings are buried in their feathers and their tail has disappeared externally. The kiwi hen lays an egg that is one quarter of her weight and, unlike most other birds, kiwis use their sense of smell rather than their sight to investigate their surroundings.

Kiwis remain fairly widely distributed in New Zealand but have disappeared from large areas, not only where the original native forest has been removed but also from some areas still forested. The North Island subspecies of Brown kiwi has even colonized some exotic pine forests and farmland with mixed scrub and pasture. The South Island brown kiwi and the Great spotted kiwi are confined to the remoter forests and mountains of the western side of the South Island. The Stewart Island brown kiwi occurs in forest, scrub and tussock grassland, and is the only kiwi active in daylight. The Little spotted kiwi, once widespread on both the North and South Islands, is now known on only three offshore islands.

The kiwi is the size of a domestic hen but its body is more elongated and has stouter,

more powerful legs. Its long, curved bill, which has openings for air passages at the tip, is used for probing the ground for food. There is no breastbone (sternum), to which in other birds the flight muscles are attached; other bones that are hollow in most birds (so as to reduce weight for flight) are only partly hollow in kiwis. Although their eyes are small for a nocturnal animal, kiwis can see well enough to run at speed through dense undergrowth.

Compared with its flightless relatives, the ostrich, rheas and emus, the kiwi is a small bird and could probably have evolved only in the absence of mammals. The New Zealand archipelago was formed 80–100 million years ago, before the evolution of efficient land mammals. When mammals appeared there was a sea barrier that prevented them from reaching New Zealand and protected the kiwis, and their ancestors, from their competition and predation. Other flightless birds (the moas) also evolved in New Zealand, but all are now extinct.

The kiwi has invested enormous energy in each large egg rather than in a clutch of many smaller eggs. Its egg is highly nutritious and not only sustains the embryo throughout the long incubation but also provides the newly hatched chick with a yolk sac as a temporary food supply.

After an egg has been laid it is believed that the egg is left unattended for several days, but once incubation begins it is the work of the male. There is some doubt as to whether parents feed their chicks; certainly within a week of their birth the chicks emerge from the nest alone and attempt to feed themselves.

The kiwi is able to detect food by smell, and uses its bill to probe amongst the forest litter, or for thrusting deep into the soil. It picks up food in the tip of its bill and throws it back to its throat in quick jerks.

Kiwis are distributed in pairs and use calls to keep in contact in the dense forest and also to maintain territories. At closer range the kiwi again uses its sense of smell rather than sight, as well as its good hearing, to detect other birds. Nonterritory holders are vigorously repelled. Breeding behavior includes loud grunting and snorting as well as wild running and chasing.

The kiwi has always been an important bird to New Zealanders. To the Maori it provided a source of food and of feathers for highly valued cloaks.

Today the peculiarity of the kiwi to New Zealand is recognized in that it has been adopted as the unofficial national emblem.

                                        JNJ

TINAMOUS

Order: **Tinamiformes**
Family: Tinamidae.
Forty-six species in 9 genera.
Distribution: S Mexico S to southern
S America.

Habitat: forest, scrub, grasslands up to 13,100ft
(about 4,000m).

Size: length 8–21in (20–53cm);
weight 16–81oz (450–2,300g).
Females are slightly larger.

Plumage: cryptic, mainly browns and grays;
usually barred, streaked or spotted; two species
have crests. Females are usually brighter,
lighter, or more barred, sometimes with
different leg coloring.

Voice: utters loud, mellow, flute-like whistles
and trills.

Eggs: usually 1–12; glossy green, blue, yellow,
purplish-brown or nearly black. Weight: 0.7–
2.4oz (21–68g). Incubation: 19–20 days.

Diet: mainly fruits, seeds, insects; small
vertebrates also recorded.

Species include: **Great tinamou** (*Tinamus
major*), **Magdalena tinamou** ⓘ (*Crypturellus
saltuarius*), **Red-winged tinamou** (*Rhynchotus
rufescens*), **Tataupa tinamou** (*C. tataupa*).

ⓘ Threatened, but status indeterminate.

▶ **Elegant crested tinamou** ABOVE (*Eudromia
elegans*), a species of tinamou almost exclusive
to Argentina. It is often encountered in groups
of 3–5 on the edges of corn fields or running
around on pasture. Hunting and the
destruction of forest habitat threaten the future
of some species, especially the Great tinamou.

▶ **An Undulated tinamou** in undergrowth.
This species (*Crypturellus undulatus*) lives in
forest and scrub in the northern half of South
America (Guyana and southern Venezuela
south to Paraguay and northern Argentina).

THE tinamous are birds restricted to the
forests and grasslands of Central and
South America, where they are thought to
have had their origins. The superficial
resemblance of certain species of this
ground-living group to gamebirds, especially the guineafowl (family Numididae), is
no indication of their true relationship, for
recent analysis of their egg-white proteins,
DNA and bone structure indicates that they
are more closely related to the rheas. Indeed,
it has been suggested that ancient tinamou
relatives actually gave rise to all ratites, even
though the breastbone (sternum) possesses
a well-developed keel, which the ratites lack.

To the casual observer tinamous
outwardly recall the guineafowl in their proportions and carriage, but differ in that the
bill is slender, elongate and slightly
decurved. Further, the rear of the body
appears arched owing to the great development of the rump feathers which normally
obscure the short tail. The legs are thick and
powerful and possess three forward-
pointing toes and one rear toe. The latter is
reduced and elevated, or even absent in
some species. Although the legs are perfectly
adapted for running, the birds soon become
tired when chased and often stumble. Their
flying ability also leaves much to be desired,
for though they have well-developed flight
muscles, their flight is clumsy and they often
collide with obstacles, which sometimes
results in injury or death.

Because of their limited running and flying capabilities, tinamous rely on their protective coloration to avoid detection. They
remain motionless with head extended,
attempting to blend in with the vegetation,
and will creep away from danger using all
available cover. Species living in more open
areas are known to hide in holes in the
ground. At all times they only break cover,
or take to the wing, at the last possible
moment. For these reasons the tinamous are
not the easiest of birds to see in their natural
environment, their presence being indicated
only by their flute-like, whistling calls,
which can be uttered day or night.

Very little detailed information is available concerning the food preferences of any
species. Some crop and stomach contents
have been analyzed, and indicate that they
feed mainly upon fruits, seeds and other vegetable matter such as roots and buds. Insects
and other small animals may also be taken,
especially by species of *Nothoprocta*, while
the Red-winged tinamou may also eat mice.

As in ratites, the sexual roles of the
tinamous are largely reversed, with the
male taking care of the eggs and young,

while the female is the most aggressive
and the main participant in the courtship
display.

Polygamy is common with the tinamous.
It is common for one or more females to lay
eggs in one nest, and occasionally a hen will
deposit her eggs in different nests, which are
being looked after by different males.

Detailed accounts of nesting are very hard
to come by. It is almost certain that the species that live in tropical forests nest in many
months of the year, while others may have
their egg-laying season governed by rainfall
and other climatic factors. What can be said
with certainty is that all are ground nesters
and either lay their eggs directly on the
ground, between roots in a shallow scrape,
or construct a nest of grass and sticks.
Clutches are said to consist of 1–12 eggs,
though the latter figure may be the result
of two females using one nest. The eggs are
relatively large and renowned for their hard,
porcelain-like gloss and vivid clear coloring.
On hatching the chicks are downy and buff
in color with darker stripes and mottles.
They are very well developed, being capable
of running soon after hatching; most species
are able to fly to some degree before they are
half grown.

During the nest period males often
become so tame that they can be picked up
off the nest. In the Tataupa tinamou the
cock will pretend to be lame in order to dis-
tract the intruder away from the nest, while
other species may cover their eggs with
leaves as in *Tinamus* species or with feathers
as in *Nothoprocta* species.

Throughout their range, tinamous are
sought after as food. This is because their
meat, although having a strange trans-
lucent appearance, is very tender and full of
flavor.   CAW

PENGUINS

Order: Sphenisciformes
Family: Spheniscidae.
Sixteen species in 6 genera.
Distribution: Antarctic, New Zealand,
S Australia, S Africa, S America N to Peru and
Galapagos Islands.

Habitat: sea water, ice, rock, islands and coasts.

Size: ranges from height 12in
(30cm), weight 2.2–3.3lb (1–1.5kg)
in the Little blue penguin to
height 32–39in (80–100cm),
weight 33–88lb (15–40kg) in the
Emperor penguin.

Plumage: most are blue-gray or blue-black
above, white below.

Voice: loud, harsh trumpeting or braying calls.

Eggs: one or two, according to genus; whitish
or whitish-green. Incubation: 33–62 days
according to species.

Diet: crustaceans, fish, squid.

Species and genera include: **Adelie penguin**
(*Pygoscelis adeliae*), **Chinstrap penguin**
(*Pygoscelis antarctica*), **crested penguins** (genus
Eudyptes), **Emperor penguin** (*Aptenodytes
forsteri*), **Fiordland penguin** (*Eudyptes
pachyrhynchus*), **Galapagos penguin** (*Spheniscus
mendiculus*), **Gentoo penguin** (*Pygoscelis papua*),
Jackass penguin v (*Spheniscus demersus*), **King
penguin** (*Aptenodytes patagonicus*), **Little blue
penguin** (*Eudyptula minor*), **Macaroni penguin**
(*Eudyptes chrysolophus*), **Magellanic penguin**
(*Spheniscus magellanicus*), **Rockhopper penguin**
(*Eudyptes crestatus*), **Yellow-eyed penguin**
(*Megadyptes antipodes*).

v Vulnerable.

▶ **Representative species of penguins.** (1) An
adult Yellow-eyed penguin (*Megadyptes
antipodes*) with two chicks. (2) A pair of
Rockhopper penguins (*Eudyptes crestatus*)
brooding a chick. (3) Little blue penguins
(*Eudyptula minor*) coming ashore. (4) Two
incubating King penguins (*Aptenodytes
patagonicus*), one arranging its egg on its feet.
(5) A pair of Adelie penguins (*Pygoscelis adeliae*)
greeting each other. (6) Adelie penguins
tobogganing, (7) leaping out of the sea,
(8) porpoising. (9) A Jackass penguin
(*Spheniscus demersus*) standing and (10) coming
ashore.

THE name penguin is used for a group of flightless birds of the southern hemisphere whose comical appearance, upright stance and waddling gait belies their abilities as the supreme swimmers and divers amongst birds. It was originally applied to the Great auk of the North Atlantic.

Europeans first heard of penguins after the great exploring voyages of Vasco de Gama (1497–98) and Ferdinand Magellan (1519–22), which discovered Jackass and Magellanic penguins respectively, but many species were not known until the southern ocean was explored in the 18th century in search of the southern continent, to be known as Antarctica.

Penguins breed in habitat ranging from the bare lava shores of equatorial islands to sandy subtropical beaches, cool temperate forests, subantarctic grasslands and antarctic sea ice. They are, however, basically adapted to cool conditions and in tropical areas only occur where cold-water currents exist, eg within the influence of the Humboldt Current along the western coast of South America and of the Benguela and Agulhas Currents around South Africa. Most species occur between 45 and 60 degrees south with the highest species diversity in the New Zealand area and the Falkland Islands; the greatest numbers live around the coasts of Antarctica and on the subantarctic islands. Winter distributions and movements are little known. Tropical and warm temperate species do not migrate.

Although penguins show a wide range in weight and size they are remarkably similar in structure and plumage, being chiefly blue-gray or blue-black above and mainly white below; species distinguishing marks (eg crests, crown, face and neck stripes, breast bands) are chiefly on the head and upper breast, being thus visible while the birds are swimming on the surface. The main chick plumages are gray or brown all over, or have one of these colors along the back and white on the sides and undersurface. Juveniles' plumage is usually very similar to that of adults, only differing in minor ways, eg the distinctiveness of ornamentation. Males are slightly larger than females, those of crested penguins notably so.

Penguins are densely covered by three layers of short feathers. They are highly streamlined, their wings reduced to strong, narrow, stiff flippers with which rapid propulsion through water is achieved. The feet and shanks (tarsi) are short, the legs are set well back on the body and are used, with the tail, as rudders. On land penguins

▲ **Grass for the nest,** carried by a Gentoo penguin. Gentoos often breed a little way inland, forming long-lasting pairs within large colonies or rookeries, which are sometimes situated on low hills. This arrangement entails much walking, in gathering grass and later in carrying food from the sea to the nest. Being adapted for fast swimming, gentoos can only waddle in a somewhat deliberate manner, but ease their task by fixing a route and turning it into a well-trodden track.

▼ **Penguin burrows,** a rookery of Magellanic penguins at Punto Tombo, Argentina.

frequently rest on their heels with their stout tail feathers forming the prop. The short legs induce a waddling gait, but on ice they can move rapidly by tobogganing on their bellies. They have comparatively solid bones and generally weigh only a little less than water, thus reducing the energy required to dive. Bills are generally short and stout with a powerful and painful grip. Emperor and King penguins have long, slightly down-curved bills, possibly adapted for capturing fast-swimming fish and squid at considerable depths.

As well as having to swim efficiently penguins also need to keep warm in cool, often near-freezing waters. For this they have, in addition to a dense, very waterproof feather coat, a well-defined fat layer and a highly developed "heat-exchange" system of blood vessels in the flippers and legs, ensuring that venous blood returning from exposed extremities is warmed up by the outgoing arterial blood, thus reducing heat loss from the body core. Tropical penguins tend to overheat easily, so have relatively large flippers and areas of bare facial skin in order to lose excess heat. They also live in burrows so as to reduce direct exposure to sunlight.

The main prey of penguins are crustaceans, fish and squid, which they chase, catch and swallow underwater. It has been suggested that they may be assisted in prey detection by a form of echolocation based on sounds produced by their swimming movement. Fish are important in the diet of inshore feeders, eg Jackass, Little blue and Gentoo penguins, and also of the deeper-diving King and Emperor penguins. Squid may predominate in the food of the King penguin and are frequently taken by Emperor and Rockhopper penguins and some *Spheniscus* species.

Krill are the principal prey of Adelie, Chinstrap, Gentoo and Macaroni penguins and other crustaceans are important to Rockhopper penguins (and probably also to the other crested penguins) and to Yellow-eyed penguins. Krill, like many minute oceanic animals (zooplankton), tend to be absent from surface water during the day, which is when penguins rearing chicks on this food are mainly at sea. However, they may still feed mainly at night (traveling to and from their colony during the day) or use their diving ability to seek prey at depth in daytime.

The Little blue penguin is unusual in feeding its chicks well after nightfall; as the smallest species it will have the shallowest diving capacity and may be more dependent on feeding around dusk when a greater proportion of its prey is near the surface. It may also be avoiding day-active predators by only coming ashore at night. In inshore-feeding species both parents usually bring food to the chick each day. Adelie, Chinstrap and crested penguin parents, however, are usually away at sea for more than a day so the chick only receives one meal per day. King and Emperor penguin chicks are fed large meals at infrequent intervals, seldom more often than every three or four days. Only in large species do meals exceed 2.2lb (1kg) but even quite young chicks of small penguins can easily accommodate 1lb (about 500g) of food. Indeed the capacity of young chicks is astounding and for much of their early growth they are little more than pear-shaped sacks of food, supported by big feet and surmounted by a small head.

Emperor penguins lay their eggs in the fall. King penguin chicks overwinter at the breeding colony but are rarely fed during this period and grow mainly during the previous and subsequent summers (see p30). Otherwise antarctic and most subantarctic and cold temperate penguins breed in spring and summer. Breeding is highly synchronized within and between colonies. Gentoo penguins and the more northerly of the crested penguins have longer breeding seasons and more variable timing. In Jackass and Galapagos penguins there are usually

two main peaks of breeding, but laying occurs in all months of the year. This is also true of most populations of Little blue penguins and in South Australia some pairs are even able to raise broods successfully twice a year. In most penguins, males come ashore first at the start of the breeding season to establish territories where they are soon joined by their old partners or by new birds that they attract to the nest site. Penguins normally mate with the partners of previous years: in a colony of Yellow-eyed penguins 61 percent of pairings lasted 2–6 years, 12 percent 7–13 years and the overall "divorce" rate was 14 percent per annum; of Little blue penguins one pairing lasted 11 years and the divorce rate was 18 percent per annum. In a major Adelie penguin study, however, no pairing lasted six years and the annual divorce rate was over 50 percent.

Macaroni penguins breed first when at least five years old; Emperor, King, Chinstrap and Adelie penguins are at least three (females) or four (males) and Little blue, Yellow-eyed, Gentoo and Jackass penguins at least two years old. In Adelie penguins very few one-year-olds visit the colony; many two-year-olds come for a few days around chick hatching but most birds visit first as three- and four-year-olds. Up to about seven years of age, Adelies arrive progressively earlier each season, make more visits and stay longer. Some females first breed at three years of age, males at four, but most females and males wait another year or two and some males do not breed until eight.

Only Emperor and King penguins lay a single egg; the rest normally lay two. In the Yellow-eyed penguin (and probably generally) age affects fertility so that hatching success in a study colony was 32 percent, 92 percent and 77 percent of eggs incubated by birds aged 2, 6 and 14–19 years respectively. In crested penguins the first egg of the clutch is very much smaller than the second; only in the Fiordland penguin do both eggs normally hatch and only one chick is ever reared—this is an extreme form of a widespread adaptation ensuring that when food is scarce the smaller chick dies quickly and does not prejudice the survival of its sibling. This system may be designed to cope with the high early egg loss resulting from the considerable amount of fighting in the closely packed colonies, which in turn presumably results from sexual selection favoring aggressive males. Alternatively, when both eggs hatch the difference in size of the chicks may ensure that only one survives for long (ie there is a form of brood reduction). Neither explanation is entirely satisfactory. In other penguins hatching is also staggered and this can promote brood reduction, usually by favoring the first hatched chick.

All penguins have the capacity for storing substantial fat reserves (especially before the period of molting and fasting) but only the Emperor, King, Adelie, Chinstrap and crested penguins undertake long fasts during the courtship, incubation and brooding periods. During fasts lasting 110–115 days for brooding male Emperor penguins and 35 days for Adelie and crested penguins up to 45 percent of initial body weight may be lost. By contrast, Gentoo, Yellow-eyed, Little blue and Jackass penguins usually change incubation every 1–2 days. Chicks grow rapidly, particularly in Antarctic species. After 2–3 weeks (6 weeks in Emperor and King penguins) the chicks in open areas form large aggregations or creches (Adelie, Gentoo, Emperor and King penguins) or small ones involving a few chicks from adjacent nests (Chinstrap, Jackass, crested penguins). Once molt is complete chicks usually start going to sea. In crested penguins there is a rapid and complete exodus from the colony (almost all leave within one week) and almost certainly no further parental care. In Gentoo penguins free-swimming chicks return to shore periodically and there obtain food from their parents for at least a further two or three weeks. Some such parental care may occur in other species but it is unlikely that chicks are ever fed by their parents at sea.

In most species, once chicks are independent the parents fatten quickly for a molting and fasting period of 2–6 weeks during which fat reserves are used twice as fast as in incubation. In Jackass and Galapagos penguins the molt period is less defined,

occurring at any time between breeding attempts. Immature birds usually complete molt before breeding birds start and at least in crested penguins the timing of this molt becomes later with age until the first breeding attempt.

Compared with other seabirds, the survival of adult penguins from one year to the next is relatively low, being 70–80 percent for Adelie, 86 percent for Macaroni, 87 percent for Yellow-eyed and 86 percent for Little blue, but 95 percent for Emperor penguins. Penguins are thus not particularly long-lived—records of 19-year-old Yellow-eyed and Adelie penguins being exceptional—and average lifespan is only about 10 years, except for Emperor penguins where it might be double this. Juvenile survival, however, is relatively high in most Antarctic species, except Emperor penguins where only some 20 percent of fledglings are reported to survive their first year, although this may be artificially low due to human interference.

Most penguins are highly social, both on land and at sea, and often breed in vast colonies, only defending the small areas around their nests. Courtship and mate-recognition behavior are most complex in

the highly colonial Adelie, Chinstrap, Gentoo and crested penguins, least so in the species that breed in dense vegetation, such as the Yellow-eyed penguin. Despite living in burrows, Jackass penguins, which usually breed in dense colonies, have fairly elaborate visual and vocal displays; those of Little blue penguins, whose burrows are more dispersed, are more restrained. The social behavior of these penguins is largely nest oriented. In contrast Emperor penguins, which have no nest site, show only behavior oriented to their partners. The great variation in the sequence and patterning of their trumpeting calls provides all the information needed for individuals to recognize each other. In King penguins the incoming bird goes near its nest site and then calls and listens for a response. King and Emperor penguins are the only penguins where the two sexes can easily be distinguished by the characteristics of their calls.

Although flightless, adult penguins have few natural predators on land because they generally choose isolated breeding sites and their beaks and flippers are effective weapons (they are, however, vulnerable to larger introduced mammals). Eggs and chicks are taken by skuas and a variety of other predatory birds. At sea Killer whales, Leopard seals and other seals and sharks catch penguins, but the extent of this predation is at most of local significance. In fact the populations of several species of Antarctic penguins (especially Chinstraps) seem to have increased appreciably in recent decades. This is attributed to the improved food supplies following the massive reduction in stocks of krill-eating baleen whales. Some King penguin populations have also increased, this perhaps being partly a recovery from when they were killed so oil could be extracted from their blubber. In the past many penguin populations were reduced (and colonies eliminated) by egg collecting for human consumption; in most cases this is not a real problem today.

Three species of penguin are presently endangered. Galapagos penguins, with a total population of about 5,000 pairs, breed only on two islands in the Galapagos Archipelago. On one they are now seriously menaced by the presence of feral dogs, although an eradication program has been started. Yellow-eyed penguins have declined to fewer than 5,000 pairs, chiefly because of changing patterns of land use and other human disturbance in the coastal dune systems of New Zealand where they breed. Fortunately populations on off-lying islands, where protection is more feasible,

▲ **Penguins in flight.** Evidence of anatomy and behavior suggests that penguins almost certainly developed from a flying bird rather than from a primitive bird that had not yet developed the ability to fly; ie the penguin's flipper is not a modified arm but a modified wing. Penguins in fact have affinities with albatrosses and petrels (order Procellariiformes). The two groups are probably derived from a common ancestor which was able to fly both above and below water (like modern diving petrels). Some members of this primitive species must have opted to perfect underwater flight and in doing so paid for their new skills in losing the ability to fly above water. Today all penguins, such as these Adelie penguins, only "fly" when diving into water.

◄ **An "ecstatic display"** is one of several kinds of displays used by penguins. Performed by males of all species, except Emperors, Little blues and Galapagos penguins, it occurs in rookeries early in the breeding season, for two reasons: firstly to attract unmated hens; secondly to intimidate other males in asserting ownership of territory. This is a Magellanic penguin.

have suffered less. Both the Jackass and the Humboldt penguins occur in highly productive oceanic upwelling systems of nutrients that support large fishing industries. Populations of these species have decreased alarmingly, initially due to egg removal and guano collection, subsequently because of competition for food; the fishing industries off the west coasts of South America and South Africa both depend, as do penguins, on anchovies and pilchards. The survival of these two species therefore depends on compromises between fish-stock exploitation and conservation.

All penguins are highly vulnerable to oil pollution. This is a particularly serious threat to the Jackass penguin, as many Jackass colonies lie near the tanker routes around the Cape of Good Hope. Thousands of Magellanic penguins have died in oiling incidents in the Straits of Magellan. Jackass penguins have been successfully cleaned and returned to their colonies where many have subsequently bred but this is a time-consuming and expensive operation. Commercial fishing practices, whether existing ones for anchovies or developing ones for krill, pose an increasing threat. JPC

Diving in Penguins

Penguins are probably better adapted for life at sea than any other group of birds. Recently reliable information on their swimming and diving abilities has become available.

Although credited with swimming speeds of up to 37mph (60km/h) all accurate measurements of normal swimming for Emperor, Adelie and Jackass penguins gave speeds of 3–6mph (5–10km/h). In short bursts and particularly when "porpoising" (a swimming motion in which penguins briefly leave the water) faster speeds may well be achieved. The purpose of porpoising is uncertain; it might confuse underwater seal predators, achieve faster speeds by reducing drag when traveling in air or allow breathing without hindering movement at a fast speed.

For Gentoo, Chinstrap and Macaroni penguins dive durations are usually 0.5–1.5 minutes, seldom exceeding 2 minutes. In Jackass and Emperor penguins, however, the mean dive time is 2.5 minutes with maxima of 5 minutes in Jackass and over 18 minutes in Emperors.

Diving depths have been measured, with "pressure-sensitive" recorders, for four species. Six Emperor penguin dives terminated at depths from 150–870ft (45–265m). Of 2,595 King penguin dives half were deeper than 165ft (50m), and two greater than 790ft (240m). By contrast of 1,110 Chinstrap penguin dives 90 percent were shallower than 150ft (45m), 40 percent less than 33ft (10m) and the deepest dive only 130ft (70m). Similarly of 19 Gentoo penguin dives 85 percent were to below 66ft (20m) and only one exceeded 230ft (70m).

How do such relatively small animals as penguins manage frequent deep diving? Diving patterns are influenced by three main factors: firstly submergence time, dictated by how long the breath can be held; secondly, the effect of increased pressure at depth; thirdly, temperature regulation, ie the ability to minimize heat loss. Breath-hold time is determined by the body's oxygen store. Penguins the size of an Adelie use about 100cc of oxygen per minute at rest and their store would be exhausted in a 2.5-minute dive. However, during dives muscles can function on a greatly reduced supply of blood and oxygen, heart beat is reduced from 80–100 beats per minute when resting to 20 beats per minute and the same oxygen store can now sustain a dive of 5–6 minutes.

Human divers who breathe compressed air are vulnerable to inert gas narcosis (the "bends") but in breath-hold diving the inert gas supply is very limited and risks are much less. Penguins on short shallow dives should have no problems but how the Emperors and Kings cope with their long dives to substantial depths is unknown.

Penguins seem well adapted for reducing heat loss during dives. However, most of their feather insulation is probably due to entrapped air and much of this is expelled under pressure during diving (as a trail of bubbles behind the bird), so penguins may need to remain very active in cold water in order to keep warm.

We know very little about how, and how often, penguins catch prey underwater. Penguins that feed mainly on krill and similar crustaceans have to catch very small prey, usually less than 1.2in (3cm) long. It was calculated that Chinstrap penguins, which averaged 191 dives per day during foraging trips when rearing chicks, need to catch 16 krill (1 every 6 seconds) per average dive. In contrast King penguins would only need to catch a single squid or fish on 10 percent of their 865 dives per trip.

The nature of the prey may also influence dive duration. Penguins feeding on relatively slow-moving, swarming crustaceans can catch many individuals even during short dives. Penguins that pursue fast-moving squid and fish may need to submerge for much longer in order to have a chance of catching them. However, they do not need to succeed often in order to satisfy their food requirements. This could explain the much longer dives of Jackass penguins, which feed mainly on surface-shoaling fish, when compared with the also shallow-diving but krill-eating Gentoo penguin. JPC

Surviving at the Extremes

Breeding strategies in large penguins

Emperor penguins, when breeding, endure the coldest conditions faced by any bird: the frozen wastes of the Antarctic sea ice, where average temperature is $-4°F$ ($-20°C$) and mean windspeed 16mph (25km/h), sometimes reaching 47mph (75km/h). Emperor penguin breeding colonies form in the fall (mid-May), when courting takes place and females each lay a single egg on the newly formed ice. The males assume the job of incubating the eggs, each holding his partner's egg on his feet for 60 days. When the eggs hatch both parents feed the chicks, from late winter and through the spring, so the young are ready for independence in the summer before the sea ice returns.

This breeding arrangement prompts two questions. Firstly, why do Emperor penguins raise their young at the worst time of year? Secondly how do the penguins survive in the winter conditions?

An answer to the first question seems to be that if Emperor penguins were to breed in the summer (a short season in the Antarctic, only four months long) they would not complete their breeding cycle before the onset of winter. Even when the chicks fledge, in late spring, they are only 60 percent of adult weight, which is the lowest proportion for any penguin, and juvenile mortality is high. The adults, however, are able to breed annually.

The means whereby Emperor penguins survive in harsh conditions are several remarkable physiological and behavioral adaptations, all stemming from the need to minimize the loss of heat and the expenditure of energy.

The body size of Emperor penguins and their shape give a relatively low surface-to-volume ratio and their flippers and bill are 25 percent smaller as a proportion of body size than in any other penguin. Heatloss is further reduced by extreme proliferation of their blood-vessel heat-exchange system (twice as extensive as that of King penguins), by recovering in the nasal passages 80 percent of the heat added to cold inhaled air, and by the excellent insulation provided by very long double-layered, high-density feathers which completely cover the legs.

Because in winter open water lies far away across the ice shelf, feeding is difficult, changeovers at the nest infrequent and long fasts (up to 120 days in males, and 64 days in females) essential. Their large size enables storage of the big fat reserves needed for this. Nevertheless the crucial adaptation is the 25–50 percent reduction in individual heat loss achieved by adults and chicks huddling

in large groups (up to 5,000 birds at 11 per sq yd, about 10 per sq m) and reducing activity to a minimum. The huddle as a whole moves very slowly downwind and windward birds move along the flanks and then into the center until they are once again exposed at the rear, so that no birds are continually exposed on the edge of the group. All this is feasible only because Emperor penguins have developed the ability to move with their egg on their feet and cover it (and the young chick) with a pouch-like fold of abdominal skin. They have also suppressed nearly all aggressive behavior.

King penguins, the other species of large penguins, have a very different solution to the problem of breeding in the short summers. They take over a year for a successful breeding attempt and cannot breed more frequently than two years in three. They have two main laying seasons, November–December and February–March, and most of the time any colony contains adults, eggs and chicks at many stages of molt, incubation and growth respectively. From the eggs laid in late November–early December chicks are reared to 80 percent of adult weight by June and fed sporadically (fasts of two months or so with an overall chick weight-loss of about 40 percent) through the winter until September when regular feeding resumes until the chicks depart in November–December. The adults then have to molt and cannot lay again until February–March. Chicks produced from these eggs are much smaller when the winter comes (and many die), and they do not fledge until the following January–February.   JPC

▲ **An army of Emperors.** As antarctic conditions become severe as many as 6,000 male Emperor penguins huddle together when incubating eggs. If eggs are to hatch successfully they must be protected perfectly by the male's pouch-like fold of skin for about two months. When crossing crevices, for example, the birds have to fall on their chests and push themselves along with their flippers.

▶ **A fat start in life.** By the time King penguin chicks hatch there is not enough time left for the chicks to reach the stage of development at which they can fledge. They therefore sit out the winter and fledge in the spring. During the last weeks of the fall they are fattened by their parents so they may have enough reserves to see them through the harshest part of winter when the parents will only feed them infrequently. By the time winter starts this chick may weigh as much as 28.6lb (13kg).

LOONS OR DIVERS

Order: Gaviiformes
Family: Gaviidae.
Four species belonging to the genus *Gavia*.
Distribution: N America, Greenland, Iceland, Eurasia.

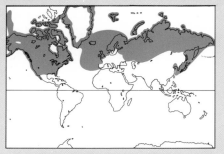

Habitat: in summer, lakes in boreal forest, taiga, tundra; most spend the winter at sea.

Size: ranges from length 21–27in (53–69cm), weight 2.2–5.3lb (1–2.4kg) in the Red-throated loon to length 30–37in (76–93cm), weight 9.7–14lb (4.4–6.4kg) in the Yellow-billed loon. Females are slightly smaller than males.

Plumage: adults of all species have white underparts. Upper parts of Common, Yellow-billed and Arctic loons are basic black with white spots on the back and wings; the Red-throated loon is sooty brown with small light spots. All species have white, vertical stripes on the neck (the pattern differing according to species). The throat of the Red-throated loon is chestnut-red. In winter adults and juveniles have gray upper parts with lighter markings. Newly hatched chicks have dense down, dark gray to black above, white on the belly.

Voice: tremolos, yodels, wails, clucks, mews, cackling. Varies considerably between species.

Eggs: usually 2 (occasionally 1, rarely 3); medium to dark brown to olive with few to many blackish spots or blotches. Weight: for eggs of Common loon 4.2–6oz (120–170g). Size: from 2.8 × 1.7in (7.3 × 4.5cm) for the Red-throated loon to 3.5 × 1.9in (9 × 5cm) for the Common and Yellow-billed loons. Incubation: 24–29 days.

Diet: mainly fish; also crayfish, shrimp, leeches, frogs.

Species: **Arctic loon** or **Black-throated diver** (*Gavia arctica*), **Common loon** or **Great northern diver** (*G. immer*), **Red-throated loon** or **Red-throated diver** (*G. stellata*), **Yellow-billed loon** or **White-billed diver** (*G. adamsii*).

Loons are aquatic predators, so highly specialized for swimming and diving that they are unable to walk properly on land. Apart from penguins of the southern hemisphere, they are the most specialized diving birds. Propelled by foot, they are fast and maneuverable under water where they readily capture fish. They regulate buoyancy by adjusting feathers, the volume of air in air sacs and the amount of air in the lungs. They nest on inland, freshwater lakes in summer. The majority migrate to coastal waters for winter, although some overwinter on large, ice-free lakes in the southern parts of their range.

Loons are mainly associated with clear, oxygen-laden (oligotrophic) lakes of the northern hemisphere, in areas with a past history of extensive glacial coverage. These include thousands of lakes in the northern forests, taiga and open tundra scraped out of rock by retreating glaciers.

Although adult loons cannot walk on land, chicks can waddle upright and have been known on rare occasions to negotiate several hundred yards between tarns or lakes while parents prompted from air or water. Loons are characteristically lone nesters within a large defended territory but colonial nesting has been documented for the Red-throated loon and the Arctic loon. Territories range in size from 15 to more than 200 acres (6–80ha).

All loons exhibit a strong preference for nesting away from the mainland shore, whether on island, bog islet, stone outcropping or log, although Arctic and Red-throated loons frequently nest in coves or promontories of small tundra lakes that lack islands.

With flight feathers renewed, small groups (packs) of loons may join others and coalesce into flocks of several hundred on certain large bodies of water prior to and during spring and fall migration. Arrival on the breeding ground is usually in singles, pairs (apparently more common in the Arctic loon) or small loosely associated groups. Territories are often reoccupied as soon as sufficient water is ice-free for landing. Loons return to the same territory and often reuse the same nest.

Courtship appears to be a prominent ritualized display only in the Red-throated loon. Copulation is secretive, on shore in the nest area. Both parents may construct the nest, incubate and tend the young. Young loons are well developed (precocial) and leave the nest within a day of hatching, weather permitting. They are brooded on the parents' backs and under a wing if weather is inclement or danger threatens. Loon chicks can dive within a day of hatching, and their expertise rapidly increases. Although chicks peck at and eat small invertebrates such as mosquitoes, black flies and a variety of aquatic insects, they are fed by both parents. Food is fresh-caught (not regurgitated) and comprised of invertebrates or fish (preferred when available) which are taken from the parents' bills. Common loon chicks are weaned from parental feeding between their 8th and 11th weeks, but they occasionally still take fish from parents until they migrate.

Adult nonbreeders and unsuccessful breeders form small social groups (usually 4–12 birds) on many lakes in summer, although certain large lakes seasonally have groups of 80–250 loons. These social groups are frequently joined by the resident parent not tending chicks. Juveniles do not join these groups. In fact they are readily attacked by strange adults.

Although loons can remain submerged for several minutes most dives last less than a minute. Underwater progress is casual while hunting but speed can be sustained while pursuing prey or fleeing. Several hundred yards can readily be traversed underwater and although most foraging occurs in relatively shallow depths with good light, ie

▲ **The streamlined, beautiful head** of an Arctic loon.

◄ **Leg movements in swimming.** Loon legs and feet are completely adapted to swimming. Only the lower part of the leg protrudes, from a position to the rear of the body that gives it great propulsive power which is transmitted by the webbed feet. In each cycle of swimming movements the head and eyes remain almost stationary in relation to the surroundings during the brief period of recovery and thrust of the legs. This allows the loon to see more readily the slightest movement of potential prey. When swimming at a moderate speed this cycle takes 0.8–1.3 seconds.

in the top 33ft (10m), Common loons have become enmeshed in nets at depths greater than 265ft (80m). Loons are visual hunters, and capture fish crosswise in the bill. As with other predators of vertebrates, atypical behavior among prey is quickly singled out for attack. Loons are opportunistic foragers; their prevalent prey is fish, of any species or size that can be captured and ingested, usually less than 7in (15cm) but reportedly even over 16in (40cm). Crustaceans such as crayfish and shrimp, leeches and frogs are also eaten. Loons appear to ingest vegetation only when ill. Digestion in their powerful gizzard is aided by pea-sized stones.

Loons are highly specialized final predators in an aquatic food web composed of complex, interdependent activities among prey and predator, from microscopic plants and animals through fishes to the loons. Hence any degradation of the environment adversely affects loons. In parts of their breeding grounds in North America and Europe they have been reduced in numbers or eliminated because of loss of nesting habitat, disturbances of nesting and brooding areas, excessive aquatic plant growth, unpredictable and extensive water-level fluctuations and toxicity. Large numbers have occasionally succumbed to botulism and considerable numbers are destroyed by oil slicks on coastal waters in winter. Acid rain is also destroying the food chain in thousands of lakes, particularly for the Common loon in eastern North America.

In spite of adversities, loons are reasonably numerous throughout much of their traditional range. JB

GREBES

Order: Podicipediformes
Family: Podicipedidae.
Twenty species in 6 genera.
Distribution: N and S America, Eurasia, Africa, Australasia.

Habitat: freshwater lakes and marshes; may use coastal waters in winter.

Size: ranges from length 13.4in (34cm), weight 4.6oz (130g) in the Little grebe to length 18.9in (48cm), weight 49oz (1,400g) in the Great crested grebe. Females are slightly smaller.

Plumage: upperparts mostly drab gray or brown shading to white on the underbelly; for breeding the head, throat and neck are often brightly colored. Some species have bright, colored tufts and crests on the head, used in courtship.

Voice: a variety of whistling and barking calls; species living in dense vegetation are often more vocal.

Eggs: usually 2–6; white or cream. Incubation: 20–30 days.

Diet: aquatic insects, crustacea, mollusks and fish.

Species include: **Atitlan grebe** E (*Podilymbus gigas*), **Black-necked grebe** (*Podiceps nigricollis*), **Colombian grebe** E (*P. andinus*), **Great crested grebe** (*P. cristatus*), **Hooded grebe** R (*P. gallardoi*), **Little grebe** (*Tachybaptus ruficollis*), **Madagascar red-necked grebe** V (*T. rufolavatus*), **Puna grebe** R (*Podiceps taczanowskii*), **Red-necked grebe** (*P. grisegena*), **Silver grebe** (*P. occipitalis*), **Slavonian grebe** (*P. auritus*), **Western grebe** (*Aechmophorus occidentalis*).

E Endangered. V Vulnerable. R Rare.

GREBES are an old group, having been inhabitants of lakes and marshes for around 70 million years, and have representative species on all continents except Antarctica.

Thanks to anatomical adaptations grebes are well suited to the rigors of aquatic life and underwater hunting. They have a dense plumage of some 20,000 feathers to keep them dry and warm. Their feet are at the extreme hind end of the body—the tail is reduced to a downy tuft—and have exceptional flexibility in the ankle and toe joints, allowing the feet to pivot in all directions and to be used, simultaneously, as "paddles" and "rudders." The lobes on the toes further aid maneuverability—a diving grebe can move at about 6.6ft (2m) a second and turn extremely quickly. Grebes can sink low in the water by expelling the insulating air from between their feathers and emptying their air sacs (reservoirs of air): this reduces the energy needed to keep them submerged and allows them to dive silently when hunting and to hide submerged when frightened. Dives typically last 10–40 seconds.

Feet placed so far back make even standing difficult: grebes only stand at the nest and, if obliged to reach nests "stranded" by falling water levels, frequently fall when trying to walk; they need a long take-off run across water to become airborne on their long thin wings, but fly quickly with rapid beats and trailing feet; they maneuver poorly in flight. Grebes rarely fly except on migration and a few species are flightless. They may migrate long distances, often flying at night, when they sometimes mistake wet roads for rivers, land on them, and become stranded.

Grebes are carnivorous, eating mainly insects and fish but also some mollusks and crustacea, taking the latter from off and around aquatic water plants or, more rarely, from the bottom. The larger species chase fish, and the Western grebe of North America spears (rather than grabs) fish with its dagger-shaped bill. Grebe species form "guilds" of aquatic carnivores, vying with each other to exploit foods more efficiently.

In Eurasia, for example, the Great crested grebe occurs mostly on open water, eating fish that it usually catches within a few feet of the surface, whereas Little grebes occur on small ponds covered with floating water-plants which they are small enough to dive among. Intermediate-sized species, such as Red-necked and Slavonian grebes, may be restricted to lake habitats where they do not compete with larger species. For

example, the Slavonian is the only grebe that breeds in Iceland and there it eats many fish as well as insects, but in Alaska it restricts its diet largely to insects and fish fry due to competition from the Red-necked grebe; similarly in eastern Siberia and Alaska a long-billed race of the Red-necked grebe has evolved which takes larger fish than its European counterpart which has to compete with Great crested grebes for food.

The courtship behavior of grebes is very striking, involving complex sequences of elaborate, ritualized postures and, particularly in *Podiceps* species, much use of the erectile feather ruffs and tufts on the head. Many elements of these complex sequences are shared by many species and considerable progress has been made both in understanding animal behavior and grebes' evolutionary histories by comparing details of their courtships. Sir Julian Huxley's study of Great crested grebe courtship (1914) was a seminal paper in animal behavior. Detailed studies of the courtship of the recently discovered Hooded grebe (1974) have confirmed its close relationship to Black-necked, Silver and Puna grebes. The crucial role that these displays serve in pair formation has been emphasized by recent findings on the Western grebe: this species occurs in two color variants (morphs) that breed in mixed colonies, but only birds of the same color morph will pair together and this segregation is achieved by each morph using a distinctly different "advertising call" to initiate courtship. An interesting feature of grebe displays is that males and females may reverse their normal roles, even to the extent of reverse mountings.

Most grebes are aggressively territorial, but some species nest in colonies. The timing of breeding is flexible—grebes seem adapted to exploit opportunistically a good food supply rather than being tied to a specific season. In Africa Little grebes may appear and start breeding within a few days of unpredictable rain storms producing temporary flood-ponds. The nests are mounds of aquatic vegetation, usually anchored in emergent waterweeds. The chicks hatch asynchronously and are brooded on their parents' backs, even when their parents dive.

Five species of grebe are listed in the *Red Data Book* including all the localized nonflying South American species: of these the Colombian grebe may well already be extinct, but the threat by a hydroelectric scheme to the only lake on which the Atitlan grebe occurs appears to have recently been lifted.   PJB

▲ **Waterborne nest.** Unable to move well on land, grebes nest on water. Their nests are simple: weeds, reeds and other vegetation piled up on aquatic plants or formed so that the nest will float on the water itself. Here a female Great crested grebe incubates her eggs, bearing a recently hatched chick on her back, and is visited by her mate.

▶ **Grebe of the north.** There are three kinds of grebe distributions: very restricted ranges, large ones encompassing latitudes from high north to low south, and intermediate ones covering large areas but restricted in latitude. The range of the Slavonian grebe belongs to the latter, the bird being restricted to northern latitudes.

◀ **Complex displays** occur when grebes are courting, though the composition of sequences differs from species to species. In the Great crested grebe mating includes: (1) the discovery display; (2) the head-shaking display; (3) preening; (4) the weed ceremony.

ALBATROSSES AND PETRELS

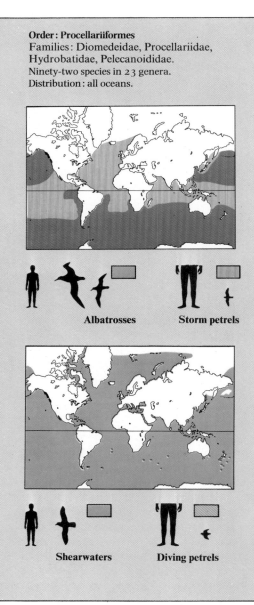

Order: Procellariiformes
Families: Diomedeidae, Procellariidae,
Hydrobatidae, Pelecanoididae.
Ninety-two species in 23 genera.
Distribution: all oceans.

Albatrosses **Storm petrels**

Shearwaters **Diving petrels**

▶ **Preening** ABOVE is one of the means by
which pairs of albatrosses, such as these Laysan
albatrosses, maintain and reinforce their bond
during the mating season. All but a few birds
have a preen gland, which is normally situated
just in front of the tail base and secretes an oily
liquid. This is then spread with the bill over the
feathers. Preen oil improves the condition of the
feathers, but exactly how it works is not
known.

▶ **Nesting** in *Diomedea* species of albatross
often takes place in large colonies, sometimes of
thousands of birds. Several species, including
the Wandering albatross seen here, build
mound-size constructions of soil or vegetation
on which to form a nest cup lined with feathers
and grasses.

THE **albatross** was the bird of ill omen, the
repository of the souls of drowned
sailors, and consequently to kill one was to
court disaster. Yet paradoxically sailors
were happy to catch and eat albatrosses to
relieve the monotony of life and diet on long
voyages. They must also have spent many
hours admiring the effortless flight of the
albatrosses that followed their ships for
hours with barely a wing-beat. Adaptations
for long-distance flight allow the albatrosses
to exploit the vast spaces of the oceans from
their restricted breeding bases on oceanic
islands. The name albatross comes from the
Portuguese *alcatraz*, used originally for any
large seabird and apparently derived from
the Arabic *al-cadous*, used for the pelican.

Albatrosses are typically associated with
the belt of windswept ocean lying between
the Antarctic and the southern extremities
of America, Africa and Australasia. The
greatest number of individuals and species
occurs between 45 and 70 degrees south,
but they also breed in temperate waters of
the southern hemisphere and a few species
have spread into the North Pacific. The
Waved albatross of the Galapagos and Isla
de la Plata off Ecuador breeds on the equator, but where the climate is under the
influence of the cool Humboldt Current.
Steller's or the Short-tailed albatross (based
on islands off Japan), the Black-footed
albatross (of the northwest Pacific) and the
Laysan albatross (from the Hawaiian archipelago) all breed in the North Pacific. No
albatrosses breed in the North Atlantic.

Albatrosses are distinguished from others
of their order (Procellariiformes) by the position of their tubular external nostrils, which
lie at each side of the base of the bill rather
than being fused on the top of the bill. They
can be split into three convenient groups:
the "great" albatrosses (three species),
which have wingspans averaging 10ft
(about 3m); nine smaller species which are
often referred to as "mollymauks" from the
Dutch *mollemok* which was originally given
to the fulmar; and the all-dark Sooty and
Light-mantled sooty albatrosses, having
relatively long wings and tails and which
are sufficiently different to warrant a separate genus.

From their habit of following ships,
albatrosses are best known as scavengers of
offal thrown overboard. They have broad
diets, including oceanic water striders and
by-the-wind sailors (plankton) but detailed
analysis of diets shows that fish, squid and
crustaceans predominate. Prey is caught
mainly by seizing at the surface, but occasionally by plunging in the manner of gannets. They also feed during darkness, when
many marine organisms come to the surface. The proportions of prey types differ
between species and these profoundly affect
the breeding biology of the species.

Albatrosses are long-lived, with an
average life-span of 30 years, but slow
breeders. They are physiologically capable
of breeding at three or four years but they
do not usually start for several years after
this. Some may not breed until 15 years old.
When they first mature birds appear on the
breeding grounds for a short while towards
the end of the breeding season, and thereafter spend more time ashore courting prospective mates. When a pair has been
established they usually remain together
until the death of one, and "divorce" occurs
only after several breeding failures.

At the beginning of the breeding season the male arrives at the colony first and mating occurs on the female's reappearance. Most albatrosses nest in colonies, sometimes numbering thousands of pairs with close-packed nests, but Sooty and Long-mantled sooty albatrosses nest alone on cliff ledges. In several species the nest is a pile of soil and vegetation which may be so large that the adults find difficulty in climbing on. The tropical albatrosses make a scanty nest and the Waved albatross shuffles about with its egg on its feet.

The single egg is incubated in alternate shifts of several days by both parents, from about 65 days in the smaller species to 79 days in the Royal albatross. The newly hatched chick is brooded at first and later guarded. Throughout its life in the nest it receives regular feeds from the parents. Once brooding has finished the adults remain ashore only long enough to identify their chicks and transfer a meal of undigested marine animals and lipid-rich oil derived from the digestion of prey. Black-footed albatross chicks frequently wander up to 100ft (about 30m) from the nest and seek shade during the day, but they rush back when a parent arrives with food. Fledging takes from 120 days in Black-browed and Yellow-nosed albatrosses to 278 days in the Wandering albatross. The extremely long nesting period of the latter (356 days including incubation) means that it can attempt to breed only in alternate years

The 4 Families of the Order Procellariiformes   E Endangered.

Albatrosses
Family: Diomedeidae
Fourteen species in 2 genera.
Subantarctic, S America N to Galapagos Islands, S Africa, S Australia and New Zealand, Pacific N to Japan. Islands used for breeding and as bases. Size: ranges from bill–tail length 27–37in (68–93cm), wingspan 70–101in (178–256cm) in the mollymauks to bill–tail length 43–53in (110–135cm), wingspan 98–138in (250–350cm) in the great albatrosses. Plumage: white with dark wingtips; white with dark brow, back, upperwing and tail; uniform darkness. Eggs: 1; white. Incubation: 65–79 days. Diet: fish, crustacea.

Species include: **Amsterdam albatross** (*Diomedea amsterdamensis*), **Black-browed albatross** (*D. melanophris*), **Black-footed albatross** (*D. nigripes*), **Gray-headed albatross** (*D. chrysostoma*), **Laysan albatross** (*D. immutabilis*), **Light-mantled sooty albatross** (*Phoebetria palpebrata*), **Royal**

albatross (*D. epomophora*), **Sooty albatross** (*Phoebetria fusca*), **Steller's albatross** or **Short-tailed albatross** E (*Diomedea albatrus*), **Wandering albatross** (*D. exulans*), **Waved albatross** (*D. irrorata*), **Yellow-nosed albatross** (*D. chlororhynchos*).

Shearwaters and petrels
Family: Procellariidae
Fifty-four species in 12 genera.
All oceans. Size: length 10–34in (26–87cm); wingspan maximum 6ft (about 2m); weight 5oz–8.8lb (130g–4kg). Plumage: most species black, brown or gray, and white; a few are all light or dark. Voice: unmusical; often nocturnal cacophony at colonies. Eggs: 1; white. Incubation: 43–60 days. Diet: fish, squid, crustacea, offal.

Species include: **Audubon's shearwater** (*Puffinus lherminieri*), **Blue petrel** (*Halobaena caerulea*), **cahow** or **Bermuda petrel** E (*Pterodroma cahow*), **Dark-rumped petrel** (*P. phaeopygia*), **Greater shearwater**

(*Puffinus gravis*), **Manx shearwater** (*P. puffinus*), **Northern fulmar** (*Fulmarus glacialis*), **Short-tailed shearwater** (*Puffinus tenuirostris*), **Snow petrel** (*Pagodroma nivea*), **Southern fulmar** (*Fulmarus glacialis*), **Southern giant petrel** (*Macronectes giganteus*). Total threatened species: 8.

Storm petrels
Family: Hydrobatidae
Twenty species in 8 genera.
All oceans except Arctic seas. Size: length 5.5–10in (14–26cm); wingspan 12.6–22in (32–56cm); weight (0.9–2.4oz (25–68g). Plumage: chiefly dark brown, black or gray and white. Voice: some species "purr" and have chuckles at breeding colonies. Eggs: 1; white sometimes with speckles. Incubation: 40–50 days. Diet: small fish, squid, plankton, fish scraps.

Species include: **Hornby's storm petrel** (*Oceanodroma hornbyi*), **Leach's storm petrel** (*O. leucorhoa*), **Least storm petrel** (*Halocyptena microsoma*),

Madeiran storm petrel (*O. castro*), **Wedge-rumped storm petrel** (*O. tethys*), **White-faced storm petrel** (*Pelagodroma marina*), **White-throated storm petrel** (*Nesofregetta albigularis*), **Wilson's storm petrel** (*Oceanites oceanicus*).

Diving petrels
Family: Pelecanoididae
Four species of the genus *Pelecanoides*.
Subantarctic, S America as far N as Peru, S Australia, New Zealand. Marine, breeding on islands and coasts. Size: bill to tail length 7–10in (18–25cm), wingspan 11.8–15in (30–38cm), weight 3.4–4.7oz (105–146g). Plumage: black above, white below. Eggs: 1; white. Incubation: 45–53 days. Diet: small marine organisms.

Species: **Common diving petrel** (*Pelecanoides urinatrix*), **Georgian diving petrel** (*P. georgicus*), **Magellan diving petrel** (*P. magellani*), **Peruvian diving petrel** (*P. garnotii*).

since, after breeding, it must have a "rest" period during which it molts. At least six species are known to breed biennially. These include all the "great" albatrosses, the two sooty albatrosses and the Gray-headed albatross along with the mollymauks (see box).

Breeding colonies of albatrosses are protected by their isolation on islands with no natural predators, but discovery by seafarers led to losses through egg-collecting and the killing of adults, followed by massive depredations for feathers which were used in clothing and bedding. Steller's albatrosses were almost wiped out by feather-collectors; huge numbers of birds were killed; and a tiny colony of 20 pairs on Toroshima, off Japan, contains the survivors. The Laysan albatross became a conservation problem when Midway Atoll was turned into a military airbase. The birds nested around the runways and installations and there were many deaths from collisions with aerial wires and aircraft.

Albatrosses face more insidious threats at sea. Contamination by oil spills and chemical pollution can occur, and albatrosses are known to suffer as "incidental catches" in fishing operations. As southern seas become exploited by the world's fishing fleets there is also the possibility that direct competition for krill or other marine species will affect the albatrosses, as well as other animals.

RWB/PAP

The **shearwater** family has one of the widest distributions of any bird family, ranging from the Snow petrels which nest 150mi (about 250km) inland in Antarctica to the Northern fulmar which breeds as far north as there is land in the Arctic. Although several species are localized and rare, others are abundant and undertake extensive migrations. Overall they are an extremely successful family. Some eat plankton, others dead whales, but the bulk catch small fish and squid at the sea surface or by underwater pursuit. Although there is a great variation between species in plumage and habits, the family divides neatly into four groups: fulmars, prions, gadfly petrels and true shearwaters.

The fulmars are a cold-water group, only venturing into the subtropics along cold-water currents. There are five species in the southern hemisphere, which is where the group probably evolved because the single northern species (the Northern fulmar) is closely related to the Southern fulmar. Most species are medium-sized, but the two sibling species of giant petrels (wingspan 6ft, 2m) are as large as some albatrosses.

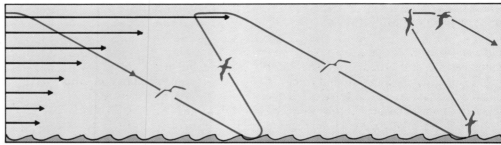

▲ **Riding the wind.** Albatrosses are adapted more for gliding than for flying, and have developed a gliding practice that makes best use of wind conditions in the southern seas. They take advantage of the phenomenon whereby wind near the sea surface moves at a slower speed than higher currents thanks to drag on the sea surface.

An albatross glides downwind from a height of about 50ft (about 15m), losing height. Just before it hits the water it turns into the wind and is blown back up to its original height by increasing wind speed.

▼ **Representative species of albatrosses and petrels.** (1) A Light-mantled sooty albatross (*Diomedea palpebrata*) with chick. (2) A Southern giant petrel (*Macronectes giganteus*) feeding on a dead seal. (3) A Cory's shearwater (*Puffinus diomedea*) with chick. (4) A Great shearwater (*Puffinus gravis*). (5) An immature Black-browed albatross (*Diomedea melanophris*).

There is speculation that the albatross shot in Coleridge's "Rime of the Ancient Mariner" (1798) was, in fact, a giant petrel. Fulmars' bills are large (enormously so in giant petrels) and broad. They once probably fed mainly on plankton, but some species now eat waste from fishing and whaling fleets; the exploitation of this new food resource has led to spectacular increases in numbers. Fulmars are fairly active on land and giant petrels can walk with upright shanks (tarsi); all other groups in this family shuffle with shanks flat on the ground. In flight they alternate flapping and gliding.

Prions (including the Blue petrel) are another southern group and breed mainly on subantarctic islands, but move into slightly warmer waters at other times. These small birds (length 10in, 26cm) all look very similar, blue-gray above, white below with a dark "W" across the wings. All eat small plankton which they filter out with plates (lamellae) on the bill, but the bill dimensions vary greatly suggesting subtle differences in diet. Some species pick fish from the surface while those with broader beaks hydroplane their way through the surface water.

Prions congregate in areas of high plankton density and vast flocks typically wheel low over the sea. They were once known as whale birds because they frequently occurred in the presence of whales.

Gadfly petrels are larger species (length 10–18in, 26–46cm) and are difficult to identify as some species have different color phases or variations. Most are black (or gray) and white above and white below with white faces; others are all dark. The short and stout bill with a powerful hook and sharp cutting edge is used for gripping and cutting up small squid and fish. They occur in the southern and tropical oceans. Some are restricted to single islands (eg the cahow) while other species roam far and wide. They are strong fliers and typically arc high above the sea. Their movements are imperfectly known but some Pacific species migrate across the equator from one hemisphere to another.

The true shearwaters and petrels are small to large birds (length 10.6–21.6in, 27–55cm); most are dark above and black or white underneath. Many species have a

black cap and only one species has white on the head. Shearwaters are widespread and very mobile and pose considerable taxonomic problems; for example, should the similar, but not identical, black-and-white shearwaters breeding in the northeast Atlantic, Mediterranean, Hawaii, east Pacific and New Zealand be considered subspecies of the Manx shearwater or separate species? (A shearwater ringed in Britain was once recovered in Australia, and the whole of the British population migrates to South America each year: distance is thus

5

4

3

no barrier to dispersal. Indeed colonies are sometimes formed far outside the normal range, and during the last 20 years the Manx shearwater has started to breed off the coast of North America.)

Shearwater bills are proportionately longer and thinner than those of other groups but they still eat mainly fish and squid. Prey is caught either by the bird crashing down onto it or by swimming after it underwater.

All the species in the family are colonial to a greater or lesser extent. Sometimes this is due to limited suitable habitat; for example, Antarctic-nesting Southern giant petrels are forced to nest on the few patches of stones kept snow free by the wind, but it usually is by choice as birds enter and try to nest in seemingly overcrowded areas even with apparently suitable, but unused habitat nearby. Colony sites are as diverse as the species themselves, but safety from predators is a prerequisite.

Of the fulmars only the Snow petrel nests under cover; other species make a scrape on a cliff ledge or incubate the egg in the open. Birds discourage intruders by spitting or regurgitating foul-smelling oil, hence the old name of "stinker" for the giant petrel. Colonies tend to be small and nests dispersed. All the prions nest underground among boulders or in burrows they dig themselves; colonies may be very large. Except for a few surface-living species on Pacific islands, gad-fly petrels and shearwaters nest in burrows or under rocks. Some line the nest chamber with vegetation; others make a mere token of a nest. Typically colonies are large and found on islands, less commonly among forests or high on mainland mountains. Whereas open nesters come and go from their nests by day, most burrow nesters are nocturnal at the colonies, so as to escape predators. It has recently been demonstrated that some species locate their burrows by smell.

Breeding is remarkably uniform throughout the family. Birds return to the colonies at least a few weeks prior to nesting and reclaim the nest sites used the previous season. Pairs usually remain together from one season to the next, and probably meet again at the nest sites. Adult survival is extremely high (at least 90 percent per annum) and pairs persist for many years. When "divorces" occur, they usually follow unsuccessful breeding. In the weeks prior to laying there are many noisy aerial displays and pairs spend days together at the nest. Many species have a "honeymoon" period, when the female leaves the colony for

about two weeks to feed so as to lay down reserves for the large egg. In some species the male is also away preparing himself for taking the first long incubation stint. However, in others he returns periodically to check the nest site.

In most species breeding is annual and synchronized. The most extreme case is the Short-tailed shearwater, whose colonies span 11 degrees latitude; all of its eggs are laid during a 12-day period with the peak always occurring between 24 and 26 November. In tropical species, which frequent the colonies throughout the year, eggs may be laid in all months. In a few species individuals breed at less than annual intervals but in most species pairs still breed annually. Even more rarely birds at adjacent colonies breed annually but are out of phase.

All species lay a single, very large white egg which varies from 6 percent (in the Giant petrel) to 20 percent (in prions) of the female's weight. Tropical species lay proportionately larger eggs than temperate or polar species, probably because food is often short so that the chick needs bigger food reserves at hatching to carry it over any shortage. Both sexes have a single large central brood patch (ie an area denuded of feathers and rich in blood vessels for transferring heat from parent to egg) and incubate in turn for spells of 1–20 days. Often the male takes the first and longest stint, presumably to let the female go back to sea to recover from laying. Lost eggs are very rarely, usually never, replaced. Eggs are tolerant of chilling, especially those safe in the uniform temperature of a burrow, but chilling can increase the incubation period by up to 25 percent.

The incubation period is long but the range (43–60 days) is less than expected given the great range of egg size (0.9–8.4oz, 25–237g). The chick is brooded for the first few days, but may then be left in the burrow to allow both adults to forage. It is fed on a soup of partly digested fish, crustacea, squid etc, and on stomach oil. Growth is rapid until the young may be much heavier than the adult. Burrow-living chicks are often deserted and complete their development on stored fat.

The young, eggs and adults of many species were once considered delicacies and were eaten in large numbers, and their fat was used extensively. Human predation has declined but not stopped. For instance, Great shearwaters are still killed at the colonies on Tristan da Cunha and in wintering grounds in the North Atlantic. Some shearwaters are

Storm petrels are the smallest and most delicate of seabirds. Their name may be derived from their habit of sheltering in the lee of a ship during severe storms and a corruption of St Peter since several common species appear to walk on the water while feeding.

Absent from brackish water and the Arctic, storm petrels can otherwise be found throughout the oceans. They are most abundant in the cold waters around Antarctica and in areas of marine upwelling, like the Humboldt Current off Peru. Some species occur only in the most desert-like areas of low biological productivity of the central tropical oceans, where there is apparently little food. A few species have very restricted distributions, others undertake long migrations. Wilson's storm petrel which breeds around Antarctica spends its non-breeding time throughout the Indian, central Pacific and Atlantic oceans north to Greenland. Storm petrels are not worried by man and many species feed in ships' wakes and a few come around fishing boats to pick up scraps.

Storm petrels are immediately recognizable by their fairly small but strongly hooked beak, pronounced tubular nostrils which are fused together, and a steep forehead. Despite the absence of color, many are striking birds with almost black plumage and white rump. Others are beautiful shades of brown and gray. The family is clearly divisible into two groups which presumably evolved in different hemispheres but which now overlap in the tropics. Species of the northern group, typified by Leach's storm petrel, are black and white and most have pointed wings, relatively short legs and feed by swooping down and picking food from the surface, rather like terns. Species in the southern group typified by the White-faced storm petrel, have more variable plumage (including species with several color forms), rounded wings and long legs which often are held down as the birds bounce or walk on the sea-surface as they feed.

All species are colonial and most breed on isolated islands lacking ground predators. However, Hornby's storm petrels breed well inland high in the Andes. Except for the Wedge-rumped storm petrel, all species visit colonies at night or, in high latitudes, at lowest light intensity. Pairs defend a burrow among rocks, tree roots or (rarely) under a bush and remain together from one season to the next. In temperate regions breeding is fairly well synchronized and seasonal while in the tropics it often appears prolonged with birds present throughout the year. However, in the Galapagos Islands the Madeiran storm petrel has two breeding

▲ **Horny pincers.** This Hall's giant petrel (*Macronectes halli*) feeds only at sea, including in its diet fish and squid. Not only is its bill powerful and tough but is also equipped with sharp hooks for holding prey.

◄ **Screams, wails and choking sounds** are among the vocalizations produced by members of the family of shearwaters and petrels. They enable individuals to recognize each other (especially at night), and perhaps also, as with these pairs of Northern fulmars, to assert the possession of territory.

known as muttonbirds and the young of one species, the Short-tailed shearwater, are still harvested commercially for their meat; however, there is a strict quota and the harvest has no effect on the population. In contrast several gadfly petrels are seriously threatened by habitat destruction and introduced predators. The cahow or Bermuda petrel is a typical example. Occurring only in Bermuda it once lived inland where it was hunted for food and then killed by pigs, cats and rats. A few pairs survived on offshore rocks but their breeding success was very low because of competition with tropic birds for nest-sites. Management has prevented this and the species just hangs on. The Dark-rumped petrel is similarly threatened at both its nesting areas, in the Galapagos by rats and pigs, dogs and farming, in Hawaii by mongooses and rats. Several species of shearwaters and petrels will need help if they are to survive.   MPH

seasons a year due to two quite separate populations each of which breeds annually but at a different time.

The single white egg is laid on the ground and incubated for 1–6 days by each bird in turn for a total of 40–50 days. If lost the egg is only very rarely replaced that season, probably because the egg is so large (up to 25 percent of the female's weight) that it would take too long to produce another.

The young is fed a mixture of partly digested food and stomach oil. It fledges alone, and at night, after 59–73 days. Although fed less frequently near to fledging it is not, as is often said, deserted and the adults may visit the burrow after it has left.

Storm petrels eat mainly planktonic crustacea, squid and fish and oily scraps picked up in flight (indeed storm petrels rarely sit on the water).

In some species many immatures visit other colonies before they breed (usually 4–5 years) and these can even be attracted to other places by playing tape recordings of the purring calls. The potential conservation value of this has been demonstrated by the National Audubon Society of the USA who persuaded Leach's storm petrel to nest in artificial burrows on an island where they had never bred before.   MPH

One of the amazing sights in the southern seas is of a small flock of **diving petrels** flying through a steep wave, plunging in one side and coming out the other, or erupting from the depths of the sea without check. This is possible thanks to the adaptation of wings for swimming underwater. Diving petrels are a southern equivalent of the auk family, resembling the Little auk in particular; both have small wings for swimming underwater and a whirring "bumblebee" flight. There is even a remarkable similarity in the structure of wing bones.

Breeding is confined to cool waters north of 60 degrees south and up the Western side of South America, where the sea temperature is influenced by the cool Humboldt Current. Unlike many other petrels, diving petrels do not appear to make extensive movements, even outside the breeding season; they are usually seen in waters over the continental shelf near the breeding area.

The four species of diving petrels are very

▼ **Representative species of storm and diving petrels.** (1) A Gray-backed storm petrel (*Garrodia nereis*). (2) A Common diving petrel (*Pelecanoides urinatrix*). (3) A Wilson's storm petrel (*Oceanites oceanicus*). (4) Georgian diving petrels (*Pelecanoides georgicus*) flying into waves. (5) Head of a White-faced storm petrel (*Pelagodroma marina*).

similar in size and plumage, which makes identification difficult unless the bird is in the hand and the variable amounts of gray or white on the upper side can be seen. Only the Magellan diving petrel is distinctive with its white collar; it also has a distinguishable juvenile which lacks the white fringes on feathers on the back.

Diving petrels chase their prey by swimming underwater and feed mainly within the upper 33ft (10m). The diet consists of small marine organisms, but detailed analysis has been made only on Common and Georgian diving petrels at South Georgia. There Georgian diving petrels fed their chicks 76 percent krill (by volume) with lesser amounts of amphipod and copepod crustaceans, while Common diving petrels delivered 68 percent copepods and lesser amounts of amphipods and euphausids.

Breeding has similarly been described in detail at South Georgia for Georgian and Common diving petrels. Diving petrels nest in burrows, reexcavated each season. The birds fly in at night, presumably to avoid predation by skuas. The Georgian diving petrel tunnels into bare stony soil above the level of vegetation, whereas Common diving petrels nest in peaty, often waterlogged, soil beneath stands of tussock grass at lower levels. The birds are heard calling at night; the Georgian diving petrel makes a series of harsh "squeaks," the Common diving petrel utters a two-syllable phrase, rendered as *kuaka*, the Maori name of the species.

The Georgian diving petrel lays a single egg between 7 and 31 December which it hatches in late January. The Common diving petrel hatches on average 29 days earlier than the Georgian. Incubation spells last one to three days. After hatching, chicks of the Common diving petrel are brooded for at least 11 days, but Georgian chicks are covered for five days less. The chicks are fed on most nights by one or both parents. The feed contains very little stomach oil, unlike that of other members of the order, and is little digested, possibly because the feed is delivered so quickly after capture. Peruvian diving petrels nest under boulders, and have suffered as islands have been stripped of guano (excrement). The Magellan diving petrel appears to nest in peaty soil.

Colonies of diving petrels can be extensive; there are an estimated two million breeding pairs of Georgian diving petrels on South Georgia and the only current threat is that of predation by introduced rats. For the Peruvian diving petrel, however, the status is unclear. Only a few breeding sites are known; some have been destroyed by the clearance of guano and the future of the species is a cause for concern. RWB/PAP

PELICANS AND GANNETS

Order: Pelecaniformes
Families: Pelecanidae, Phaethontidae, Sulidae,
Phalacrocoracidae, Anhingidae, Fregatidae.
Fifty-seven species in 7 genera.
Distribution: worldwide.

Pelicans   Tropicbirds   Darters

Gannets   Frigatebirds   Cormorants

▶ **Representative species of pelicans and
gannets.** (1) A Brown pelican (*Pelecanus
occidentalis*), the most colorful of pelicans.
(2) A Reed cormorant (*Phalacrocorax africanus*),
widespread in Africa. (3) A male Great
frigatebird (*Fregata minor*) with his throat-
pouch inflated. (4) A male Peruvian booby
(*Sula variegata*) pointing to his mate in the sky.
(5) Head of a Spotted shag (*Phalacrocorax
punctatus*). (6) A Cape gannet (*Morus capensis*).
(7) A White-tailed tropicbird (*Phaethon
lepturus*). (8) An African darter (*Anhinga rufa*)
swimming.

▶ **Pelicans afloat** OVERLEAF. A gathering of
Australian pelicans.

WITH their long bill, saggy throat
(gular) pouch, large size and
lugubrious manner **pelicans** have attracted
man's attention for centuries. The pelican
has served as a symbol for Christian piety,
based on a myth that the adult slits its own
breast to feed its starving young with blood.
The origins of this myth are obscure. Today
the image of a pelican is one of the most
widely used animal caricatures for commercial enterprises, such as hotels,
restaurants, toys and books.

Pelicans are primarily birds of warm
climates, although the desert regions where
some species live become cold at night.
Breeding occurs mainly in isolated areas
away from mammalian (and especially
human) predation and disturbance.
Because pelicans eat fish exclusively they
must breed near a ready and abundant fish
supply. However, with their good flying ability and aptitude for using thermal updrafts
they may commute hundreds of miles
on a daily basis from their protected nesting
areas to lakes with abundant fish. They eat
fish ranging from under an ounce to 1.1lb
(0.5kg) which may be over 1ft (30cm) long.

The pelican family is divided into two
groups, based on color of plumage and nesting habitats. The first group of basically all-
white birds (Australian, Great white,
Dalmatian and American white pelicans)
nest on the ground in dense colonies. The
second group (Brown, Pink-backed, and
Spot-billed pelicans) have predominantly
gray or brown plumage and nest in trees.
All species have distinct pouch and facial
skin colors, which become intensely vivid
prior to the breeding season and serve as
both attractants and indicators of sexual

readiness. Males are larger in all species,
most noticeably in their weight and bill
length. The young of all species are very
noisy, yet adults are essentially silent.
Young have either black or white down,
according to species.

Courtship activities of all species are similar, with the male picking out the nest site
and performing an "advertising" display
which attracts a female and which is distinct
in each species. Pelicans do not have a
highly developed behavioral repertoire,
probably because of the restrictions of having such a long bill. Once a pair bond is
formed overt communication between
members is minimal. Though pelicans are
always colonial and often nest in clumped
groups, there does not appear to be any
established social hierarchy. Interactions

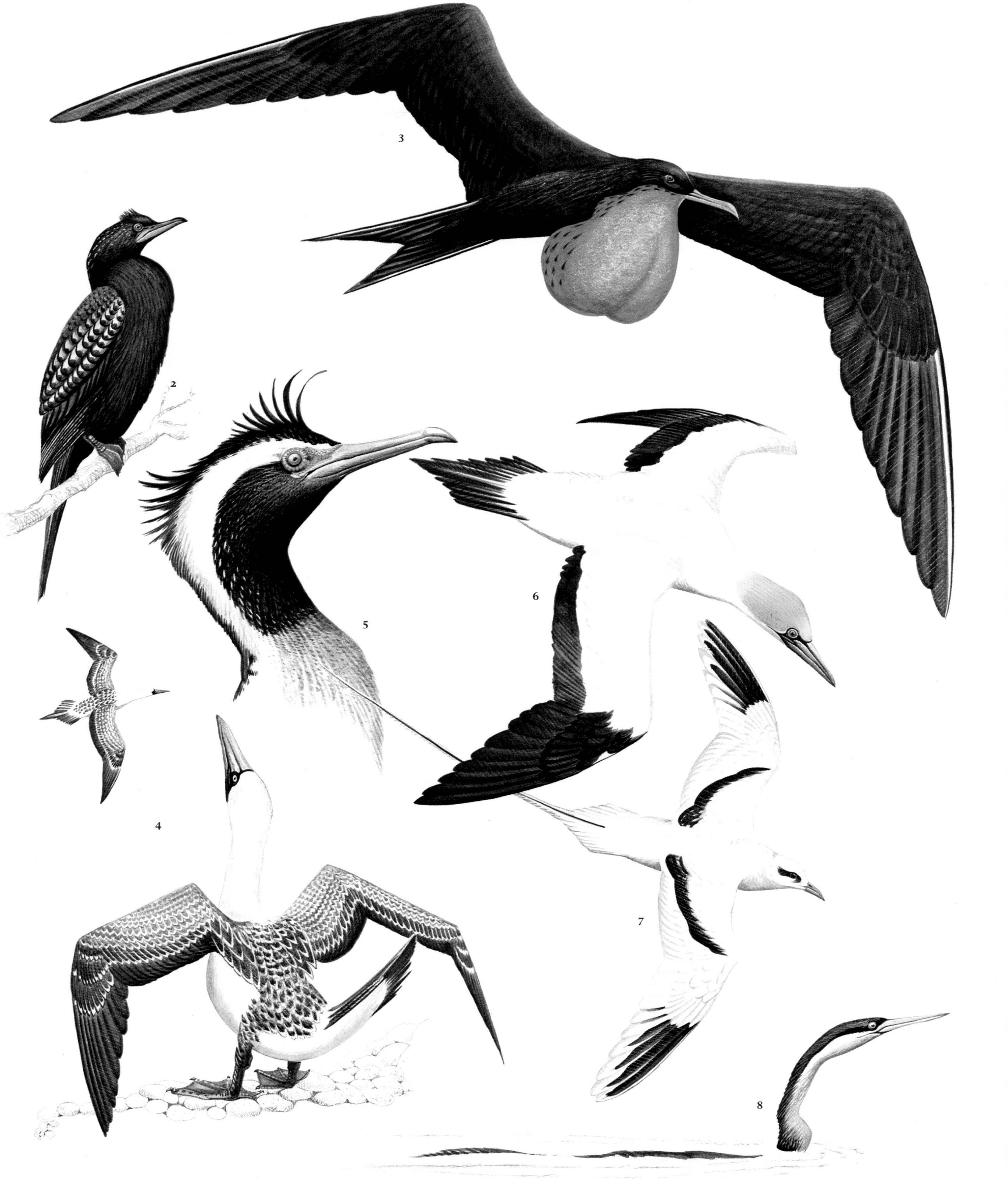
3
2
6
5
4
7
8

occur merely between individual birds. After the male has gathered the nesting material and the female built the nest, members of the pair cooperate in all nesting activities, including incubation and feeding of the growing chicks. Young are not fed once they fly away from the nesting colonies, although in the ground nesters individual young may receive food when they have wandered far from the actual nest site, but only from their own parents.

The marine Brown pelican feeds exclusively by diving for fish, sometimes from great heights. The other species either feed individually from the water's surface or "communally" by herding schools of fish and then synchronously scooping them up. Whole fish are fed to nestlings. Contrary to the famous lines about the pelican by Dixon Lanier Merritt ("it can keep in its beak enough food for a week") fish are not kept in the pouch for any length of time. The pouch is used as a dip net to catch fish, which are soon swallowed into the stomach, at the center of gravity, so that the birds can maintain their balance while flying.

Pelicans are long-lived, one living in a zoo for 54 years. It is known that in the wild many pelicans live 15–25 years. Most individuals probably begin to breed at three or four years of age. Food supply is the overwhelming factor involved in the onset and success of breeding. In tropical climes nesting can occur throughout the year. Temperate species nest in the "spring," when daylength increases. However, temperature is an important controlling factor; cold inhibits nesting.

The length of the pelican pair bond is unknown, but monogamy during the breeding season is essential because both members of a pair must meet the food requirements of the rapidly growing young. Occasionally two or three young can be raised. However, the more usual situation is the raising of only one young and some species virtually never raise more than one. Eggs are laid asynchronously with two or three days between eggs. Incubation begins with the laying of the first egg and lasts the same time for each egg. Thus the first sibling to hatch has advantages of age and size when feeding: these older chicks can take most of the food supply from the adults. If the parents cannot supply sufficient food for all the nestlings the smaller young starve. The adults must also bring enough food to enable the young to lay down stores of body fat for when they are first independent and developing the coordination of nerve and impulses and muscles necessary for feeding

▲ **Diving for fish.** All pelicans catch fish in their throat pouch but only the Brown pelican dives into water to take its prey. Each dive seems to be made to capture a particular fish. On sighting its prey (1), the pelican enters a dive, pulling back its wings to form the wings and back into the shape of a triangle (2 and 3). As the bill enters the water, legs and wings are thrust back, increasing speed (4).

As it comes into the water the pelican positions the mandibles of its beak above and below the fish whilst the throat pouch expands (5), trapping the fish. The bird then pulls its body and head above the water, enabling water to drain from the pouch. The bill is then lifted from the water and the fish swallowed. Since the water in the pouch can weigh more than the bird, it has to drain the pouch before it can move. It can take the pelican almost a minute to drain the water.

themselves. The vast majority of the young do not survive their first year out of the nest.

Two species of pelicans, the Dalmatian and the Spot-billed, are among the more endangered large birds of the world. Only 500–1,400 breeding pairs of Dalmatians still exist, in 19 colony sites between eastern Europe and China. Half the population breeds in the USSR. This species has been declining in both numbers and the extent of its range for the past century. Predation and human disturbance in colonies and flooding of nests appear to be the major factors causing the population decline.

The Spot-billed pelican is presently confined to four known colonies in India with fewer than 400 pairs and 23 colonies in Sri Lanka with 900 pairs. This species was once widespread in Asia with many nesting sites having thousands of pairs. Pesticides are implicated in the recent decline, but habitat destruction and disturbance in colonies by humans are also major problems. A decline in food availability is also a factor.

Little is known about either species and only concerted efforts at conservation and research will preserve these magnificent birds. EAS/RWS

Gannets and **boobies** (or sulids)—large seabirds breeding from the Arctic circle through the tropics to the edge of sub-Antarctica—are notable for their dramatic plunge-diving, gaudy colors, teeming colonies and boldness (often to their undoing). All species share a basic body-plan, adapted for plunge-diving and for catching fish underwater: a tapered body, long wings and tail, a long bill with serrations on the cutting edges and a sharp point, occluded nostrils and shock-absorbing air sacs. Refining this uniform arrangement, however, there has been a wide range of further adaptations in response to different climates and habitats. Ecological adaptations are particularly visible in breeding arrangements. Where food supplies are abundant, reliable and easily exploited adults are able to feed larger broods. The Peruvian booby, which lives near the richest fishing area in the world, the Humboldt upwelling off Peru and northern Chile, usually raises three or four young. Blue-footed boobies, which live on the fringes of the upwelling areas, often have two or three young. All other members of the family usually raise just one young, though two of the tropical boobies (the Masked and Brown boobies) often lay two eggs, but within a few days of hatching one chick will always kill the other, regardless of the availability of food. This adaptation

seems to ensure that one stronger chick, rather than two weaker ones, has the opportunity to become independent. The laying of a second egg also ensures that a chick will survive should the first to hatch die from temporary famine or some other cause. (Famines are a recurring but unpredictable feature of tropical seas.) The other two tropical species of boobies (the Red-footed and Abbott's boobies) lay a single egg but provide for the survival of their offspring by producing large eggs with greater food reserves, so the chicks are more robust when they hatch. Also, the free-flying young continue to be fed for several weeks or months. The gannets also lay single eggs, but as they live where food is relatively abundant they feed their chicks well enough for them to become independent at an earlier stage than boobies, ie when they become free-flying. Until they become proficient at hunting for food the young of these species live partly off reserves of fat.

In temperate areas (eg where the Atlantic gannets live) breeding is a seasonal activity, but in the tropics, where climate and the availability of food do not occur in seasonal patterns, boobies may lay in any month.

The availability of food also influences the frequency with which sulids breed, which (for successful cycles) varies from once every nine or ten months in the Brown and Blue-footed boobies to once every two years in Abbott's booby.

▲ **Pelicans en masse.** These Great white pelicans live and breed in colonies that can vary in size from as few as 50 birds to as many as 40,000.

◄ **Pelicans in pod.** Three weeks after hatching pelican chicks become able to walk. There then follows a period of 8–10 weeks when they live in groups or "pods." Each chick, however, continues to be fed by its own parents, who provide regurgitated liquid matter in their bills. By this means chicks put on so much weight that they become heavier than an adult. At this point they are deserted and have to fly out into the world alone. These are Brown pelican chicks.

Sulids may expect to live about 20 years, though some individuals may last as long as 40 years. (The normal life span of most boobies is slightly less than that of gannets.)

After they have fledged (at about 90 days in the Atlantic gannet but about 150 days in Abbott's booby) all young sulids except gannets remain dependent on their parents for a further period of weeks or months. They then spend a period as nomads. Breeding normally begins within 2–5 years. Boobies generally breed at a younger age than gannets, and females at a younger age than males. Both gannets and boobies usually return to their natal colonies to breed, engaging in conspicuous displays when reestablishing their territories and forming pairs. After Atlantic gannets have begun to breed they normally attempt to breed every year, for as long as they retain their mate. Ninety-five percent of gannets remain faithful to their partner and to their nest-site. All species of booby except Abbott's booby,

however, change both partner and site from time to time, occasionally taking "rest" years. (It is not known whether partners remate after such a break.) Between breeding cycles all adult gannets and boobies disperse.

Today all species of gannets and boobies are having to cope with a number of difficulties, principally disturbance, pollution, introduced predators and the effects of man on their food supply, and are doing so with differing success. The Australasian and Atlantic gannets are increasing, the latter at about 3 percent per year, but the African gannet is probably declining. The Masked, Brown and Red-footed boobies have had to face extensive slaughter of adults and young, perhaps for tens of thousands of years. In this connection the tree-nesting Red-footed booby may have been at an advantage over the ground-nesting Masked and Brown boobies and is more numerous. The Peruvian booby is a classic case of a sea

The 6 Families of Pelicans and their Relatives

Pelicans
Family: Pelecanidae
Seven species of the genus *Pelecanus*.
East Europe, Africa, India, Sri Lanka, SE Asia, Australia, N America, or on near coasts and inland waters. Size: length 4.2–5.6ft (1.27–1.7m); wingspan 6.6–9.2ft (2–2.8m); weight 5.5–33lb (2.5–15kg). Males slightly larger than females. Plumage: gray or white with black primary and flight feathers; washes of pink or orange on the body; Brown pelican is gray-black. Voice: hisses and grunts; nestlings are very noisy. Eggs: 1–4; chalky white. Incubation: 1 month. Diet: fish.

Species include: **American white pelican** (*Pelecanus erythrorhynchos*), **Australian pelican** (*P. conspicillatus*), **Brown pelican** (*P. occidentalis*), **Dalmatian pelican** V (*P. crispus*), **Great white** or **European white pelican** (*P. onocrotalus*), **Pink-backed pelican** (*P. rufescens*), **Spot-billed** or **Gray pelican** (*P. philippensis*).

Gannets and boobies
Family: Sulidae
Nine species in 2 genera.
Most pantropical oceans. Islands used for breeding. Size: length 23.6–33.5in (60–85cm); wingspan 4.6–5.7ft (1.41–1.74m); weight 2–8lb (0.9–3.6kg). In some species females are larger than males. Plumage: all species have white underparts with variable amount of black or gray above; some species have brightly

colored bills, faces and feet. Voice: raucous or sonorous single or polysyllabic grunts or shouts and thin whistles. Eggs: according to species 1, 1 or 2, 2–4; plain, whitish with a limy coating that becomes stained. Incubation: 42–55 days. Diet: fish, squid, offal.

Species: **Abbott's booby** E (*Sula abbotti*), **Atlantic gannet** (*Morus bassana*), **Australasian gannet** (*M. serrator*), **Blue-footed booby** (*S. nebouxii*), **Brown booby** (*S. leucogaster*), **Cape** or **African gannet** (*M. capensis*), **Masked, Blue-faced** or **White booby** (*S. dactylatra*), **Peruvian booby** (*S. variegata*), **Red-footed booby** (*S. sula*).

Tropicbirds
Family: Phaethontidae
Three species of the genus *Phaethon*.
Tropical and subtropical oceans. Size: length 31–43in (80–110cm), including tail streamers; wingspan 35–43in (90–110cm). Plumage: white with black markings; some adults tinged rosy or gold. Sexes similar (but the greatly elongated two inner tail feathers are longer in the male, and absent in juveniles). Nest: on bare ground, or in holes in cliffs, trees. Voice: shrill screams. Eggs: 1; blotched red-brown. Incubation: 40–46 days. Diet: fish, squid.

Species: **Red-billed tropicbird** (*Phaethon aethereus*), **Red-tailed tropicbird** (*P. rubricauda*), **White-tailed tropicbird** (*P. lepturus*).

Cormorants
Family: Phalacrocoracidae
Twenty-nine species of the genus *Phalacrocorax*.
Worldwide; few at high latitudes; inhabiting inland waters and marine shorelines. Size: length 17.7–39.8in (45–101cm); wingspan 31–63in (80–160cm); weight 2–11lb (900–4,900g). Plumage: generally drab black, brown or blackish with a green sheen; some species have white breasts. Voice: grunts and croaks, but generally quiet. Eggs: 1–6; chalky blue, elongate ovoid. Incubation: 22–26 days. Diet: small fish and marine invertebrates.

Species include: **Brandt's cormorant** (*Phalacrocorax penicillatus*), **Cape cormorant** (*P. capensis*), **Double-crested cormorant** (*P. auritus*), **Galapagos flightless cormorant** R (*Nannopterum harrisi*), **Great cormorant** (*P. carbo*), **guanay** (*P. bougainvillii*), **Olivaceous cormorant** (*P. olivaceus*), **Pelagic cormorant** (*P. pelagicus*), **Pygmy cormorant** (*P. pygmaeus*), **Red-faced cormorant** (*P. urile*), **shag** (*P. aristotelis*), **Spotted shag** (*P. punctatus*).

Frigatebirds
Family: Fregatidae
Five species of the genus *Fregata*.
Pantropical oceans. Size: length 31–41in (79–104cm); wingspan 5.8–7.5ft (1.76–2.3m); weight 26.4–57.3oz (750–1,625g). Females 25–30 percent heavier than males.

Plumage: males black with varying amounts of white beneath; females black in Ascension frigatebird, other species dark brown above and on head and belly with white breast. Voice: varied rattling, whistling, cackling and bill-rattling sounds; males give resonant drumming, hooting or whistling sounds. Eggs: 1; white, chalky. Incubation: 44–55 days. Diet: mainly flying fish and squid.

Species: **Ascension Island frigatebird** R (*Fregata aquila*), **Andrew's** or **Christmas Island frigatebird** V (*F. andrewsi*), **Great frigatebird** (*F. minor*), **Lesser frigatebird** (*F. ariel*), **Magnificent frigatebird** (*F. magnificens*).

Darters
Family: Anhingidae
Four species of the genus *Anhinga*.
America, Africa, Asia, Australasia inhabiting fresh waters (lakes, lagoons, rivers). Size: length 30–39in (76–98cm), wingspan 47–50in (120–127cm), weight 2–5.7lb (0.9–2.6kg). Plumage: mixture of black, brown, gray, silver and white; males darker than females. Voice: clicking, rattling, whistling and hissing calls. Eggs: 2–6 (average 4); elliptical, pale green with white chalky outer layer and some blood streaks. Incubation: 26–30 days. Diet: mainly fish.

Species: **African darter** (*Anhinga rufa*), **American anhinga** (*A. anhinga*), **Asian darter** (*A. melanogaster*), **Australian darter** (*A. novaehollandiae*).

▲ **Bush booby.** The Red-footed booby is unusual among sulids in nesting in bushes and trees. This has had some minor consequences in its behavior; its displays, for example, are slightly less elaborate than those of ground-nesting species. What has never been explained, however, is for what reason the bird has tomato-red feet.

◄ **Cape gannets** ABOVE. Living in the hot climes of Africa, this species has several minor adaptations to facilitate heat loss, including the enlarged strip of naked black skin on the throat.

▶ **The packed multitude: African gannets** OVERLEAF. All sulids breed in colonies, ranging from a few pairs to hundreds of thousands.

▼ **Sulid displays.** All species have highly developed territorial and pair displays. Each species has evolved variants on common forms, involving exaggerated postures and movements of head, wings, feet and tail, and in some species aerial displays. Display sequences may be long and protracted. Here a male Brown booby makes a territorial display (1), male and female Atlantic gannets greet each other (2), a pair of Cape gannets attain copulation (3).

bird whose numbers are controlled by its food supply, though not in relation to its own numbers. The area where it lives is normally rich in fish, but is periodically affected by incursions of warm water (*El Ñino*) which cause cold-loving anchovies to dive to depths where the boobies cannot reach them. The birds starve in their millions. In the past they have usually been able to restore their previous numbers quickly, but recently serious overfishing by man has prevented the birds from recovering from *El Ñino*. Numbers have remained at less than one-fifth of previous highest levels.

The enigma among boobies is the tree-nesting Abbott's booby. It once nested on islands in the western Indian Ocean, but has been driven from there by human destruction of its environment. But human activity does not apparently account for the small size of the sole remaining breeding population, about 1,000–1,500 pairs on jungle-clad Christmas Island in the Indian Ocean. It now faces a threat from the clearing of jungle for phosphate mining, but the Australian government has imposed conservation measures and research is in progress for devising a policy that will protect these birds. JBN

Tropicbirds are among the most beautiful and widespread of tropical seabirds. Except when breeding they scorn land and are distributed, albeit sparsely, over vast areas of sea.

Sturdily built, tropicbirds appear larger than their body length of 18in (45cm). This is partly due to their brilliant white plumage, set off by black markings on the head, wings and upperparts, but also by the extremely thin central pair of white or red tail feathers which double the birds' length. The bill is either blood red or yellow, and stout and decurved with a vicious series of serrations on the cutting edge for holding prey. The legs are drab and very short, and webs join all four toes.

These birds forage well away from the col-

onies. When hunting they fly high, hover when they see something interesting and then plunge into the sea. The basic foods are medium-sized fish, especially flying fish (up to 8in, 20cm long) and squid, but there are great seasonal and annual differences in the proportions of each that are eaten. After diving tropicbirds spend little time underwater which suggests that they do not go deep.

Tropicbirds are colonial, partly by choice and partly because suitable nesting sites are extremely limited on oceanic islands. The colonies are very obvious as the birds have noisy communal displays in which they glide close together with wings held high and tails flowing. Breeding seasons are complex (see p54), but pairs usually remain together and reuse the previous nest site, which is typically a hole in a cliff, under a boulder or bush; less commonly it is in a hole in a tree, a palm or even on the ground. The site must be safe from ground predators and be near a convenient takeoff point as tropicbirds have such short and backwardly placed legs that they only shuffle on land. There is much fighting for nest-sites which results in the loss of eggs and chicks.

The newly hatched young is covered with thick down. If conditions are good, it may be constantly protected until two-thirds grown. However, it is often soon left as it is necessary for both adults to be away foraging if the young is to be properly fed. It is given slightly digested fish or squid by direct regurgitation, sometimes every day, often only every two or three days. The young is normally fed until it flies off alone after some 60–90 days, again according to how well it has been fed. Its plumage is similar to that of an adult except that it is more heavily marked and lacks tail streamers and bright bill coloration. Young return to the colonies after three or four years and breed at about five years.

Adults were once killed for their feathers and young were considered delicacies. Rats and other introduced predators have reduced nesting success, but most populations

1

2

3

are now probably stable. On Bermuda, White-tailed tropicbirds are a threat to the endangered cahow, as they compete for nest-sites. Luckily this species of shearwater can use slightly smaller holes, so the conservation method of putting wooden baffles into the entrances to holes has proved successful.   MPH

Cormorants are common residents of seacoasts and inland water systems, accounting for over half the species of their order. They range from the duck-sized Pygmy cormorant of the Middle East to the Great cormorant of Europe and Asia, a bird about the size of a goose. They are the most aquatic of their order, being distributed worldwide and absent from only the uttermost polar regions, isolated oceanic islands and arid lands. Their commonness caused the naturalists of antiquity to give them the name *corvus marinus* ("sea raven") which passed to us through the early French *cor marin* to the present cormorant.

Cormorants feed in inshore waters, sharing fishing grounds with humans. Their voracious appetites and preference for breeding and feeding in large groups have left fishermen through the ages with the erroneous impression that they consume valuable fish. Periodic extermination campaigns have been waged, but later studies have shown such persecution to be unjustified. Cormorants are pursuit-divers; the Great cormorant and shag feed on midwater and bottom-schooling fish, such as mullet and sardines. Other species, for example the Pelagic and Brandt's cormorants, often prefer to take various invertebrates and rockfish that live on the bottom.

The cormorants share with the rest of the pelican-like birds webbing that connects all four toes (totipalmate feet) and a throat (gular) pouch. Loose folds of skin under the throat form a small pouch, but it is not as well developed here as in pelicans, probably because it is not used to capture fish. The expandable throat area helps to accommodate and position large fish for swallowing, but it serves mainly as a signaling device and as a means for cooling down the body. These primarily dark birds overheat quickly in direct sunlight. By panting and rapidly fluttering the gular pouch, blood passing through the rich concentration of capillaries is rapidly cooled. Like all other water birds cormorants have oil glands at the base of the tail for proper feather maintenance; however, their plumage is not waterproof. The special feather structure allows water to penetrate quickly and drive the air out, enabling them to sink and dive easily. After diving the wings are characteristically spread out, possibly to dry the feathers, but this action may also be a behavioral display or a means to warm up in the sun after a cold swim.

Cormorants are often seen swimming low in water, with only their long, sinuous necks exposed. To dive, the bird rises from the water in a graceful arc and then disappears often without a ripple, only to emerge minutes later some distance away. It used to be thought that cormorants swam underwater with their wings. Not only do they rely primarily on their superbly adapted totipalmate feet for swimming, but they press their wings tightly to the body, further reducing their underwater profile.

Cormorants' feet are placed close together and set far back on the body. Their propulsive thigh muscles are relatively large and strong for the size of the body. A unique bone at the base of the skull allows them to thrust at a fish and snap the bill shut independently. Even a fiercely struggling fish can be held by the serrated, strongly hooked bill.

Physiologically cormorants are more similar to diving birds such as penguins than to other seabirds. Their body and muscles are richly endowed with blood vessels and a relatively large blood volume, so that the oxygen supply is greatly enhanced. Cormorants can endure long periods of submersion and attain great depths; Brandt's cormorants have been caught in trawling nets set 165ft (50m) deep and deeper. Only a small amount of fat is stored in the body for insulation, and little is available for energy reserves. This restricts cormorants to the warmer, more productive waters. These adaptations, which improve the diving abilities of cormorants, also give the flesh a very strong flavor. North American natives would catch and hang cormorants in trees for a few weeks to improve the flavor; the Fuegian Indians of South America apparently caught and buried guanays in specially constructed pits.

Unusually for seabirds, cormorants have the ability to lay large clutches (up to 6 eggs and more), and to lay again late in the season should conditions require. The young are completely helpless at birth, being blind and naked, only able to move their necks and bills for feeding. Areas allowing protection from land predators and close enough to feeding grounds are uncommon, and may be the reason cormorants nest in large colonies. Even when only a few

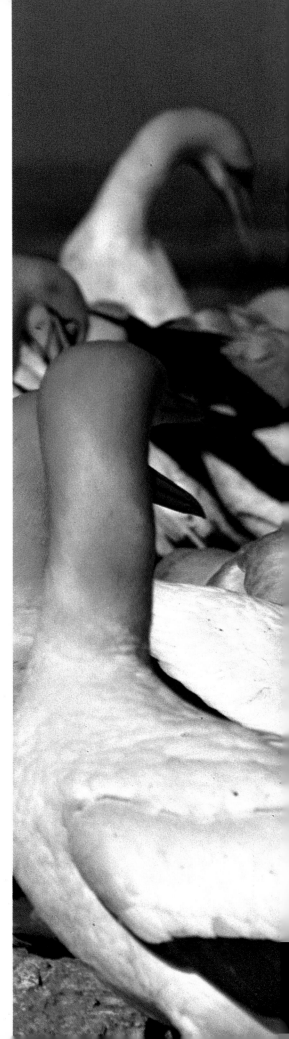

weeks into the breeding season these colonies become notoriously filthy with rotting fish and guano. In Chile, where the guanay breeds, and in South Africa with the Cape cormorant, rainfall is so rare that the guano accumulates to many feet thick and is mined as a rich source of nitrogen and phosphorus.

Although they are consummate aquatic birds, cormorants are nearly useless on land. They are able to waddle only with great effort and often trip over their own feet. The relatively small area of the wings, an advantage in moving between land and water, means that slight wind gusts while landing could cause them to overshoot and fall into a neighboring nest. Tree-nesting species like the Double-crested and Olivaceous cormorants need also to avoid branches: nests are more landing pads than egg containers.

This unsteadiness on land and crowded colony conditions may be the reason that cormorant behaviors are more complex than those of any of the other members of their order. An adult preparing to leave the nest must signal its close neighbors that it is not moving to attack. The bill is opened, displaying the colored mouth and tongue, and a short hop is taken with the wings slightly outspread. The bill is then held down, often pointed at the feet; only then does the bird leap into takeoff. When landing, the neck is brought low and the hyoid bone in the throat is depressed to enlarge the throat pouch. Each cormorant species uses a distinct set of displays for takeoff, landing, courtship and other events, but the behaviors of the entire family are similar. The displays bring attention to the bright colors of the throat, gape, eyes, sometimes feet, which stand in contrast to their drab bodies. The range of coloration for these parts of the bodies is wide, from the jade-green eyes of the Pelagic cormorant, the iridescent blue throat pouch of Brandt's cormorant, the intense carmine of the Red-faced cormorant, to the blue pouch, white breast and varicolored eyes of the Spotted shag. Different colors, different displays and slight differences in food and feeding areas allow many cormorants to live together. In Australia and New Zealand some colonies may have four species breeding together; some islands in Tierra del Fuego have even more.

Since at least the 5th century in Japan and the early 17th century in Europe cormorants have been used for sport fishing. A ring is placed around the neck, preventing the bird from swallowing. When it comes to

the surface it is hauled to the boat on a special perch and the fish are removed. Later the ring is removed so the cormorant can feed itself, but experienced birds can be trained to fish without the ring. This type of fishing is still done in the Orient, but usually for the edification of tourists.   DS-C

Frigatebirds are large seabirds, combining the soaring and gliding powers of vultures with the speed and agility of birds of prey. They nest in colonies on remote islands throughout the tropical oceans, where the males during courtship perform bizarre communal displays with huge inflated red throat-pouches. The name "frigatebird" and its alternative "man-of-war" refer to their robbing other birds of food or nest material. They are among the most oceanic of all birds, roaming far out to sea in search of food; yet their plumage is not waterproof and their legs are so tiny, and their feet so scantily webbed, that they cannot swim and have difficulty rising from the water.

Four of the five frigatebird species breed in the Atlantic; one of these now breeds only at Ascension Island and the only species not found in the Atlantic, Andrew's frigatebird, is confined to Christmas Island in the eastern Indian Ocean. Of the two most widespread species, the Great and Lesser frigatebirds, each shares about half its breeding stations with the other.

In general appearance frigates are one of the most distinctive of all seabird families. Soaring at sea, their long, angular, sharply pointed wings and long scissor-shaped tail give them an unmistakable outline. At shorter range their huge, sinuous, hook-tipped bill is equally distinctive, and the males' brilliant red throat-pouches, when inflated, adorn the trees of the breeding colony like ripe fruits.

▲ **Mother and chick:** Red-tailed tropicbirds. As inhabitants of the tropics, tropicbirds have had to establish breeding cycles in a part of the world where annual cycles are not well established. Different situations have arisen. The Red-tailed tropicbirds on Aldabra on the western edge of the Indian Ocean breed throughout the year whereas on Christmas Island on a similar latitude in the eastern Indian Ocean there is a well-defined breeding cycle. On the Galapagos Islands there is an overcrowded colony of the same species where birds lay all year round within 12.5mi (20km) of an uncrowded colony where there is a regular breeding cycle. There are no obvious reasons for these different arrangements.

▶ **Adult and young** ABOVE. Blue-eyed cormorants (*Phalacrocorax atriceps*) on Bird Island, South Georgia.

▶ **Enjoying the sun,** a Galapagos flightless cormorant. Having loose-fitting feathers cormorants emerge from water, after fishing expeditions, thoroughly soaked. Before flying again they stand in the sun, to dry them off. The Galapagos cormorant (*Nannopterum harrisi*) does the same, even though it long ago lost the ability to fly and subsequently also lost the keel to which the flight muscles were attached.

All species breed in colonies on small or remote islands. The males choose possible nest sites; usually these are in trees—up to 100ft (30m) high or more in Andrew's frigate—but where there are none, they will use bare ground, as on Ascension Island. Males display in groups of up to 30, and when prospecting females fly overhead the males spread and vibrate their wings, throw back their heads and call or clack their bills above their distended scarlet throat-pouch. When a female lands by her chosen mate they snake their head and neck across each other, occasionally nibbling at the other's feathers. The male's courtship display, especially when given in concert with the others', is more noisy, vivid and spectacular than that of any other seabird; but the subsequent repertoire of displays between paired birds is primitive and desultory. Males collect most material for the nest, which the female builds while she guards it from theft by other males; so strong is the male's drive to gather twigs at this stage that if his mate is driven away a male will even "automatically" rob twigs from his own nest.

The female's single white egg weighs 5–14 percent of the female's weight, and is incubated by both birds for a total of 6–8 weeks in shifts of up to 12 days at a time. The young chick is born naked and grows a black cape of feathers on the back while white down begins to cover the rest of the body. It grows as slowly as any seabird, spending five to six months in the nest and remaining dependent on its parents for food for several months more—over a year in one case. Frigates first breed probably at about seven years, and their reproductive output is so low that adults must live 25 years on average.

A successful breeding attempt takes more than 12 months, so adults that rear young one year cannot breed the next; thus like some of the larger albatrosses most frigate-birds probably breed successfully only in alternate years. They cannot return to the same nest-site each year, reckoning to meet their mate there, because another pair will have taken it over; the pair-bond is accordingly weak and displays—apart from at the initial frenzied courtship stage—are vestigial.

One species, the Magnificent frigatebird, shows slight but illuminating differences from the family pattern. It feeds closer inshore than the other species and apparently has a more reliable food supply, for not only are incubation shifts shorter than in any other frigate (averaging 1 day or less), but when the chick is about 100 days old the male deserts the colony leaving the female to raise their chick unaided. Probably he goes away to molt before returning for another breeding attempt with a different female, while his previous mate is still feeding their offspring, but this unique division of resources between the sexes remains to be proved with marked birds.

AWD

Darters are large slender waterbirds, somewhat like a cross between a heron and a cormorant. Head, neck and wings are heronlike, while plumage patterns, feather structure, rump and feet are cormorant-like. Darters differ from other water birds in having very long tails with corrugated outer tail feathers. They occur where there are quiet, waters in tropical, subtropical and warm temperate parts of America, Africa, Madagascar, Asia and Australasia.

The bill is dagger-shaped with each mandible having a cutting edge. The front end of this is serrated or saw-like as in gannets, boobies and tropicbirds. The bill does not have a terminal hook (unlike shags and cormorants). The head is very small, long and slender. The neck is thin and G-shaped. To reduce buoyancy the body plumage is permeable to water, as it is also in shags and cormorants. The legs are short and stout with long toes, all four of which are united in a web as in the other members of the order. Plumage patterns vary between species, sexes, ages and individuals. All are dark above. Long slender scapular and mantle covert feathers have silver, white, gray or light brown streaks, more marked in adults than in immatures. Males are blacker than females, and immatures paler than adults, mainly on the head, neck and underparts. All have dark tails. As in ducks and rails all flight feathers of the wings are shed at the same time and darters then are flightless. The tail feathers are shed gradually.

Darters are also adapted for soaring on thermal updrafts. Because of their long tails when gliding they look like flying crosses. They are further adapted for moving slowly underwater. They submerge slowly and often swim with only their head and neck out of the water, thus looking like a swimming snake, hence the popular name "snakebird." They stalk their prey underwater, often moving very slowly with spread wings and tail and coiled neck. Between the eighth and ninth neck vertebrae there is a special hinge mechanism which enables the neck to dart forward and snap up insects at the water surface, and to stab fish in the side

◄ **Different uses for the gular pouch.** In the order of Pelecaniformes the two families with the most developed throat pouches are the pelicans and frigatebirds. Whereas pelicans use their pouches for catching food, in male frigatebirds they are only inflated to attract a mate, in which this Great frigatebird has succeeded.

▼ **A passion for lakes.** For stalking prey underwater darters prefer quiet water. Though they can be found in a variety of aqueous habitats, lakes satisfy several important criteria to perfection: they provide a bounteous supply of prey, still water, vast areas free of underwater impediments and plenty of lakeside trees and islets on which to build nests. Large numbers of darters live on the natural lakes of several continents, and are quick to colonize man-made lakes. This colony of African darters lies on Lake Naivasha in Kenya.

Piracy by Frigatebirds

Weak legs, tiny feet and non-waterproof plumage restrict frigatebirds to feeding at, or above, the surface of the sea. Their feeding technique is a spectacular swoop to just above the surface, the bill snapping down and back to pluck a flying fish or squid from the jaws of a pursuing tuna. They use the same method to pick up floating nest material, and can snatch a twig from glass-calm water without making a ripple. It takes years to perfect the technique sufficiently for a frigate to be able to take time off, as it were, to breed, and it is not surprising that some of them take the shortcut of waiting for other birds to catch the food and then robbing. This piratical behavior is so conspicuous around some colonies that frigates have the reputation of acquiring most of their food this way, but usually it is mostly young birds, or individual specialists, which force other birds to disgorge their prey. Adult males also chase birds—often of their own species—to rob them of nest material. As a feeding technique piracy is especially valuable to frigates because the depth at which they can feed for themselves is so limited; by robbing species which can dive below the surface, they effectively increase the depth of water they can exploit. AWD

with the bill slightly open. A stabbed fish is usually shaken loose, flipped into the air and swallowed head first. The same darting and stabbing mechanism is used in defense to stab at the eyes of predators and unwary human molesters.

The comfort movements of darters (ie movements designed to put the feathers in place) are like those of other birds and include also a spread-eagle extension of the wings, similar to that of cormorants and some species of shag.

Darters are more territorial than other kinds of pelecaniform birds, and may defend not only small resting and nesting sites but substantial feeding, resting and nesting areas. They do, however, intermingle with other kinds of water birds at roosts and nesting colonies. Long-distance flights are usually made by "spiraling up" on thermal updrafts and then gliding down to the next updraft. When taking off from water both feet kick together as in other pelican-like birds. Sometimes they climb up trees and bushes before takeoff.

Breeding starts with a male selecting a nest-site and claiming a territory round it, which may even include as much as a whole tree. He decorates his nest-site with a few fresh green leafy twigs, and displays to attract his mate and to ward off other darters from his territory, but not to repel other species of birds. Females select a displaying male and his nest-site including its approaches. The male's advertisements include wing-waving in which the partly closed wings are alternately raised, and twig-grasping, in which a nearby twig or stick is grabbed with the bill and shaken vigorously. After pair-formation the female builds the nest with material brought to it mainly by the male. Breeding may occur at any time during the year.

New nests consist of a base of mainly green twigs, a cup of about 150 dry sticks and a lining of leaves. Often an old nest is used as a base. The nest is usually built in the fork of a tree branch over water, but sometimes in bushes or reeds; it is always near water.

The first egg is laid 2 to 3 days after the start of a new nest by a pair, and subsequent eggs laid at intervals of 1 to 3 days. Incubation starts as soon as the first egg is laid and lasts for 26–30 days (average 28 days). Eggs in a clutch hatch at intervals of 1–4 days. The parents take turns in guarding the nest, from the start of building until the chicks are at least one week old. Relief takes place at least three times a day, usually at dawn, at noon and at dusk. At the nest-site the parents greet each other with several recognition displays by the bird on the nest and signals by the bird outside the nest before departure and before arrival. Some of these displays are very similar to those of other pelecaniform birds and herons. As long as the chicks are at the nest they are guarded, even during the night.

The chicks are fed a fluid of partly digested fish which flows down the inside of the upper bill. Larger chicks take food directly from the parent's throat. Small chicks are fed six to nine times a day. When they are two weeks old they are fed twice a day. When they are five weeks old they are fed only once a day.

Darters only incidentally come into conflict with man. None of the four species is in immediate danger of extinction. Locally darters depend on the availability of suitable waters to fish in. They readily colonize man-made lakes, and in New Guinea they increased in numbers following the introduction of the African fish *Tilapia* to the southern lowlands. Some darters become caught in nets set for fish. In Southeast Asia darters have been used for fishing in a manner similar to that practised by cormorants there and elsewhere. GFvT

HERONS AND BITTERNS

Family: Ardeidae
Order: Ciconiiformes (suborder Ardeae).
Sixty species in 17 genera.
Distribution: worldwide but absent from high
latitudes.

▶ **The Japanese night heron,** a relation of the cosmopolitan Black-crowned night heron. In the breeding season night herons feed during the day as well as at night.

Ⅰ N Europe and North America herons steal
fish from ornamental ponds in suburban back gardens and have learned to raid fish farms whenever they are left unprotected. In tropical rice-growing countries they feed on insects and amphibians and greatly benefit the hard-pressed farmers. This highly diverse and adaptable family of birds can be either harmful or beneficial to man. Unfortunately, their fish-stealing habits have led to much persecution.

Herons are long-billed and long-legged wading birds, with short tails and long, broad wings. All are highly specialized predators adapted for the capture of live (usually aquatic) prey, which is often large compared with the heron. Prey are stalked with a variety of techniques, but always ending with a rapid stab to catch the animal. They preen themselves using special feathers that crumble to a powder which is rubbed into the other feathers. The claw of the third toe is flattened for combing out the powder.

The **day herons** show a tremendous range of form, coloration and behavior patterns, from the huge Goliath heron to the smaller egrets and the Squacco heron. Some are black, others white, while some, such as the Chestnut-bellied heron, are very brightly colored. Some breed singly, while many come together in huge colonies, and on the feeding grounds some species are highly territorial, while others feed together in flocks.

The best-known and most widespread heron in the Old World is the Gray heron, most northerly populations of which migrate southward during the winter to find ice-free waters. Its equivalent in the New World is the Great blue heron, which breeds as far north in Canada as the Great Lakes and south to Honduras and the Caribbean. In Trinidad and South America, this

---

The Heron Family   ☑ Vulnerable.

Day herons
Subfamily: Ardeinae (tribe Ardeini)
Thirty-four species in 8 genera.

Worldwide except at high altitudes. Temperate and tropical areas near fresh or salt waters. Size: 15–55in (39–140cm); males usually larger than females. Plumage: a wide variety, ranging from pure white in many egret species, to bright chestnut and green in the Chestnut-bellied heron. Geographical variations in some species are very marked. Voice: a loud croak, grunt or hiss. Many are silent outside the breeding season, but in colonies of breeding birds the general hubbub of sound is quite loud. Nests: mostly in trees (some on ground) and most species colonial nesters. Eggs: 2–7, usually pale blue, sometimes white; incubation period 18–30 days; nestling period 35–50 days. Diet: mainly fish, amphibians, small mammals, birds and insects. Species include: **Cattle egret** (*Bubulcus ibis*), **Chestnut-bellied heron** (*Agamia agami*), **Chinese** or **Swinhoe's egret** (*Egretta eulophotes*) ☑, **Cocoi heron** (*Ardea cocoi*), **Goliath heron** (*A. goliath*), **Gray heron** (*A. cinerea*),

Great blue heron (*A. herodius*), **Green-backed heron** (*Butorides striatus*), **Squacco heron** (*Ardeola ralloides*).

Night herons
Subfamily: Ardeinae (tribe Nycticoracini)
Eight species in 3 genera.

N and S America, Europe, Africa, Asia. Wetlands, marshy areas, mangroves and woodlands near water. Size: 20–28in (50–70cm) long, weight 21–28oz (600–800g); sexes similar. Plumage: usually contrasting gray and black or brown and black; sexes similar; juveniles speckled brown. Nests: in trees, bushes or occasionally in reedbeds. Eggs: 2–5, white or bluish-white; incubation period 21–26 days; nestling period 6–8 weeks. Diet: omnivorous; mainly fish and small birds and mammals. Species include: **Black-crowned night heron** (*Nycticorax nycticorax*), **Boat-billed heron** (*Cochlearius cochlearius*), **Japanese night heron** (*Gorsachius goisagi*), **Nankeen** or **Rufous night heron** (*Nycticorax caledonicus*).

Tiger herons
Subfamily: Ardeinae (tribe Tigrinorthini)
Six species in 4 genera.

New Guinea, W Africa, C and S America. Marshlands, wetland forests in the tropics. Size: mostly 24–32in (60–80cm) long; males generally larger than females; Zigzag heron only 12in (30cm). Plumage: brown, barred and striped in concealment patterns. Voice: a bittern-like "boom." Nests: usually in trees overhanging water. Eggs: usually 1 or 2, whitish, blotched red. Diet: fish, amphibians. Species include: **White-crested tiger heron** (*Tigriornis leucolophus*), **Zigzag heron** (*Zebrilus undulatus*).

Large bitterns
Subfamily: Botaurinae
Four species of the genus *Botaurus*.

One species each in Eurasia, Australia, N America, S America. Reedbeds. Size: 24–34in (60–85cm) long, weight 14–67oz (400–1,900g); males usually larger than females. Plumage: tawny brown, streaked

black; sexes similar. Eggs: usually 3–6, olive brown; incubation period 25 days; nestling period 40–55 days. Diet: fish, amphibians, small mammals, insects. Species: **American bittern** (*B. lentiginosus*), **Australian bittern** (*B. poiciloptilus*), **Eurasian bittern** (*B. stellaris*), **South American bittern** (*B. pinnatus*).

Small bitterns
Subfamily: Botaurinae
Eight species of the genus *Ixobrychus*.

Worldwide. Reedbeds, marshy grasslands. Size: 11–23in (27–58cm) long, weight 3.5–7oz (100–200g). Plumage: cream, tawny chestnut, brown and black; sexes markedly different, with males showing more contrast (black/brown and cream) than females (creamy-brown, streaked black). Eggs: usually 3–6, white or pale blue-green; weight 0.35–0.5oz (10–15g); incubation period 14–20 days; nestling period 28–30 days. Species include: **Black bittern** (*I. flavicollis*), **Least bittern** (*I. exilis*), **Little bittern** (*I. minutus*).

▲ **A pair of Purple herons** with young among the reeds. More slender than Gray herons, Purple herons (*Ardea purpurea*) forage in swamps and usually nest in reedbeds.

▶ **Poised to stab,** OVERLEAF a Gray heron waits at the water's edge, its neck held coiled into an S-shape, ready to shoot out when prey is spotted.

heron is replaced by the Cocoi heron, which, though widespread, is by no means as common as the other two species, nor has it developed distinct local races as have the Gray and Great blue herons.

These large herons have strong bills. When they fly they tuck in their long necks but let their long legs trail out behind them. Their wing beat is slow, but they are capable of flying very long distances.

All three species have blue, gray or blackish heads and bodies with some white and heavily marked white necks. The bills and legs vary in color according to the season, from yellow to dark brown, and during the brief period of courtship turn to deep pink or red. Long plumes on the head, neck, breast and back develop well before the breeding season, assuming their most luxurious color, length and texture when courtship commences.

Just as the plumage varies from light gray basic plumes in the Gray Heron to various shades of blue in the Great blue heron, so do the different races of these two species vary geographically in color and pattern of plumage. The most extreme form is the "Great white heron." Until recently, it was considered to be a separate species, but interbreeding with Great blue herons has now been proved. It is now accepted that birds living in an entirely marine tropical habitat lose much of their darker markings with age until the final plumage becomes all white, or nearly so.

The day herons all nest colonially, mostly, but not always, in trees. Sometimes they join huge colonies of mixed species of egrets, storks, ibises, spoonbills, and other water birds. When nesting is complete the young of the year fly off in all directions, although northern birds do not remain long in their summer breeding areas before moving further south in search for their very varied diet of fish, amphibians, small mammals, crustaceans and insects, as well as snakes and sometimes small birds.

It is this ability to adapt to such a wide variety of diet, as well as to make use of reed-beds, sandy beaches and even stone walls for their nests, which has enabled them to survive in an increasingly hostile environment.

Tiger herons take their name from their strikingly barred or striped plumage. They have also been called tiger-bitterns as a result of their bittern-like postures and "booming" calls. Some live in dense tropical forests, where their solitary breeding habits and camouflaged plumage have kept many aspects of their biology a mystery. Few nests have been recorded of the six species in this group, but these have always been in trees, particularly by rivers. Dates of breeding strongly suggest that river height and rainfall may be important factors in determining the onset of breeding. All species are nocturnal feeders.

Night herons are very stocky birds with relatively short, thick bills and short legs. They are principally nocturnal feeders with large eyes but, particularly during the breeding season, they also feed by day.

The Black-crowned night heron is the most cosmopolitan of all herons, occurring in a wide range of non-arid habitats throughout the world (in Australasia it is replaced by the Nankeen night heron). It is the best-known of the night herons, being both gregarious on the feeding areas and a colonial breeder. Although an attractive bird to watch, it has the nasty habit of eating the eggs and young of other herons in the colony.

The Boat-billed heron, with its curious slipper-shaped bill, may be most closely related to the Black-crowned night heron, and occurs from Mexico south to Argentina. Recent evidence suggests that this largely nocturnal feeder captures its prey by touch rather than sight, the shrimps and small fish of its diet perhaps being sucked in by rapid bill movements.

Both groups of **bitterns** are solitary, mainly daytime feeders, stalking their prey with great stealth. Most have brown plumage, often very heavily streaked to camouflage them in their reedbed habitats. Their bills are yellowish and they have green feet. The largest are very stocky birds, while the Least bittern is the smallest heron. When disturbed, they freeze motionless, their bill pointed toward the sky.

The larger species can handle very large fish, while small fish, frogs and insects are taken by them all. The Eurasian bittern is famed for its "booming" call during the breeding season, which can be heard from distances up to 3mi (5km) away. The eggs are laid in a nest of reeds which is usually suspended over open water. The chicks leave the nest some time before fledging, and clamber out in the reeds.

Many different styles of breeding can be seen among the heron family. Most species are monogamous, the pair-bond being of at least seasonal duration. The Eurasian bittern male, however, may mate with up to five females during a single breeding season, and in such cases probably takes no part in incubation or raising the young. Most bitterns are solitary nesters, while egrets and some herons nest colonially, sometimes in huge numbers. On the feeding areas they also show a wide range of habits, some such as the bitterns being solitary, while many of the other species are highly gregarious, congregating in enormous numbers in good feeding places.

Breeding is often timed to coincide with peaks in food abundance. Nests are simply constructed of twigs or reeds, often being no more than a simple platform on which to lay eggs. Most species start incubation immediately after the first egg has been laid,

resulting in the eggs hatching over a period of time. This gives the first chick a great advantage over the others, and may be important in maximizing breeding success. The chicks are fed by their parents until they fledge, although many will leave their nests within a few days of hatching, to clamber around the vegetation near to the nest. All are fed by regurgitation.

Herons are very resilient—no family of birds has suffered predation on a greater scale. The ruthless slaughter of egrets at their breeding colonies to obtain the plumes for the adornment of ladies' hats caused the

▲ **Mantling.** A black heron (*Egretta ardesiaca*) creates a cowl over the water while hunting for fish. The shadow may attract fish, which may believe they are fleeing into cover, or enable the heron to see them better.

▶ **Frozen in the reeds,** a Eurasian bittern on its nest demonstrates its brilliantly effective camouflage. When the neck is held upright its markings blend perfectly with the reeds.

Herons and Fish Farming

Gone are the days when the wily wild trout was stalked by the fisherman along the streams of Britain and Ireland or in the Great Lakes and the rivers of North America. Today's sportsman fishes from a river stocked with fish specially reared on a farm and some species of trout, notably the North American Rainbow, are economically grown under captive conditions for the supermarket and restaurant trade. To meet this demand fish farms have sprung up quickly and often experimentally, in open ponds by the sides of rivers, or artificially created pools with no form of protection, both in Europe and America.

The highly adaptive heron was not slow to discover this rich new resource. In Britain the

Gray heron has become an expert at robbing unprotected fish farms, and defenses against it have proved extremely difficult. At most farms, predators include ospreys, cormorants, mink, gulls, kingfishers and above all human poachers, but herons as the most conspicuous visitors have taken most of the blame. Although the heron is a protected species in Britain, as elsewhere, it is nevertheless shot by fish farmers when they can prove its destructive effect.

In the late 1970s it was estimated that no fewer than 4,600 Gray herons were shot annually in England and Wales—when the adults were breeding birds, the young at the nest died of starvation. As the total breeding population of these two countries in 1979

was only 5,400 pairs, the level of the destruction clearly indicates that the species is in grave danger. When cold weather and other natural causes reduce breeding success, the additional loss due to shooting may make it impossible for the population to sustain itself as a breeding species in Britain.

Following a two-year study by the Royal Society for the Protection of Birds, carried out with the full cooperation of the majority of the country's 250 fish farms, and continuing work by other conservation bodies, inexpensive deterrents such as steeper banks, lower water levels and, most effectively, cords and chains spread around the pools have proved very successful in discouraging the herons from fishing at the farms.

death of millions of adults and young and whole populations to be wiped out. The Royal Society for the Protection of Birds in Britain and the Audubon Society in America owe their existence to the outcry caused by this devastation.

In spite of this, herons have survived and in many areas even prospered. But the wetland habitats that they require have been destroyed at a greater rate than any natural habitat other than forests.

There are some herons, however, which have not been able to adapt. Highly specialized feeders needing, as all such species do, a very special set of circumstances, have reached dangerously low numbers, but the species involved are fortunately few, and are outnumbered by the species that have expanded.

The one most endangered, the Chinese or Swinhoe's egret, has been found nesting in pitifully small numbers in Hong Kong, and this is the only known colony in the whole of China, although recent reports from North Korea indicate increasing numbers nesting on islands there. The plume hunters obviously massacred most of the birds of this species and its remnant population found difficulty in recovering. They can only feed in salt water estuaries and virtually all of these have been utilized to grow rice right down to the water's edge. Mangroves and other vegetation have been eradicated to provide high-intensity cultivated paddy fields.

This trend is noticeable in other parts of Asia, although the peoples of southern Asia and India do not cultivate as intensively as the Chinese. Small herons can live almost next door to man in villages and towns. Feeding at dusk and dawn and hiding in deep foliage, the small bitterns, the Green-backed heron, and the often tamer, confiding pond herons (*Ardeola* species) have adapted easily to populated areas. Almost every zoo and park contains its resident, free-roaming population of these birds, and many cheekily steal the food from the troughs of captive animals.

As the forests of South America have been destroyed and cattle ranching expanded, so have the African emigrant Cattle egrets prospered. Originally arriving in South America probably in the first few years of this century, this species has spread rapidly. As their numbers have risen, they have moved northward into North America, and spread throughout the plains and ranches of the USA, which only 40 years ago had never seen this aggressive little heron.

JH

STORKS AND SPOONBILLS

Families: Ciconiidae, Threskiornithidae, Scopidae, Balaenicipitidae
Order: Ciconiiformes (suborders Ciconiae, Balaenicipites).
Fifty species in 25 genera.
Distribution: see maps and table.

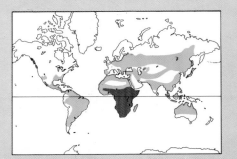

Storks   Hammerhead stork

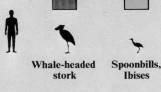

Whale-headed   Spoonbills,
stork   Ibises

▶ **Part of the furniture.** This church in Spain is festooned with nests of the White stork. Despite the ancient associations between storks and human habitations, many European villages have only a single pair of storks and even these are disappearing in many areas.

▶ **The gaping bill** of a Yellow-billed stork. Despite the scientific name (*Ibis ibis*), this is a stork not an ibis.

THE White stork has long been a symbol of pilgrimage and continuity in European and Islamic cultures. It nests happily close to people in villages, makes long migrations, but shows great fidelity to its nest-site. Such reliability has always appealed to human beings and perhaps led to the folk tale, which originated in Germany and Austria, that storks deliver babies. At any rate, storks are a reassuring presence.

Storks are large to very large wading birds having long legs, long bills, a stately upright stance and striding gait. They are birds of wetlands and water margins, as well as fields and savannas. They prefer warm continental climates and tend to avoid cool and damp regions. As a result, they are widespread in the tropics and subtropics, whereas few occur in temperate regions. The greatest numbers of stork species are found in tropical Africa (eight species) and tropical Asia (nine). White and Black storks are particularly widespread, nesting in Europe, East Asia, North Africa and southern Africa. Both species spend most of the year in Africa or India. The White stork inhabits cultivated countryside, whereas the Black stork tends to avoid areas of human activity.

Storks have long, broad wings and are strong fliers. They fly with their necks outstretched, except for the species of adjutants, which retract their head. Most storks alternate flapping flight with soaring in warm air-currents (thermals). Such currents are only found over land, which restricts the migration routes. Storks nonethe-less can engage in remarkable aerobatics, such as diving, plummeting from the sky, and flipping over in flight. The Black stork, having relatively narrow wings, relies more on flapping flight than on soaring.

The bills of storks are long and heavy. Most are straight but those of wood storks are downcurved, and that of the jabiru is slightly upcurved. Wood storks, adjutants, and the jabiru lack feathers on their heads. The sexes look similar, but males are noticeably larger than females. Dark irises distinguish male Black-necked and Saddle-bill storks from the yellow-eyed females. Air sacs lie under the neck skin, and the marabou and the Great adjutant have long, bare, pendent throat sacs. Juvenile plumage is dull, reaching full development over the first year. Nestlings of the otherwise white Maguari stork are black, probably as camouflage. The African open-bill stork is black, whereas the closely related Asian species is white.

The colors of the bill, together with the bare skin of the head and legs, are characteristic for each species, and they intensify during courtship. The breeding Maguari stork has a striking blue-gray bill, becoming maroon near its red face. The jabiru has a pink neck band that changes to deep scarlet when it is excited.

Most storks feed alone but also will form large flocks when food is abundant. They walk, wade, or run about, grabbing prey with thrusts of their bills. A typical stork will walk slowly across fields with its neck extended and head down looking for prey. The White stork's diet during nesting is varied, including aquatic vertebrates, insects and earthworms. On its African winter ground, this stork is known as the Grasshopper bird because it follows locust swarms. White storks also follow mowing machines. The Black stork is more closely associated with marshy margins of streams and pools where it feeds on fishes. The White-bellied stork often hunts in large flocks, especially near grass fires and locust swarms.

The adjutants are largely scavengers and carrion-eaters. They are well known for their attendance at carcasses, along with vultures and hyenas. Although not adept at tearing flesh, their size and large bills allows them to steal bits of meat from nearby vultures. Requiring over 25oz (700g) of food per day, marabou frequent predator kills, domestic stock yards, plowed fields and rubbish dumps, as well as drying pools that

Feeding by Touch

Most birds feed by sight, first observing a potential food item and then grabbing it with their bills. Storks, spoonbills and ibises also have an alternative foraging strategy, using the sense of touch rather than sight. Although all these birds can feed by sight, and some, such as the typical storks, do so customarily, spoonbills, wood and open-bill storks, the jabiru and most ibises usually feed by touch, and other species do so on occasions.

When a bird feeds by touch, it responds when an unseen prey animal encounters its open bill by immediately snapping it shut. In the American wood stork, this happens within 25 milliseconds, one of the fastest reflexes among vertebrates. Touch-feeding is probably facilitated in part by sensitive touch receptors under the horny covering of the bill. Or the bill snap may be stimulated by the jaw muscle being stretched by a prey item. Feeding by touch can be remarkably effective, and permits feeding in very turbid water, muddy pools, dense underwater vegetation or at night.

contain the natural prey necessary to raise young. Marabou are attracted from great distances to grass fires, where they march along the fire front. The size range of their prey varies greatly. Marabous stand at termite mounds eating swarming insects, but also take quite large prey, killing young crocodiles, young and adult flamingos, and small mammals. The Greater adjutant was formerly common in Indian cities, where it consumed refuse that included human corpses.

The four species of wood storks feed by touch, wading slowly with their partially opened bills inserted in shallow water (see box). The bill of the open-bill storks is used for dealing with mollusks, especially large water snails. The bill tip is inserted into the opening of the shell, cutting the snail's muscle, which permits extraction of the body. An open-bill may ride on a swimming hippopotamus to capture the snails it stirs up. The Black-necked stork sometimes feeds by running back and forth, jumping and wing-flashing. The largest New World stork, the jabiru, feeds by touch, wading slowly and periodically inserting its open bill into the water.

By soaring, storks can forage long distances from their colonies and roosts. The White stork, wood storks and adjutants are particularly adept at reaching high altitudes, and then gliding toward distant feeding sites. This behavior helps birds locate places of concentrated food, where many birds may forage together. In East Africa as many as seven species of storks may feed in the same location.

Most storks undertake seasonal population movement; several species (eg the White-bellied stork from North to South Africa) migrate across the equator. The migrations of the European storks have been known since biblical times. European White storks use two migratory routes, one down the Iberian Peninsula, the other across the Middle East through Egypt, both avoiding the long sea crossing of the Mediterranean. All storks, even those from Europe and Asia, therefore spend most of their year in the tropics; some yearling White storks remain in Africa throughout their first summer. The population movements of other species are less long-distance migrations than population shifts in response to feeding conditions and rainfall patterns.

The nesting cycle of all storks is strongly seasonal, apparently determined by food supplies. Only the White and Black storks regularly leave the tropics to nest, during the temperate spring and summer. The American wood stork nests during the dry season when prey are concentrated in drying pools and are easily captured using touch to guide them (see box). Other species of wood storks nest during the wet season, when most food is available in their situation. The marabou nests in the dry season when carrion and drying pools become available, while the White-bellied stork is

▼ **Representative species of storks and spoonbills.** (**1**) Roseate spoonbill (*Platalea ajaja*), showing the broad, flattened bill characteristic of spoonbills. (**2**) Black stork (*Ciconia nigra*), a species similar in many ways to the White stork, but which lives in more wooded areas. (**3**) Whale-headed stork (*Balaeniceps rex*) in its freshwater swamp habitat. (**4**) Hammerhead (*Scopus umbretta*), showing the extreme wedge-shaped head that gives it its name. (**5**) Marabou (*Leptoptilos crumeniferus*) with its large throat pouch. (**6**) Glossy ibis (*Plegadis falcinellus*). (**7**) Sacred ibis (*Threskiornis aethiopica*), a species that was revered in Ancient Egypt. (**8**) White stork (*Ciconia ciconia*) performing the "Up-Down" display on the nest.

considered a "rain bringer:" in Ethiopia it nests during the first heavy rains, which produce a flush of its insect food.

Wood stork colonies may exceed tens of thousands of nests, whereas many European villages have only a single White stork family nesting there. Most storks nest in trees, but they may also use cliffs or nest on the ground. Non-colonial tropical species, such as Saddle-bill storks, may remain paired year-round, and White storks often re-pair because both birds are attracted to the nest of the previous year. Nests are situated near sites providing suitable food supplies; drying pools for American wood storks; carrion-producing rangeland for marabou; agricultural fields for White storks.

The nest site, selected by the male, is defended against all intruders. The male gives advertisement displays, and the attracted female responds with appeasement behavior (see pp74–75). Differing between the species, advertisements may consist of up-down movements, calls and bill-clattering. In its extreme form, a stork bends its neck backwards until its head touches its back. In some species, this posture forms a resonance chamber in the throat that amplifies the sound of snapping its two mandibles.

Even newly hatched young behave in this way. Both parents incubate and feed the relatively helpless young by regurgitating food onto the nest floor. Storks may also regurgitate water over their eggs and young, presumably to cool them.

Nesting success is determined by prey availability and weather conditions. Wood storks only fledge young when high densities of food remain available throughout the entire nesting season. White stork nesting success is poor in years or locations having very high rainfall.

Some populations of storks have undergone massive population decreases. As a harbinger of good fortune and many children, the White stork has been protected in Europe for centuries, and has been censused longer than any other bird. Nonetheless, between 1900 and 1958, western European populations decreased by 80 percent, and by 92 percent between 1900 and 1973. Storks no longer nest in Sweden or Switzerland, and occur only in small numbers in other countries. The reasons for the decrease are not certain, but the following factors have been suggested: cooler and wetter summers; loss of nest-sites; pesticide poisoning; hunting on the winter grounds; changing agricultural practices. The last hypothesis is of interest in that it is possible that storks had previously increased in Europe following deforestation; populations have decreased as modern agriculture has destroyed more and more foraging sites. Hunting pressure in wintering areas in Africa is also certainly an important cause of their decrease.

The Greater adjutant population has been critically reduced throughout its range. The Milky stork, confined to the mangrove forests of southeast Asia, is in jeopardy because of habitat destruction. Some species, such as the Black-necked stork, are rare over wide ranges, while others such as the Asian open-bill stork, are numerous, but only locally. Although remaining abundant in South and Central America, the American wood stork has decreased in southern Florida, because of ecological changes in the vast

► **The Saddle-bill stork,** a large species found from Ethiopia and Senegal to South Africa.

► **Unusually elegant** and serene for fledglings, BELOW three young White storks bask on their nest. They will almost certainly return close to this same nest-site after their first migration.

The 4 Families of Storks and Spoonbills
E Endangered. V Vulnerable. R Rare.

Storks
Family: Ciconiidae
Seventeen species in 9 genera.
Southern N America, S America, Africa, Eurasia, Australia, East Indies. Habitat: marshes, savannas and fields. Size: 30–60in (75–150cm) long; to 4–20lb (2–9kg); 57–126in (145–320cm) wingspan. Plumage: chiefly white, gray and black, some with pink tinge. Voice: bill-clatter; various species also hiss, moo, whistle, peep and grunt. Nests: platforms made of sticks in trees or on cliffs; one species nests on buildings. Eggs: usually 3–5 (the Saddle-bill stork lays one), white becoming stained with age; incubation period 30–50 days; nestling period 7–18 weeks. Diet: fish, insects, carrion, depending on species.

Species include: **African open-bill stork** (*Anastomus lamelligerus*), **American wood stork** (*Mycteria americana*), **Asian open-bill stork** (*Anastomus oscitans*), **Black-necked stork** (*Xenorhynchus asiaticus*), **Black stork** (*Ciconia nigra*), **Greater adjutant stork** (*Leptoptilos dubius*), **Jabiru stork** (*Jabiru mycteria*), **Lesser adjutant stork** (*Leptoptilos javanicus*), **Maguari stork** (*Euxenura maguari*), **marabou** (*Leptoptilos crumeniferus*), **Milky stork** V (*Ibis cinereus*), **Painted stork** (*Ibis leucocephalus*), **Saddle-bill stork** (*Ephippiorhynchus senegalensis*), **White-bellied stork** (*Ciconia abdimii*),

White-necked stork or **Woolly-necked stork** (*C. episcopus*), **White stork** (*C. ciconia*), **Yellow-billed stork** (*Ibis ibis*).

Spoonbills and ibises
Family: Threskiornithidae
Thirty-one species in 14 genera.
Southern N America, S America, southern Europe and Asia, Africa, Australia. Habitat: marshes, lake shores, plains, savannas. Size: 19–43in (48–110cm) long. Plumage: chiefly white, brown, or glossy black; the Scarlet ibis is red; the Roseate spoonbill is pink. Some, eg the Sacred ibis, the Straw-necked ibis, have modified display plumes on their neck, back or crest. Voice: honks, croaks; can bill clatter; one ibis yelps. Nests: platforms of sticks or reeds in trees, marsh plants, or on cliffs, often with an inner lining of leaves. Eggs: usually 2–5; white or blue, some with darker spots; incubation period about 21 days; nestling period 20–30 days. Diet: insects, crustaceans, carrion and other animal material.

Species include: **African spoonbill** (*Platalea alba*), **American white ibis** (*Eudocimus albus*), **Australian white ibis** (*Threskiornis molucca*), **Bald ibis** R (*Geronticus calvus*), **Black-faced spoonbill** (*Platalea minor*), **Black ibis** (*P. papillosa*), **Buff-necked ibis** (*Theristicus caudatus*), **Giant ibis** R (*Pseudibis gigantea*), **Glossy ibis** (*Plegadis falcinellus*), **Green ibis** (*Mesembrinibis cayennensis*), **hadada** (*Bostrychia hagedash*), **Hermit ibis** or **waldrapp** E (*Geronticus eremita*), **Japanese ibis** E (*Nipponia nippon*), **Oriental ibis** (*Threskiornis melanocephala*), **Puna ibis** (*Plegadis ridgway*), **Roseate spoonbill** (*Platalea ajaja*), **Royal spoonbill** (*Platalea regia*), **Sacred ibis** (*Threskiornis aethiopica*), **Scarlet ibis** (*Eudocimus ruber*), **Straw-necked ibis** (*Threskiornis spinicollis*), **Wattled ibis** (*Bostrychia carunculata*), **White-faced ibis** (*Plegadis chihi*), **White spoonbill** (*Platalea leucorodia*), **Yellow-billed spoonbill** (*P. flavipes*). Total threatened species: 6.

Hammerhead
Family: Scopidae
Sole species *Scopus umbretta*.
Hammerhead, hamerkop, or Hammerhead stork.

Africa south of the Sahara. Habitat: found near water; even small ponds are sufficient. Prefers open woodland to forest. During and after rains it may move seasonally to areas which are normally dry. Size: length about 20in (50cm). Plumage: dark brown; bill and legs black. Voice: usually silent, but utters wide range of high notes when flying or during courtship. Nests: an enormous domed structure built of sticks, weeds, grass, usually in a tree overhanging water at varying heights; the domed entrance is plastered with mud. Eggs: 3–7, white becoming mud-stained; average weight 0.95oz (27.6g); incubation period 30 days. Diet: amphibians, especially frogs, but also fish and invertebrates. Often scavenges near human habitation.

Whale-headed stork
Family: Balaenicipitidae
Sole species *Balaeniceps rex*.
Whale-headed stork or shoebill.

Swamplands of southern Sudan and western Ethiopia south through Uganda to southern Zaire and Zambia. Possibly to be seen in western Kenya (rarely) and more recently in Botswana. Habitat: fresh water swamps with tall vegetation of reeds, tall grass and papyrus. Feeds in pools and channels within the swamp. Size: length about 47in (120cm). Plumage: head gray with lighter crown. Slate gray wings with black tips. Belly nearly white. Adult bill color varies between pink and yellow, immature birds being darker. Legs black. Voice: usually silent. Frequent bill-clattering; at the nest, gives a high "gull-like" mew. Nests: on floating vegetation in deep water; sometimes on termite mounds which have become flooded. A large flat nest of reeds and other vegetation collected from nearby. Eggs: 1–3, usually 2, white. Diet: mainly fish, amphibians and reptiles, but also small birds and mammals.

Everglades marsh. The inability to obtain sufficient food to raise their young has caused continuous reproductive failure in this stork population. Thus protection of wetland habitat, and other feeding sites, is essential for conservation of storks.   JAK

Ibises and spoonbills are medium-sized birds having distinctive down-curved or flattened bills. Most species are highly social, nesting, feeding, and flying in large groups. A formation of ibises gliding to their chosen night roost before a setting sun is a memorable sight. In most areas several species occur together: as many as seven in the Venezuelan *llanos*.

The most distinctive features of these birds are their bills. Ibises have long, thin, down-curved bills; spoonbills have long, broad bills, flattened at the tip. Both characteristically lack feathers on their faces; the Sacred ibis lacks feathers over its entire head and neck. Most are uniformly colored and have distinctive ornamentations, such as the elongated secondary feathers of the Sacred ibis, bright red skin color of the American white ibis, or the colored head tubercles of the Black ibis. Males are generally larger than females. The juveniles of White and Scarlet ibises have gray-brown backs for a year.

Ibises are an ancient group, the fossil record of which goes back 60 million years. The divergence of spoonbills from ibises represents the fundamental radiation within the group. Although fossils are few,

subfossils from Hawaii and Jamaica demonstrate the repeated evolution of flightlessness on islands. These island representatives may have become extinct in relatively recent times, because of man.

As birds of marshes, swamps, and savannas, both ibises and spoonbills feed on a variety of insects, frogs, crustaceans and fishes. Both feed primarily by touch rather than by sight (see p65). Ibises use their long bill for probing in soft mud, holes or under plants. Ibis species that are typically aquatic tend to have longer bills than terrestrial species. They catch slow moving or bottom-dwelling prey. The American White ibis specializes in eating crayfish and fiddler crabs; the Hermit ibis feeds on terrestrial insects and worms; the Sacred ibis often feeds on carrion scraps and associated insects. It also eats pelican and crocodile eggs broken by predators. Spoonbills usually swing their open bill from side to side in the water. The width of its bill is an aid for capturing prey, especially fish and aquatic insects.

Most species nest colonially, some at sites that can include tens of thousands of birds. Other species, such as the hadada, nest in isolation, but even this species is social when not breeding.

The nesting cycle is usually two to three months, with re-nesting sometimes occurring after a failure. Most species place their nests in bushes, but considerable variability occurs in placement. The American White

ibis nests on trees, bushes, reeds, or on the ground in marshes and swamps. Hermit and Bald ibises nest on cliffs; the hadada sometimes nests on telegraph poles. Black ibises take over raptor nests. The Buff-necked ibis nests in single pairs in palm trees in Venezuela, on cliffs in the puna and on the ground in colonies in Argentina. Isolated places, such as trees or islands surrounded by open water or marsh, are often chosen for nesting, as ground predators are less likely to occur there.

During pair formation, coloration and display accessories, such as the throat pouch of the American White ibis and black plumes of the Sacred ibis, are at their seasonal peak. In the few species studied, the male chooses a potential nest-site from which it advertises, using bill pointing and bowing displays. Females attempt to land near the male, who at first repulses them. When he accepts a female, the pair engages in mutual bowing and display preening. Solitary species use loud vocalizations to maintain contact, and may remain paired all year round. The common name of the hadada reflects its distinctive call.

The male usually gathers nest materials, which he ritually presents to the female, and both sexes defend the nest-site. Copulation takes place at the nest, and in some species "extra-marital" copulations are frequent. Both sexes incubate and feed the young regurgitated food, which the nestling

▲ **A flock of African spoonbills.** In flight, when the bill is seen side-on, spoonbills and ibises look similar. Both will travel long distances to find food when their swamps and marshes dry up.

◄ **As if dyed** from head to rump, a group of Scarlet ibises in their resplendent plumage, roosting in a tree. They are joined here by a few American white ibises, whose distribution extends north into the southern USA.

Nomadic Waders

Several species of ibises show remarkable nomadic tendencies. The Straw-necked ibis and White ibis of Australia depend on aquatic food made available by suitable water conditions. During droughts, both species disperse widely, but they concentrate to nest in intermittently flooded swamps after heavy rains bring forth an abundant supply of invertebrate food. Because such rains are unpredictable in their location, season and amount, nomadic migrations permit ibises to locate those water conditions suitable for breeding. As a result, except in areas of dependable food supplies, the size and location of ibis colonies vary.

The American white ibis undertakes similar population movements. Foraging flocks of White ibis wander over the vast inland marshes of southern Florida during the course

of a year, remaining in areas where water is sufficiently shallow for foraging. As the flooded area contracts in the dry season, ibis follow the receding water, establishing a succession of night roosts near current feeding grounds. This population shift enables ibises to use most of the available habitat during the course of the year. If food supplies persist, such a roost may become a breeding colony.

Other characteristics also adapt ibises for nomadic life. They can rapidly begin nesting when conditions are suitable and can complete nesting within 2–3 months. Flock-feeding assists the birds in finding and using sites of short-lived food supplies. A variable nesting schedule and an ability to skip nesting completely are also adaptations of some ibises to make the best use of variable food supplies. As a result, some species are able to occupy highly changeable habitats and to maintain large populations.

obtains by inserting its bill down the parent's gullet. Young later leave the nest and, in colonial species, roost in groups. Fledging success depends on food supplies. Nesting failure at any stage is not uncommon when food supplies give out.

As a result of dependence on temporarily variable food supplies, local conditions determine breeding seasons. For example, the Sacred ibis has quite different breeding schedules in various parts of Africa, coinciding with local seasonal rainfall patterns. The nesting schedule in one area may vary from year to year. The Australian White ibis is particularly nomadic, nesting when and where water conditions become suitable (see box). In each case, water conditions determine food availability. Not all species in an area nest at the same time. In

Venezuela, the Green ibis nests in the wet season, but the Buff-necked ibis nests in the dry, presumably because of different choices of prey, although such dietary differences have not been established.

The migrations of ibises have figured prominently in the annual activities of various peoples. It is possible that the occurrence of Sacred ibis along the Nile was associated with the seasonal floods crucial to farming. Similarly, along the Euphrates, the Hermit ibis's return in spring was celebrated by a festival.

The high degree of sociability of most ibises and spoonbills is exposed in flocking and coloniality. Many species fly in compact flocks or in long undulating lines, alternating flapping and gliding flight. When feeding, most species form aggregations at suitable foraging sites, often with other wading bird species. In such situations, they tolerate other birds in close proximity and often move in unison. Communal roosts are located near feeding grounds, which may be shared with herons, storks and cormorants. Specific roost sites may be temporary, lasting only as long as nearby food supplies, or may persist for years.

The conservation of ibises and spoonbills depends on their protection and habitat preservation. The Sacred ibis, a seasonal resident along the Nile for millennia, has been absent from Egypt since the first half of the 19th century. The Hermit ibis had nested in the alpine area of central Europe from at least the Stone Age into the 17th century but is now confined to small areas of North Africa and the Middle East. Hunting, despite protective laws, led to its decline, hastened by habitat change. This ibis was lost from Europe very early, and it was not until the end of the 19th century that it was found to be extant in Asia Minor. These populations total less than a thousand birds. The most endangered ibis species is the Japanese crested ibis. Fewer than two dozen individuals are known to survive in China and Japan. The species was widely distributed in these two countries until the early 20th century, and in Korea until World War II. It is possible that loss of suitable habitat—pine forests surrounded by swamp land—may have contributed to its demise. The Giant ibis, only found in lowland Southeast Asia, is also nearing extinction, and Black-faced spoonbills are becoming very scarce.   JAK

The **hammerhead**, though often called "stork," is not a close relation of that family and is a distinctive species. Usually, it has been included in the heron family, but it is sometimes linked to the flamingos because it has a free hind toe; its true taxonomic position is as yet unclear.

Usually seen in pairs, this all-brown bird is common throughout the African savanna, even feeding at pools by the roadside. Its name derives from the crest extending behind the head. The toes are partly webbed. Its short tail and huge wings enable it to glide and soar easily, which it does with its head stretched forward. Usually when disturbed it will fly only a short distance. It is a sedentary species which remains in a well-defined territory, although some pairs will move to normally dry areas when the seasonal rains fill dry holes and ditches. Wherever man-made dams or canals are built, the hammerhead will quickly arrive and if trees are not available it will build its huge nest (often several in a season) on a wall, bank, cliff or sometimes even on the ground.

Hammerheads are also to be seen in group ceremonies, usually near a nest. They can involve a number of birds together and as many as ten birds may call loudly while running round each other in circles, a male

▼ **The hammerhead's huge nest** attracts many other species. Verreaux's eagle owls have been known to take over the nest, and when completed Gray kestrels or Barn owls often evict the rightful owners. Smaller mammals such as genets sometimes take up residence. Monitor lizards will eat the eggs and snakes occupy the nests, making it dangerous to investigate too closely. Even during occupation by the hammerheads, small birds such as weaver birds, mynas and pigeons will attach their nests to the main nest. Old nests are quickly occupied by other hole-nesting birds such as the Egyptian goose, the Pygmy goose or the Knob-billed duck. Thus the presence of this species provides nesting sites for numerous species which otherwise would find no suitable place for breeding in the area.

▲ **The flaking bill** of a Whale-headed stork. The huge bill is adapted for feeding on fish such as lungfish and gars and also frogs and perhaps young turtles, crocodiles and small mammals.

and the body plumage within a month. While both birds feed the young, they leave them for long periods, presumably being enabled to do so because of the thickness of the nest walls which protect them. When the young are fully fledged, they remain near the nest for another month, using it to roost in at night.

A disproportionately large bill and head give the **Whale-headed stork** both its name and an oddly unbalanced look. This large stork-like bird has some of the characteristics of herons, storks and pelicans, but has no direct affinity to any of these families, so is placed in a family of its own.

The Whale-headed stork is bulky and slow moving; when it feeds it stands with its bill, which is hooked at the end, pointed downwards. It then stretches its neck and hurls itself forward with wings outstretched and gulps its prey. The prey is ground apart by a scissoring action of the mandibles and accompanying vegetation is discarded. A large drink of water is taken after the meal is consumed.

The Whale-headed stork seldom travels far, preferring a favorite piece of marsh in which to fish, and not moving unless forced to do so by changing water conditions. It does, however, fly up on the thermals like a stork, though it tucks in its neck like a heron. It usually fishes alone, but will join with others of its own species, as well as herons and storks, in feeding in pools which are drying out, and where the large fish stocks can be easily harvested.

Both sexes incubate the eggs, often standing to turn them with bill or feet, and in hot weather pouring beakfuls of water over them to cool them. Greeting at the nest by a pair is done by bill clattering and bowing in a manner similar to that of storks. The young have silvery-gray down. Their heads are large, but the bill takes some time to develop its extraordinary shape. Early feeding of the chick is by regurgitating food onto the floor of the nest, but later whole prey are left and the chick swallows them whole. It is most unusual for more than one Whale-headed stork chick to be successfully reared each year.

Like many highly specialized large birds which require very special habitats, the Whale-headed stork is becoming dangerously low in numbers. While it is not persecuted by native populations, the drainage of wetlands, disturbance by cattle and the robbing of nests by zoos has reduced its numbers alarmingly and probably only 1,000–2,000 still remain over the vast area of its African habitat. JH

sometimes mounting a crouching female and sometimes pretending to copulate without actually doing so. Crests are raised, wings fluttered and a chorus of cries continues for several minutes.

True mating is usually done at a completed nest site, often on top of the nest, using displays similar to those used during the larger gathering of birds. When the eggs have been laid, both birds share incubation, although very frequently partly incubated clutches will be abandoned. When the young hatch they are covered with gray down, but quickly develop feathers, with the head and crest completed within 17 days

Up-down, Flying Around
Courtship and relationships among storks

"Advertising Sway," "Flap-Dash," "Flying Around," "Gaping," "Up-Down"—these are all names given to forms of courtship display found in storks. These gestures are as repeatable and consistent as bill-shape and plumage patterns, and can be used to assess evolutionary relationships, some gestures being considered more derived and others more primitive. The advertisement display of the White stork has been well known for centuries, and was illustrated in 13th-century manuscripts.

The most typical, and in some storks the most remarkable, courtship behavior is the *Up-Down*. It is a greeting issued when one member of a pair returns to its nest. In giving the display a stork raises then lowers its head in a characteristic stylized manner. Although present in all storks, it differs importantly among species. The head movement is usually accompanied by a vocalization, such as the bill-clattering of the typical storks. The amount of bill-clattering differs among the species of this group. The White stork has a loud, resonant bill-clatter that may last ten seconds or more; yet the Black stork clatters only infrequently. Such a difference in the display suggests that within the group of typical storks these two species are not closely related. The White stork also differs from the other typical storks in that its *Up-Down* is not accompanied by whistling. The typical storks are distinguished from other groups of species by uniquely sharing a *Head-Shaking Crouch*, in which the male crouches on its nest and shakes its head from side to side as if saying "no," which is probably also the message of the display, since it is given as another bird approaches its nest.

The *Up-Down* behavior is simplest in the wood storks. It consists mainly of raising the head and gaping the bill, then emitting hissing screams as the head and bill are lowered. The display differs among the four species, forming an evolutionary sequence. The American wood stork does not snap its bill during the display; the Yellow-billed stork gives a single or double snap; the Painted stork gives double or triple snaps; the Milky stork gives multiple snaps. The wood storks share three displays that are unique among storks: *Flying Around*, in which a male that has just accepted a female leaves its nest and flies in a circle before returning; *Gaping*, in which a bird holds its parted mandibles open; and *Display Preening*, in which the male pretends to comb the feathers on its wing with its bill. The displays of the open-bill storks strongly resemble those of wood storks, especially their simple *Up-Down* and also their copulation clattering, in which a male during copulation clatters his mandibles while knocking them against the bill of the female. Because of such resemblances, the wood storks and open-bill storks are thought to be more closely related to each other than they are to other storks. Open-bills also have a unique display, the *Advertising Sway*, in which a displaying male bends its head down between its legs and repeatedly shifts its weight from one foot to the next.

Differences in the details of the *Up-Down* display among closely related storks demonstrate important distinctions not otherwise obvious. The *Up-Down* of the adjutants includes moving the bill to vertical, accompanied by mooing and squealing. The marabou and Greater adjutant are similar-looking birds, which do not overlap in range. Their displays differ, however, in that marabous first throw their head upward and squeal with the bill near vertical, before pointing it downward and clattering loudly. The Greater adjutant clatters while the bill is pointed upward. The difference in this important pair-bonding display suggests that the birds would not interbreed should their ranges overlap, and so are best considered as separate species.

The Black-necked and Saddle-bill storks display infrequently because of their long-lasting pair bond. The *Up-Down* of the Black-necked stork is a spectacular greeting that includes rapid fluttering of fully extended wings and clattering of bills, but the head is not raised. These two species and the jabiru share a distinctive display given on the foraging grounds, the *Flap-Dash*, in which a bird dashes wildly through the water while vigorously flapping its wings.

Comparative behavioral observations have discovered distinctive traits from which relationships among the storks can be deduced. The distribution of these traits corresponds to other differences and similarities in morphology, plumage, and foraging habits, which support and confirm the relationships suggested by courtship displays. JAK

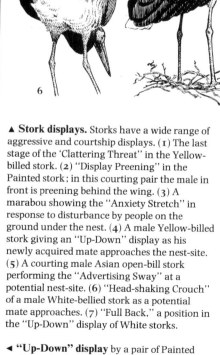

▲ **Stork displays.** Storks have a wide range of aggressive and courtship displays. (**1**) The last stage of the 'Clattering Threat" in the Yellow-billed stork. (**2**) "Display Preening" in the Painted stork; in this courting pair the male in front is preening behind the wing. (**3**) A marabou showing the "Anxiety Stretch" in response to disturbance by people on the ground under the nest. (**4**) A male Yellow-billed stork giving an "Up-Down" display as his newly acquired mate approaches the nest-site. (**5**) A courting male Asian open-bill stork performing the "Advertising Sway" at a potential nest-site. (**6**) "Head-shaking Crouch" of a male White-bellied stork as a potential mate approaches. (**7**) "Full Back," a position in the "Up-Down" display of White storks.

◄ **"Up-Down" display** by a pair of Painted storks on the nest.

FLAMINGOS

Family: Phoenicopteridae
Order: Ciconiiformes (suborder Phoenicopteri).
Four species in 3 genera.
Distribution: around the world in a wide range
of tropical and warm temperate sites, some at
high altitude.

Habitat: shallow salt or soda lagoons and lakes.
Plumage: pink, sexes similar.

Size: 31–57in (80–145cm) long
and 4.2–6.6lb (1.9–3kg), females
smaller.

Nest: mud-built mounds.
Eggs: usually single, white, weight about 3.5oz
(100g); incubation period 28 days, nestling
period 75 days.
Diet: algae and diatoms, aquatic invertebrates,
particularly crustaceans and mollusks.

Species: **James' flamingo** (*Phoenicoparrus
jamesi*), **Lesser flamingo** (*Phoeniconaias minor*),
Andean flamingo (*Phoenicoparrus andinus*).
Subspecies: **Caribbean flamingo** (*Phoenicopterus
ruber ruber*), **Chilean flamingo** (*P. r. chilensis*),
Greater flamingo (*P. r. roseus*).

▶ **Bills tucked under** ABOVE in their
characteristic style, these Caribbean flamingos
are feeding by filtering food organisms from the
water and mud taken in by their bills.

▶ **"Head Flagging"** in a group of Greater
flamingos. This is the first stage in their
ritualized group displays.

▶ **Flamingo twilight** OVERLEAF. A colony of
Greater flamingos, picked out by the late sun.
The dull brown plumage of the young birds in
the foreground contrasts markedly with the
pink-flecked white of the adults.

WHETHER flamingos are thought to be
bizarre or beautiful depends on their
numbers: individually they are rather
grotesque, but two million pink birds
massed around the edge of Lake Nakuru in
Kenya's Rift Valley make a breathtaking
spectacle.

Fossils suggest that flamingos once
ranged through Europe, North America and
Australia, as well as in areas where they are
found today, but the group now occurs only
in isolated pockets, mainly in the tropics and
sometimes at high altitudes. They are
unusual in feeding on the microscopic blue-
green algae, diatoms and invertebrates that
live in alkaline salt and soda lakes.

Flamingos have large bodies with long
legs for wading, long necks and small heads.
Their pink and crimson plumage, with black
secondary and primary wing feathers,
makes them conspicuous and unmistakable. The Caribbean flamingo is the
brightest (as are the Caribbean ibis and
spoonbill among their respective families)
and there is a single molt of the feathers of
wing and body per breeding cycle. Legs, bills
and faces are brightly colored red, pink,
orange or yellow. The rather small feet are
webbed and the birds can use these webs to
swim and to stir up debris from the mud by
trampling. Males are larger than females,
markedly so in some species, but this is the
only obvious difference between the sexes.
At hatching, the chick has gray down, a
straight, pink bill and swollen pink legs,
both of which turn black within a week.
Juveniles in first plumage are gray, with
brown and pink markings, and their legs
and bills are black. When fully grown, bills
are turned down in the middle, with the
upper jaw small and lid-like and the lower

one large and trough-like; both are fringed
and lined with filtering comb-like structures
called lamellae, and the tongue is thick and
spiny.

The feeding method of flamingos is
characteristic and peculiar. The bill is held
upside-down in the water and the tongue
acts as a piston so that water and mud are
sucked in along the whole gape and expelled
three or four times a second past the filtering
lamellae. In the small Lesser, James' and
Andean flamingos, which have deep-keeled
bills, very fine particles, such as algae and
diatoms are retained, and coarse particles
are kept out by stiff excluder lamellae. The
"shallow-keeled" Caribbean, Greater and
Chilean flamingos are larger and feed
mainly on invertebrates such as brine flies
(*Ephydra*), shrimps (*Artemia*) and mollusks
(*Cerithium*), which they obtain from the bottom mud, normally by wading in shallow
water, more rarely while swimming, and
sometimes by upending like ducks. The brilliant red color of flamingo plumage derives
from the rich sources of carotenoid pigments
(similar to the pigments of carrots) in the
algae that the birds consume either directly
or secondarily. Blue-green algae are also an
extremely rich source of protein, and dense
blooms of the planktonic algae *Spirulina
platensis* are associated with the gathering
of huge flocks of Lesser flamingos in East
Africa; success in breeding probably
depends on such blooms.

Flamingos are an ancient group, the fossil
evidence for which goes back to at least the
Miocene epoch (about 10 million years ago).
Their classification is still controversial.
Usually they have been considered a
suborder of the storks (Ciconiiformes) and
their egg-white proteins resemble those of

herons (Ardeidae). On the basis of behavior and feather lice they have seemed most like waterfowl (Anseriformes), but recently affinity with the waders (Charadriiformes) has been stressed because of supposed similarities between flamingos and the Australian banded stilt. The Caribbean flamingo seems to show more "primitive" displays than the other two subspecies of *Phoenicopterus ruber*, while the Chilean flamingo seems to be sufficiently different from the other two that it is treated, by some authorities, as a separate species. Andean and James' flamingos differ from the Lesser flamingo in having no hind toe, or "hallux", but all three have a more specialized feeding apparatus than the larger flamingos of *Phoenicopterus.*

Flamingos appear to be monogamous and can be very long-lived: 50-year-old birds are probably not unusual in the wild. The pair bond is strong and often sustained from one season to the next. They tend to be rather erratic in breeding, and whether they nest or not depends mainly upon rainfall and the effect it has on the food supply of the adult birds. The nest mound is made of mud and may be 12in (30cm) high, thus giving protection from flooding and from the often intense heat at ground level. Nests are built by male and female using a simple technique of drawing mud towards the feet with the bill. The single large chalky egg is incubated by both sexes in turn and, after hatching, the chick remains in the nest for some days. Here it is fed by its parents on a secretion from the glands of the upper digestive tract or crop (see box). The Caribbean flamingo chick can feed itself from 4–6 weeks of age but, in at least the Greater and Lesser flamingos, parental feeding continues until fledging, by which time the bill of the chick is hooked as in the adult and the youngster is capable of independent feeding. After they leave the nest, the young move into large creches which in the Lesser flamingo may contain as many as 30,000 birds; parents apparently find their own chick in the group and feed it alone, recognizing it by its calls. The young bird is fledged in about 11 weeks and gradually loses the gray juvenile color over two or three years but will not display and breed until it is fully pink. Flamingos did not nest successfully in zoos until the importance of good feather color of the adults was realized, and an effort made to increase the carotenoids in the diet. Carrots, peppers, dried shrimps and other such items were tried initially; today synthetic canthaxanthin is added to the food, and the large

Phoenicopterus flamingos are breeding more regularly in captivity.

The birds are highly gregarious at all stages of their life-history and the displaying and nesting colonies are noisy affairs. Breeding in small numbers is almost unknown; an exception is provided by the Caribbean flamingo, whose isolated population on the Galapagos islands occasionally nests in groups of only 3–5 pairs. Group display seems to bring all the birds of the colony to the same readiness to mate and thus ensures rapid and synchronized egg-laying in a potentially unstable breeding habitat.

It is interesting that the founder of systematic biology, Linnaeus, described the Caribbean flamingo as the typical flamingo

Flamingo's Milk

Two groups of birds, flamingos and pigeons, feed their young on "milk". Compared with pigeon milk, the secretion from the crop of the flamingo has somewhat less protein (8–9 percent versus 13.3–18.6 percent) and more fat (15 percent versus 6.9–12.7 percent). There is almost no carbohydrate in either case. About 1 percent of flamingo milk is made up of red blood cells whose origin is unknown. Thus bird milk is similar in nutritional value to that of mammals.

As with mammalian milk, secretion is controlled by a hormone called prolactin. In birds, the hormone causes a proliferation of the cells of the crop gland in males and females, so that both sexes feed their offspring, whereas in mammals "nursing" is only ever a female task. Flamingos have been studied extensively in captivity and it has been found that a few birds that are not parents produce milk, and even seven-week-old chicks can act as foster-feeders for smaller orphaned birds. The persistent begging calls of the youngster seem to stimulate hormone secretion. Milk is not produced until the crop is cleared of food, so that food items themselves are never regurgitated.

The crop milk of the flamingo contains initially large amounts of canthaxanthin (the pigment that colors the adult feathers), which gives the milk a bright red color. This pigment is stored in the young bird's liver and not in the down nor in the juvenile plumage, which is gray.

Parental feeding of this specialized kind seems to be an adaptation to ensure that the young obtain enough food, especially protein. The high alkalinity of the water in which the adults feed, their unusual feeding habits and bill structure, and the fact that they may nest some distance from their food source, probably encouraged the evolution of crop milk manufacture. The system is successful only because the clutch size of the flamingo is so small (usually a single egg), even smaller than in most pigeons.

◄ **Flight of the flamingo.** Chilean flamingos at 13,000ft (4,000m) high in the Andes, near the limit of their range for height.

► **Flamingo displays** are similar to the preening and stretching movements that the birds adopt in everyday activity. The displays are only more stiffly performed, more contagious amongst members of the group, and given in predictable sequences. "Head Flagging" followed by "Wing Saluting," in which a bird spreads its wings to the sides and folds them again, is common. The general effect is a flash of black in a pink field. (**1**) "Wing Salute" in Chilean flamingo. (**2**) "Wing Salute" in Greater flamingo. A 'Twist-Preen' may then follow (**3**): a Caribbean flamingo twists its neck back, flashing a wing forward to expose the black primaries, and appears to preen behind the wing with its bill. In the "Inverted Wing Salute" (**4**), given here by a Greater flamingo, the bird bends foward and the wings are flashed partly open and held above the back. Mating displays between male and female are, on the other hand, almost non-existent and quite inconspicuous.

▼ **Inelegant feeders.** All flamingos feed with their bills upside-down. These are Lesser flamingos, the smallest species.

of the family Phoenicopteridae, and not the European Greater flamingo with which one might have thought he was more familiar. Early travelers to the West Indies must have produced the specimens that he described. They also returned with myths about the incubating postures of the birds: they were said to sit while dangling their legs in front of the mud nest mounds, whereas they fold them under in exactly the same way that other birds do. The color of flamingo feathers fades gradually in sunlight and this perhaps has been one reason why large numbers have not been taken in the past for the plumage trade, but their tongues were once pickled as a rare delicacy, and flamingo fat is still considered a cure for tuberculosis by some Andean miners. The development of salt and soda extraction works has been a particular threat in various parts of the

world, but in the Camargue in southern France and Bonaire (an island in the Lesser Antilles, off the coast of Venezuela) for instance, man-made lagoons have been created by the salt industry and are being accepted by the birds with considerable success. Natural predators are few because flamingos tend to live in inhospitable places where the water is so alkaline that the lagoons are often barren of vegetation and surrounded by almost desert-like wastes.

All the flamingos are vulnerable to habitat change and exploitation. James' flamingo is rare, but the crimson Caribbean flamingo is perhaps more threatened because it breeds in only four main colonies around the Gulf of Mexico (Yucatan, Inagua, Cuba and Bonaire), and is in great demand by zoos. Many birds die when they are caught—they tend to travel badly and are susceptible to stress upon arrival. So far, the three smaller species have bred seldom or not at all in captivity, and birds are still taken from the wild for the zoo trade in regrettably large numbers. JK

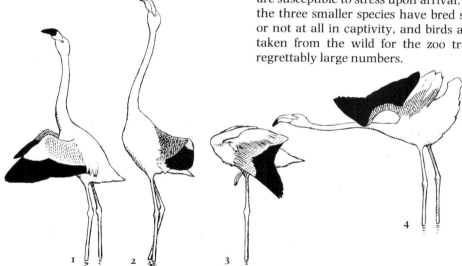

Order: Anseriformes
Families: Anatidae, Anhimidae.
One hundred and fifty-two species in 43 genera.
Distribution: worldwide except Antarctica.

Swans, Geese, Ducks   Screamers

Swans, geese and ducks

Family: Anatidae
One hundred and 49 species in 41 genera.
Total threatened species: 12.
Distribution: worldwide except Antarctica.
Habitat: chiefly coastal, freshwater wetlands.
Size: 12–59in (30–150cm) long, weight 8.8oz
(250g) to 33lb (15kg) or more.
Plumage: very variable, majority show some
white, combinations of black and white
frequent, some all white or all black; also grays,
browns and chestnut common; green or purple
gloss often on head or on wing-patch. In some
genera males bright, females dull camouflaged
brown, but sexes similar in others.
Voice: some genera very vocal (usually quack,
cackle, whistle or hiss), others mostly silent or
with soft calls connected with display.
Nests: majority a platform of vegetation,
occasionally on rocky ledge or tree crown;
some in already existing holes in trees.
Eggs: 4–14; white, creamy, pale green, blue,
unmarked; incubation 18–39 days; young
leave nest early, self-feeding except for Magpie
goose; fledging period 21–110 days.
Diet: wide variety of animals and plants,
including fish, mollusks, crustaceans, insects
and their larvae, and aquatic and terrestrial
vegetation—leaves, stems, roots and seeds.

Screamers

Family: Anhimidae
Three species in 2 genera.
Distribution: South America.
Habitat: open wet grasslands and marshes,
shallow lagoons.
Size: 28–37in (70–95cm) long, weight 4.4–
11lb (2–5kg).
Plumage: black, gray, brown; sexes similar.
Voice: loud screams.
Nests: large platform on ground near water.
Eggs: 2–6; whitish tinged buff or pale green;
incubation 40–45 days; young leave nest early,
self-feeding; fledging in 60–75 days.
Diet: vegetation.
Species: **Black-necked screamer** (*Chauna
chavaria*), **Crested screamer** (*C. torquata*),
Horned screamer (*Anhima cornuta*).

THE waterfowl (swans, geese and ducks)
have, for thousands of years, provided
man with eggs, meat and feathers. He has
hunted them, pursued them for sport, and
domesticated them. More recently, he has
become aware of the aesthetic pleasure
which they can give, and of the need to conserve both them and their habitats.

The waterfowl and the screamers are
birds of water and wetlands. Nearly all of
them nest on or beside fresh water, but
several species (eg Brant goose, steamer
ducks, scoters) live much of their lives in
estuaries and on shallow seas.

Unlike the screamers of South America,
waterfowl are found on every continent
except Antarctica, and on all larger, and
many very small, islands. A few species,
including the Hawaiian goose and some
subspecies, or races, of other species, are
numbered only in hundreds, and may be
confined to a single island. Others are
extremely numerous, perhaps occurring in
millions, and are distributed very widely.
Different distribution patterns may result
from great adaptability to a considerable
range of habitats and food, as in the case
of the mallard, or be linked to long-distance
migration, eg the White-fronted goose, or be
the consequence of some chance colonization of an oceanic island, followed by the loss
of any migratory instinct and gradual evolution to fit the conditions found there, as in
the Laysan teal in the Pacific, the Kerguelen
pintail in the Indian Ocean and the Falkland
Islands flightless steamer duck in the south
Atlantic. Two species of waterfowl are
restricted, apart from vagrants, to Europe,
12 to Asia, 18 to Africa, 10 to North

▲ **Male Black swan incubates the clutch,** taking turns with his mate. In nearly all other species of the family, incubation is largely by the female. Like other swans and geese, Black swans (*Cygnus atrata*) are often faithful to their mate for many years. Both build the bulky waterside nest, and share the care of the young, often through their first winter. Unlike other swans, the Australian Black swan usually nests in colonies.

◄ **Duckweed feast for mallard ducklings.** As well as "dabbling" just under water, they scoop up mouthfuls of surface water and then strain out the tiny leaves, seeds and insects that form their diet. The familiar mallard is widespread in the Northern Hemisphere, and is the ancestor of most domestic breeds of duck.

America, 30 to Central and South America, and 25 to Australasia. The remaining 50 species of waterfowl occur more widely, in two or more continents. The Hawaiian goose is placed in a separate species, but all other forms on small oceanic islands are treated, in most classifications, as subspecies of mainland species.

Waterfowl are essentially aquatic birds, and so have a generally broad body, flattened underneath, a medium to long neck, and shortish legs with webbed feet. The bill is usually rather broad and flattened, with a horny "nail" towards the tip which in some species ends with a slight hook. The sides of the mandibles, in most species, have comb-like lamellae for straining food particles from the water, while the tongue is rather thick with short, spiny teeth along its edges, used in grasping and manipulating food items. Most ducks have their legs set

well back on the body, some very far back, and so progress on land can be slow and awkward. However, the many species which feed underwater (eg diving ducks, sea ducks, stifftails) are thereby able to move quickly and to maneuver well. A very few ducks (eg Red-breasted merganser) also use their wings underwater, but generally the wings are held tight to the body when diving. Geese and sheldgeese are generally more terrestrial, especially when feeding—their longer legs are placed more centrally beneath the body, they stand more upright and walk with ease.

Screamers are goose-like in overall shape, though they have a heavier body not unlike that of a turkey, and very broad wings. Their long, thick legs end in large feet with long toes which have only very slight webbing at the base. Their bill is quite different from any waterfowl species, being short, down-curved, ending in a distinct hook, and lacking any lamellae. Screamers rarely, if ever, swim, but use their long-toed feet to best advantage when walking over floating mats of vegetation. Their hooked bill is used for grasping and tearing off plant leaves and stems. The main plumage coloring is gray, black and white. Screamers are noisy birds, and their display appears to include a soaring flight on their broad wings, with frequent calling.

The **waterfowl** are divided here into eleven tribes based mainly on internal features, such as the skeleton, but also on external features—for example, the type and pattern of plumage both in adults and the downy (less than three-week-old) young—and, through fairly recent studies, on behavior, particularly the displays that accompany the formation and maintenance of pairs.

The **Magpie goose** of Australasia is the only member of the tribe Anseranatini. It shares features with the screamers, particularly the overall long-legged, long-necked shape and the reduced webbing between the toes. The bill is more typically waterfowl-shaped, though deep and broad at the base, and rising into a steep forehead ending in an enlarged dome to the head. The flight is steady and direct on broad, slow-flapping wings. The plumage of the Magpie goose is black and white, as it is in many waterfowl, but the wing feathers are not molted all at once as in nearly all other waterfowl, and so the birds do not become flightless during their wing molt. In contrast to all other waterfowl, Magpie goose parents feed their young, passing food items from bill to bill.

Whistling ducks (tribe Dendrocygnini)

have a wide distribution throughout the tropics and subtropics. Most are confined to rather small ranges, which do not overlap. The Fulvous whistling duck, however, has a most extraordinary distribution for a bird, occurring in the Americas, East Africa and Madagascar, and southern Asia; yet across all this enormous but discontinuous range there is no detectable variation of form.

Whistling ducks are mostly quite small, long-legged birds with an upright stance. They get their name from their high-pitched whistling calls. An alternative name for them is "tree ducks," from their fairly general habit of perching on branches. They have broad wings and are maneuverable fliers rather than fast ones. As well as walking well on land, they both swim and dive. The plumage is the same in both sexes, often highly patterned, particularly with brown, gray and fawn. The flank feathers of the Fulvous and three other species are enlarged in showy ornaments, and the downy young have a distinctive plumage quite unlike that of any other waterfowl except the Coscoroba swan. The unique feature is a pale yellow or white line running right round the head

under the eyes; the head is dark-capped. After copulation the whistling duck pair indulges in a mutual display, both sexes performing similar actions.

The **swans and "true" geese** (tribe Anserini) conduct a mutual display before copulation, and also a "triumph" ceremony after a rival male has been successfully driven off. The 15 species of geese are confined to the Northern Hemisphere, their place in the Southern Hemisphere being taken by the sheldgeese. Three of the six swan species are confined (apart from introductions) to the Northern Hemisphere, and three occur only south of the Equator. The swans include the largest of the waterfowl, over 6.6ft (2m) in wingspan, and weighing up to 33lb (15kg) or more. They are very long-necked but comparatively short in the leg, and not very mobile on land. In contrast, the geese are able to walk and run well; their moderately long legs being more centrally placed on their bodies. Their necks are medium to long. Both swans and geese are powerful fliers, and several undertake regular migrations covering thousands of miles.

The swans have either all-white plumage,

The 11 Tribes of Swans, Geese and Ducks
$\boxed{V}$ Vulnerable. $\boxed{Ex}$ Extinct. $\boxed{I}$ Threatened, status indeterminate.

Magpie goose
Tribe: Anseranatini
Sole species *Anseranas semipalmata.*

Whistling ducks
Tribe: Dendrocygnini
Nine species in 2 genera.
Species include: **Fulvous whistling
duck** (*Dendrocygna bicolor*).

Swans and true geese
Tribe: Anserini
Twenty-one species in 4 genera.
Species include: **Barnacle goose**
(*Branta leucopsis*), **Bewick's or
Whistling swan** (*Cygnus columbianus*),
Brent goose or **brant** (*Branta bernicla*),
Coscoroba swan (*Coscoroba coscoroba*),
Hawaiian goose $\boxed{V}$ (*Branta
sandvicensis*), **Mute swan** (*Cygnus
olor*), **Snow goose** (*Anser caerulescens*),
White-fronted goose (*A. albifrons*).

Freckled duck
Tribe: Stictonettini
Sole species *Stictonetta naevosa.*

Shelduck and sheldgeese
Tribe: Tadornini
Sixteen species in 7 genera.
Species include: **Egyptian goose**
(*Alopochen aegyptiacus*), **Ruddy-headed
goose** $\boxed{V}$ (*Chloephaga rubidiceps*),
shelduck (*Tadorna tadorna*).

Steamer ducks
Tribe: Tachyerini
Three species of the genus *Tachyeres.*
Species include: **Falkland Islands
flightless steamer duck** (*Tachyeres
brachyapterus*).

Perching ducks and geese
Tribe: Cairinini
Thirteen species in 8 genera.
Species include: **Comb** or **Knob-billed**
goose (*Sarkidiornis melanotos*),
Hartlaub's duck (*Pteronetta
hartlaubii*), **Mandarin duck** (*Aix
galericulata*), **Muscovy duck** (*Cairina
moschata*), **Pygmy goose** (*Nettapus
coromandelianus*), **Spur-winged goose**
(*Plectropterus gambensis*).

Dabbling ducks
Tribe: Anatini
Forty species in 5 genera.
Species include: **Cinnamon teal** (*Anas
cyanoptera*), **Eurasian widgeon** (*A.
penelope*), **mallard** (*A. platyrhynchos*),
pintail (*A. acuta*), **Pink-headed duck**
(*Rhodonessa caryophyllacea*), **Torrent
duck** (*Merganetta armata*).

Diving ducks
Tribe: Aythyini
Sixteen species in 3 genera.
Species include: **canvasback** (*Aythya
valisineria*), **South American pochard**
(*Netta erythrophthalma*), **Tufted duck**
(*Aythya fuligula*).

Sea ducks and sawbills
Tribe: Mergini
Twenty species in 8 genera.
Species include: **Brazilian
merganser** $\boxed{I}$ (*Mergus octosetaceus*),
Common eider (*Somateria mollissima*),
Common scoter (*Melanitta nigra*),
Labrador duck $\boxed{Ex}$ (*Camptorhynchus
labradorius*), **Long-tailed duck** or
oldsquaw (*Clangula hyemalis*), **Red-
breasted merganser** (*Mergus serrator*).

Stifftails
Tribe: Oxyurini
Eight species in 3 genera.
Species include: **Black-headed duck**
(*Heteronetta atricapilla*), **Ruddy duck**
(*Oxyura jamaicensis*).

---

or some combination of black and white, varying from white with black outer wings to black with white outer wings. The geese are more variable, with some species black and white, other predominantly gray or brown. The sexes are similar in all species.

The **Freckled duck**, only representative of the tribe Stictonettini, is rather duck-like in overall shape, and has comparatively short legs. Male and female are similar in plumage, being mottled gray-brown all over, though the male gets a reddish bill during the breeding season. There are sufficient structural and behavioral similarities to place this tribe next to the Anserini.

The **shelducks and sheldgeese** (tribe Tadornini) comprise one genus of shelducks (seven species, one probably extinct), four genera of sheldgeese (eight species), and two other single-species genera. Shelducks occur worldwide except for Central and North America, but the others are confined to the Southern Hemisphere, with the single exception of the Egyptian goose. They are medium-sized birds, the sheldgeese upright in stance, and all feed on land as well as in the water.

Plumage is very variable in this group, though the majority of species have a green speculum (patch on outer half of the secondaries) which is iridescent, and white wing coverts. Other common colors include some white, black, chestnut and gray. The sexes are similar in some species, but completely contrasting in others. The displays show some similarities with those of the geese. Some, if not all, sheldgeese molt their wing feathers sequentially (like the Magpie

goose, see above); furthermore, the wing molt may occur only every other year.

The **steamer ducks** (tribe Tachyerini) are often lumped together with the preceding tribe. They are confined to southern South America, where they lead a predominantly aquatic life, often round the coasts. Two species have such short wings that they are completely flightless, while the third flies infrequently and weakly. All are very sturdily built, with short necks and legs and powerful bills. Steamer ducks get their name from their habit of threshing over the water like a paddle-steamer's wheel, using wings and legs in order to move more quickly, when escaping from danger. Their plumage is predominantly gray and the sexes are alike.

The **perching ducks and geese** (tribe Cairinini) are a somewhat varied collection of small and medium-sized ducks, and some larger goose-like birds. They can perch on branches and other structures, an ability rare or absent in nearly all other waterfowl. Most are hole-nesters, and their young have sharp claws on their feet and rather stiff tails, both used in climbing out of the holes soon after hatching. Perching ducks and geese occur mainly in tropical and subtropical latitudes, extending into the temperate zone in a few cases (eg mandarins). The sexes are dissimilar among smaller species (eg pygmy geese), which show a wide variation in coloring, from dull brown to bright chestnut, green and white. Among larger species (eg Comb duck, Spur-winged goose) the sexes are alike in plumage, but the males are usually considerably larger than the

▶ **Seeing off a rival gander,** one male Canada goose intercepts and threatens another. There are 10 or more subspecies—the larger ones known as "honkers"—but all have a black head and neck and contrasting white cheek patches.

▼ ▶ **Representative species of ducks.**
(1) Mandarin duck (*Aix galericulata*).
(2) White-faced tree duck (*Dendrocygna viduata*).
(3) Red-breasted merganser (*Mergus serrator*).
(4) Ruddy duck (*Oxyura jamaicensis*).
CONTINUED OVERLEAF.

1

females. Black and white, the former often glossed with green, predominate.

The **dabbling ducks** (Anatini) are the largest tribe of waterfowl. The great majority are small, short-legged, aquatic birds, feeding on the surface of the water or, by up-ending (dabbling), just beneath it. One species, the Torrent duck, of which there are a number of well-marked geographic races, is highly adapted for living in the fast-flowing streams of the Andes in South America; it has a very streamlined shape, sharp claws for gripping slippery boulders, and a long stiff tail used for steering in the fast-rushing water. Dabbling ducks occur throughout the world, including remote oceanic islands, from where a number of non-migrating subspecies (eg Laysan teal, Andaman teal, and Rennell Island gray teals) have been described. Many other dabbling ducks (eg pintail, teal, widgeon) are highly migratory and fly long distances; the smaller species are also very maneuverable in the air, and take off from the water almost vertically.

In many species the male is brightly colored, generally with an iridescent speculum in the wing, while the female is a well-camouflaged brown. Brown, green, chestnut, white and pale blue all occur

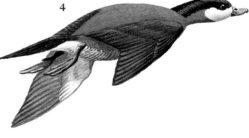

frequently. Displays involve complex movements by the male, which show off his plumage to best advantage. The female is much less demonstrative and mutual display movements are absent or rare.

The **diving ducks** (tribe Aythyini) have a worldwide distribution and are principally freshwater species, though some winter on the coasts, and obtain their food by diving. To facilitate this, their short legs are set well back on their generally plump bodies; they only rarely venture onto land. To become airborne usually involves a take-off run over the surface of the water, accompanied by rapid wing beats. Although males have different coloration from females, they are not especially brightly colored; gray, brown and black are the commonest colors. They lack the speculum of the shelducks and other members of the family, but often have a whitish wing stripe. Iridescence is quite frequent on the dark head and chest. Their displays are relatively simple.

The **sea ducks and sawbills** (tribe Mergini) here include the eiders, which are sometimes separated into their own tribe, the Somaterini. Most are principally saltwater species, diving for their animal food, though several breed beside fresh water. Most are restricted to the Northern Hemisphere, but the Brazilian merganser occurs in South America, and another species (now extinct)

Lead Poisoning

The poisoning of waterfowl that swallow lead shotgun pellets in mistake for grit or seeds has caused increasing concern, particularly in the United States and Canada and, more recently, in Europe. Intensive shooting beside small flight ponds and over marshland areas produces a build-up in the mud and soil of pellets which remain virtually intact and, unless they sink through the subsoil, available to birds for many years. As a result, the chances of a feeding bird finding a pellet at such sites can become quite high. In certain circumstances, the provision of plenty of grit can alleviate the problem, but a single pellet, taken into the gizzard and there ground down by grit particles so that the lead enters the bloodstream, is sufficient to cause the death of a duck. These deaths reached such high levels in parts of the United States that a ban on the use of lead shotgun pellets has been progressively introduced in recent years.

Substitutes made of alloys or stainless steel have not proved entirely satisfactory, because of problems with ballistics, gun barrel wear, etc, and opposition to the ban may yet bring about its reversal.

A second source of lead causing waterfowl deaths is the weights used by anglers fishing in rivers, canals and standing freshwaters. Discarded or lost lengths of line may be eaten by birds such as Mute swans as they pluck underwater vegetation. Some anglers have become accustomed to throwing away the fine end-line with its lead weights after each day's fishing. Two or three lead weights (or a single large ledger weight) are quite enough to poison a bird the size of a Mute swan. In some river systems of Britain this species has been virtually wiped out by lead poisoning. After much publicity and discussion, lead substitutes are now being investigated and may soon be in general use.

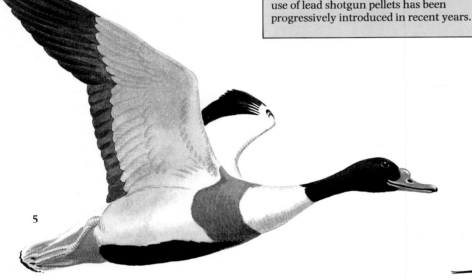

5

6

once occurred on islands south of New Zealand. Many are rather bulky and heavily built, requiring a long take-off for their rather labored flight. Some of the small species are much more agile and fast moving. Almost all are sexually dimorphic, with the males mainly black or black and white, though often with iridescent green or blue heads, or with pastel coloring of green and blue. Displays by the males are often quite elaborate and vary greatly between species. The females are much less demonstrative.

The eleventh tribe, the **stifftails** (Oxyurini), are mostly found in the Southern Hemisphere, with just two occurring in the northern. They are small, dumpy birds, with tails of short, stiff feathers, used for steering underwater. Their legs are set very far back on their bodies and movement on land is limited. Males are mainly dark chestnut or brown, often with black or black and white heads, while many species have a bright

blue bill. The females are generally dull brown. Flight on their short stubby wings is rapid and direct, after a long take-off run. The displays by the males are relatively elaborate. Whereas most waterfowl molt their wing feathers (and become flightless) once a year, most if not all stifftails carry this out twice a year.

The closest relatives of the waterfowl and the screamers are the flamingos, and possibly the curassows, but the fossil record is not sufficient to reveal their precise origin. Between members of the waterfowl family (despite the division into tribes) relationships remain close; this is demonstrated by the very large number—over 400—of hybrids recorded between species, the majority of which have occurred in captivity, but some also in the wild. A number of inter-tribal hybrids have occurred.

Grazing on land and plucking vegetation from the water are the commonest feeding methods of geese, swans, sheldgeese and screamers. Some species also dig for roots of plants in soft mud and many geese and sheldgeese, and some swans, have adapted to feeding on agricultural land, at first by grazing grass and growing crops but more recently picking up waste grain, beans, maize and potato tubers. Some of the dabbling ducks, too, graze on land, while most take many seeds from the surface of the water as well as small insects. None of the vegetarian waterfowl or screamers have bacteria in the gut to help them digest cellulose. The nutrients they obtain from plant leaves and stems are restricted to the cell juices, obtained by breaking down the cell walls in their gizzards with the aid of small particles of grit, which they ingest for the purpose. These species have to feed long, often the majority of daylight hours in temperate winter latitudes, in order to obtain sufficient food. The plant remains pass through the gut in still recognizable form, and it is usually possible to identify the species of plants eaten.

While the grazers are known to select the most nutritious parts of the plant, such as the growing tips of grass leaves, dabbling ducks are much less selective, taking in relatively large quantities of surface water through the tip of their bills, and pumping it out of the sides through the comb-like lamellae with the aid of their tongues. The trapped particles, seeds and insects, are then swallowed at intervals.

Diving ducks feed on underwater plants and invertebrates of all kinds, generally in fairly shallow water a few feet deep. The sea ducks and sawbills may dive much deeper, the latter pursuing and catching fish and large free-swimming invertebrates, while the former prize mollusks from rocks, or catch crabs and other crustaceans in shallow water or soft mud. Their bills are large and powerful, well adapted for crushing the shells of such prey. Some of the shelducks also feed in a marine environment, sifting tiny mollusks and crustaceans from the mud in estuaries, while the steamer ducks use their strong bills to prize mussels from tideline rocks.

The stifftails feed exclusively underwater. They swim along the bottom, sifting through the silt with their lower mandible just entering it, and catching animal prey.

The lifespan of many waterfowl is greatly affected by man's hunting activities. While, if not hunted, the geese and swans are quite long-lived, with 20 years not uncommon, heavy shooting pressure can reduce life expectancy to no more than 5–10 years at most. The majority of dabbling ducks, diving ducks, small sea ducks and stifftails mature at one year old, and have a life expectancy thereafter of 4–10 years, this being greatly affected by whether or not they are quarry species of man. Most swans do not mature until they are 3–4 years old, and geese, sheldgeese and shelducks until they are 2–3. Similarly, the eiders and larger sawbills are commonly not mature until at least two years of age. Screamers probably also do not breed until they are 2–3.

The great majority of species breed annually, but some from the Southern Hemisphere may breed only every other year, or are adapted to await favorable conditions before attempting to breed, for example during the irregular rains in parts of Australia. In some years arctic-breeding species may, over wide areas, fail to breed (see p92).

The waterfowl show a wide range of variation in the maintenance of the pair bond and in parental care. Swans and geese mostly pair for life, and while only the female incubates the eggs, both parents look after the young, often throughout the first winter of their lives, the family only splitting up at the start of the following breeding season. This period may well include a long migration to winter quarters, the young birds thus being shown the route and resting areas by example, a pattern which often leads to highly traditional use being made of certain haunts over many years. Thus White-fronted geese have wintered in England on the Severn at Slimbridge since the 18th century, if not earlier.

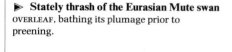

▶ **Stately thrash of the Eurasian Mute swan** OVERLEAF, bathing its plumage prior to preening.

◀ ▼ **Representative species of ducks** CONTINUED. (5) Shelduck (*Tadorna tadorna*). (6) Pintail (*Anas acuta*). (7) Common eider (*Somateria mollissima*). (8) Tufted duck (*Aythya fuligula*).

Almost all the ducks only pair for the breeding season, though pairing may take place during the previous fall, as in the case of many dabbling ducks, through to the spring, as in many diving and sea ducks. The pair bond usually breaks as soon as the female has begun incubation. She generally rears the young until they can fly, before deserting them, though some diving duck females may abandon their young when only half grown. "Creche care" of several broods by a few females takes place in some of the sea ducks, and in some shelducks.

The pair bond and parental care in stiff-tails are both very short lived, and most young fend for themselves almost from the day of hatching, as in the case of the offspring of the Black-headed duck, which parasitizes other ducks' nests.

Screamers are closest to the swans and geese in their reproductive behavior, with a life-long pair bond and both parents looking after the young until well after they fledge.

The great majority of waterfowl are gregarious, some of them highly so. Swans, geese and sheldgeese are almost always found in flocks away from the breeding grounds, and some species even breed in colonies. A solitary individual can generally be assumed to be a lost straggler. Among these species, flock size is very variable, from a few tens to a hundred thousand or more.

Flocks of swans and geese comprise family units, pairs and immature non-breeding birds, while flocks of dabbling and diving ducks are frequently made up principally of males or of females, with considerable geographical separation between the sexes. In most species of the Northern Hemisphere, females winter further south than males, which leave the breeding grounds first.

The emphasis on conservation of waterfowl has moved in recent years from protection of individual species to a recognition of the vital importance of their wetland habitat. A few species, notably the Hawaiian goose, have been the subject of successful captive-rearing programs aimed at boosting small or declining wild populations.

While conservation measures are required for probably most species of waterfowl, there are circumstances in which they can be regarded by man as pests, particularly of agriculture, and to a lesser extent fisheries. While locally this can be important, worldwide it is not a major problem. The extinction in 1875 of the Labrador duck and the almost certain recent extinction of the Pink-headed duck of India and Nepal, are reminders that there is much to be done if no more species are to disappear. MAO

A Race to Breed

Factors affecting breeding success in arctic-breeding geese

About 18 species or subspecies of geese breed in arctic regions, before migrating south to winter in more temperate latitudes in North America, Europe and Asia. The arctic summer is extremely short—there may be only eight weeks free of lying snow, the migrating geese may travel thousands of miles, and the food supplies they find on arrival at the breeding grounds can be scant or non-existent. In some years bad weather conditions may prevent successful breeding altogether.

Arctic-breeding geese have adapted to surmount these difficulties. Virtually all are smaller than close relatives that breed further south. Their own food requirement and that of their young is reduced, and they produce smaller eggs which require less time to incubate. Clutch sizes too, tend to be smaller, again shortening the time needed for laying. The goslings are able to feed throughout the long arctic day and so grow at a faster rate and can fly at a younger age than their southern relatives. Finally, geese are relatively long-lived birds, taking two or three years to reach maturity. Those years when no young are produced do not, therefore, seriously interfere with the overall population level, provided they do not occur too often.

It used to be thought that the weather conditions on the breeding grounds, particularly when the geese arrive and when the eggs are hatched, were the most important factors determining the success or otherwise of a season. For example, the geese may arrive to find the breeding grounds completely snow-covered. It has been found that, after waiting for a week to 10 days for the snow to clear, the geese give up all attempt at breeding; the egg follicles inside the females are reabsorbed without any eggs being laid. On other occasions severe storms of rain or snow at the time of hatching, or when the goslings are very small, are known to have caused numerous deaths.

Recent work, particularly on Snow geese in North America and, more recently still, on Barnacle geese in Europe, has shifted the focus of attention to the period immediately before the arrival at the breeding grounds, namely the spring. Migrant birds lay down fat deposits prior to their long flights as, during them, they will have less opportunity to feed. Geese are no exception, but it is now known that the arctic-breeding species lay down reserves not just for the migration itself but also, in the case of the female, for the production of eggs, and, for both parents, to tide them over until the vegetation on the breeding grounds has started to grow, often 2–3 weeks after their arrival.

A few species or populations remain on the southern wintering grounds through the spring before making a single long migration to the breeding grounds. Most geese, however, move at least some distance along their route, then stop for a few weeks, before undertaking the final stage of the migration. The advantage of finding a more

▲ **Within a flock of Snow geese,** family parties of pairs and immature non-breeding birds stay together as units. Groups of families tend to form larger groups within the flock.

◄ **Snow goose and goslings.** In arctic-breeding geese the birds arrive on the breeding grounds with sufficient resources (fat layers) to be able to lay eggs and incubate them before grass is available for them to feed. This enables them to raise young in the short, harsh arctic summer.

► **Migration route of Barnacle geese** in northern Europe, between their wintering grounds on the Scottish–English border and summer breeding grounds in the Norwegian island group of Svalbard (Spitsbergen), high in the Arctic (to 80°N). On their way north the geese stop off in Norway to feed up on succulent new growth of grasses, laying down food reserves that are vital for successful breeding. On the return journey, Bear Island is an important staging area.

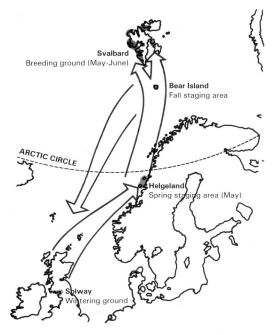

Svalbard
Breeding ground (May-June)

Bear Island
Fall staging area

ARCTIC CIRCLE

Helgeland
Spring staging area (May)

Solway
Wintering ground

northerly spring feeding place seems to stem from the fact that faster-growing vegetation is more nutritious. In temperate wintering latitudes the grass may be past its peak growth-rate well before the geese can move on to the breeding grounds. However, further north the grass will still be at its growing peak. Barnacle geese wintering on the Solway in Scotland leave in late April, then spend most of May at staging places in northern Norway, before reaching their breeding grounds in Svalbard as soon as conditions there become favorable, in late May and early June.

However, even with this timetable things can go wrong. A delayed spring on the wintering grounds and, particularly, the spring feeding areas, can so reduce the vital food intake that on arrival at the breeding site some birds lack sufficient reserves to lay any eggs, while others lay smaller clutches than usual. The layers may subsequently give up if they cannot find enough food during the short breaks in incubation, which normally occur twice a day. Starving females have even died on the nest.

The conditions during the growing period of the goslings are still of great significance, whether the season has started well or poorly. Losses to bad weather or predation can be serious in many years. Finally, the fall migration must be undertaken when the young may have been on the wing for only a few weeks. Little is known about possible losses during their first long journey, but there is some evidence that they could be heavy when the migrating flocks meet strong headwinds or storms.

There is certainly no single most important factor governing breeding success of arctic-nesting geese. As more work is done, on both sides of the Atlantic, our understanding of the relative importance of the various hazards is becoming clearer. MAO

BIRDS OF PREY - THE RAPTORS

Order: Falconiformes
Families: Accipitridae, Cathartidae, Falconidae,
Pandionidae, Sagitariidae.
About 286 species in 80 genera.
Distribution: worldwide except Antarctica and
a few oceanic islands.

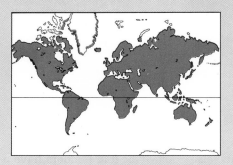

► **Proudly perched** on a rocky ledge, a
Common buzzard, the most common European
bird of prey, surveys his habitat.

▼ **Unprepossessing contrast** to the grandeur of
most birds of prey is provided by the vultures.
These are Lappet-faced vultures feeding on a
zebra carcass in South Africa.

FALLING like a dive-bomber, its wings folded back, an osprey dissolves into a cauldron of spray as it hits the surface of a lake. Moments later, it struggles from the water, shaking off the spray to reveal a fish firmly gripped in one of its talons. High drama like this is typical of birds of prey, one of the most exciting groups of birds, yet one which has suffered greatly at the hands of man.

The birds of prey or raptors (from the Latin, meaning plunderers) form a large and highly varied group of five families, but they all share the same specializations for finding food, and for holding and tearing apart the bodies of other animals: acute vision, strong legs and feet, mostly equipped with sharp, curved claws, and a hooked beak. There are two strategies for killing prey: most of the Accipitridae kill with their claws and use their beaks to tear up the prey; the true falcons grasp their prey with their claws and kill it with a blow from their beak. Most birds of prey sometimes take carrion, and for the vultures this is their main food. Although most have a varied diet, some are highly specialized, such as the Everglade kite, which feeds only on a single species of snail.

The condors are the most dramatic of the **New World vultures**—they are among the largest flying birds, with wingspans of up to 10ft (3m). New and Old World vultures are similar in appearance but are not closely related. Like the cranes, to which they may be related, New World vultures have perforated nostrils. The head and upper neck are bare of feathers, usually highly colored, and the larger species have a ruff of fluffy or lance-shaped feathers round the base of

the neck. The toes are long, and the claws are only slightly curved, not well adapted for grasping prey.

The Andean condor is still widespread, but the California condor is almost extinct, with fewer than 30 individuals left in the wild, all in one area of California. It is not clear what has caused the decline of the California condor, but persecution, including poisoning and shooting, have been major factors. Such a huge bird presents a tempting target for a trigger-happy hunter and, being carrion-feeders, the birds are easily killed by poisoned meat baits. Widespread poisoning campaigns to eliminate ground squirrels and jackals from certain areas have also taken their toll. Condors have a very low reproductive rate, producing at most only one chick every second year. Each young then develops for six or more years before it can itself breed. In an attempt to prevent extinction, four eggs were recently taken into captivity and hatched there. This did not affect the wild population, because the pairs concerned simply produced another egg for themselves some weeks later. Together with previous birds, there are now a total of nine California condors in captivity, in the San Diego and Los Angeles Zoos. The eventual aim is to breed the species in captivity for future release to the wild. The program will benefit from experience gained with the related Andean condor, which has already been bred very successfully in captivity.

The fossil record indicates that the New World vultures were formerly found in Europe too, and that species even larger than condors used to exist. One specimen, *Teratornis merriami*, from the Pleistocene (about 2 million years ago) of the southern United States, was truly massive. It weighed up to 33lb (15kg), had a large head and body, and a wingspan up to 24.5ft (7.5m). Some modern species inhabit mainly open habitats, while others are found in forest.

Some of the forest dwellers are unusual among birds in using smell, as well as sight, to locate their food. As well as carrion, most species eat eggs and some eat fruit and other vegetable matter. Certain species frequent rubbish dumps and abattoirs.

New World vultures nest in cliff-caves or tree-holes, and lay only one or two eggs, dependent on species; nestlings are fed by regurgitation. All species are long-lived.

Like a cross between a stork and a raptor, the **Secretary bird** is an oddity, having a whole family to itself. It has long stork-like legs—the bird is up to 3.3ft (1m) high, with a wingspan up to 6.6ft (2m)—and the long

THE 5 FAMILIES OF BIRDS OF PREY

E Endangered. V Vulnerable. R Rare.

New World vultures
Family: Cathartidae
Seven species in 4 genera.
S Canada to tip of S America. Mainly open habitats but some in forests. Size: length 23.5–47in (60–120cm); weight 2–31lb (0.9–14kg). Plumage: brownish black with paler patches on the underside of the wings, except King vulture which is mainly cream and white. Species include: **Andean condor** (*Vultur gryphus*), **California condor** E (*V. californianus*), **King vulture** (*Sarcoramphus papa*), **Turkey vulture** (*Cathartes aura*).

Secretary bird
Family: Sagittariidae
Sole species *Sagittarius serpentarius*.
Africa south of the Sahara. Savanna and other open habitats. Size: length 49–59in (125–150cm); weight 7.5–8.8lb (3.4–4kg). Plumage: pale gray with black wing quills, rump and thighs.

Osprey
Family: Pandionidae
Sole species *Pandion haliaetus*.
Osprey or Fish hawk
Worldwide. Primarily coastal; also lakes and rivers. Size: length up to 24.5in (62cm); weight 2.6–4.2lb (1.2–1.9kg). Plumage: dark brown above and white beneath.

Falcons, falconets and caracaras
Family: Falconidae
About 60 species in 10 genera.

Typical falcons
Thirty seven species of the genus *Falco*.
All continents except Antarctica. Size: length 10–24in (25–60cm); weight 4–70oz (110–2,000g). Plumage: enormously variable, but most species are darker above than below; reds, browns and blue-grays are frequent colors. Species include: **American kestrel** (*Falco sparverius*), **Common kestrel** (*F. tinnunculus*), **Eastern red-footed falcon** (*F. amurensis*), **Eleonora's falcon** (*F. eleonorae*), **Gray falcon** (*F. ardosiaceus*), **gyrfalcon** (*F. rusticolus*), **Laggar falcon** (*F. jugger*), **Lanner falcon** (*F. biarmicus*), **Lesser kestrel** (*F. naumanni*), **Mauritius kestrel** E (*F. punctatus*), **Peregrine falcon** V (*F. peregrinus*), **Prairie falcon** (*F. mexicanus*), **Red-footed falcon** (*F. vespertinus*), **Saker falcon** (*F. cherrug*), **Seychelles kestrel** (*F. araea*) R, **Sooty falcon** (*F. concolor*).
Total threatened species: 4.

Pygmy falcons and falconets
Genera: *Spiziapteryx* (1 species; Argentina), *Polihierax* (2 species, Africa), *Microhierax* (5 species, tropical Asia).
Size: length about 6in (15cm); weight 1.4–2.1oz (40–60g). Plumage: strongly contrasting dark above and whitish below, often with orange or reddish patch on upper or lower surface. Species include: **African pygmy falcon** (*Polihierax semitorquatus*), **Philippine falconet** (*Microhierax erythrogonys*).

Forest falcons
Five species of genus *Micrastur*.
New World tropics. Size: length 12–24in (30–60cm), including tail; weight 6.7–26.5oz (190–750g). Plumage: slate gray or dark brownish above, whitish or orange below; barred tail; some forms barred on the breast.

Laughing falcon
Sole species *Herpetotheres cachinnans*.
Tropical S America. Forest. Size: length 16in (40cm). Plumage: dark above; buff below.

Caracaras
About 9 species of genera *Milvago*, *Phalcoboenus*, *Daptrius* and *Polyborus*.
C and S America. Open country, forest or savanna. Size: length 14–24in (35–60cm); weight 10–56oz (280–1,600g). Plumage: mainly dark; some species with pale below or on head; others finely barred, above and below.

Sparrowhawks to Old World vultures
Family: Accipitridae
Two hundred and seventeen species in 64 genera.
Total threatened species: 11.

Kites and honey buzzards
Thirty-one species in 17 genera.
Distribution: all continents except Antarctica. Size: length 12–27in (30–70cm). Plumage: enormously variable, but most species darker above than below. Species include: **Bat hawk** (*Macheiramphus alcinus*), **Black kite** (*Milvus migrans*), **Everglade kite** (*Rostrhamus sociabilis*), **Letter-winged kite** (*Elanus scriptus*), **Red kite** (*Milvus milvus*), **White-tailed kite** (*Elanus leucurus*).

Fish eagles
Eleven species in 3 genera.
Distribution: all continents except S America and Antarctica. Size: length 24–47in (60–120cm); weight 4.4–14.3lb (2–6.5kg). Plumage: most species have striking color patterns, with dark brown and white. Species include: **African fish eagle** (*Haliaeetus vocifer*), **Bald eagle** (*H. leucocephalus*), **Palm-nut vulture** (*Gypohierax angolensis*), **White-bellied sea eagle** (*Haliaeetus leucogaster*), **White-tailed eagle** V (*H. albicilla*).

Old World vultures
Fourteen species in 8 genera.
Europe, Asia and Africa. Size: length 24–55in (60–140cm). Plumage: mainly brown or dark with bare heads and necks. Species include: **African white-backed vulture** (*Gyps africanus*), **Asian white-backed vulture** (*Gyps bengalensis*), **Bearded vulture** (*Gypaetus barbatus*), **European black vulture** (*Aegypius monachus*), **Egyptian vulture** (*Neophron percnopterus*), **Griffon vulture** (*Gyps fulvus*), **Lappet-faced vulture** (*Aegypius tracheliotus*), **Rüppell's griffon** (*Gyps rueppellii*).

Snake eagles
Twelve species in 5 genera.
Africa, Europe, Asia. Size: length 16–24in (40–60cm); weight 2.2–4.4lb (1–2kg). Plumage: usually gray or brown. Species include: **bateleur** (*Terathopius ecaudatus*).

Harrier hawks and crane hawk
Three species in 2 genera.
Africa, S America. Size: 20–24in (50–60cm); weight 11–21oz (300–600g). Plumage: adults gray, young brown. Species include: **Crane hawk** (*Geranospiza caerulescens*).

Harriers
Ten species of the genus *Circus*.
All continents except Antarctica. Size: 18–22in (45–55cm); weight 10–21oz (290–600g). Plumage: males usually grayish or black-and-white; females and young brownish. Species include: **Australian spotted harrier** (*Circus assimilis*), **Hen harrier** or **Marsh hawk** (*C. cyaneus*), **Marsh harrier** (*C. aeruginosus*), **Montagu's harrier** (*C. pygargus*).

Goshawks and sparrowhawks
Fifty-three species in 5 genera.
All continents. Size: length 12–28in (30–70cm); weight 3.5–70oz (100–2,000g). Plumage: generally gray or blackish above, white or reddish barred below. Species include **Cooper's hawk** (*Accipiter cooperii*), **Goshawk** (*A. gentilis*), **Lesser sparrowhawk** (*A. gularis*), **sparrowhawk** (*A. nisus*), **Sharp-shinned hawk** (*A. striatus*).

Buzzards, buteonines and harpies
Fifty-three species in 14 genera.
All continents. All habitats from tropical forest to arctic tundra. Size: length 18–39in (45–100cm); weight 1.1–10.1lb (0.5–4.6kg). Plumage: mainly brownish gray. Species include: **Broad-winged hawk** (*Buteo platypterus*), **Common** or **Steppe buzzard** (*B. buteo*), **Harpy eagle** R (*Harpia harpyia*), **Harris's hawk** (*Parabuteo unicinctus*), **Monkey-eating eagle** E (*Pithecophaga jefferyi*), **Red-tailed hawk** (*Buteo jamaicensis*), **Rough-legged buzzard** (*B. lagopus*), **Swainson's hawk** (*B. swainsoni*).

Booted eagles
Thirty species in 9 genera.
All continents except Antarctica. Size: 18–39in (45–100cm). Plumage: usually plain brown; specialized forest species often strongly barred with black and white. Species include: **Golden eagle** (*Aquila chrysaetos*), **Indian black eagle** (*Ictinaetus malayensis*), **Martial eagle** (*Polemaetus bellicosus*), **Tawny eagle** (*Aquila rapax*), **Verreaux's eagle** (*A. verreauxii*), **Wedge-tailed eagle** (*A. audax*).

▲ **Nest of Secretaries.** These Secretary birds are building their large nest on the top of an acacia, the flat crowns of which provide an ideal platform. Note the heavily feathered upper leg.

black-tipped plume-like feathers at the back of the head resemble pen quills, hence the name. It also has two very long central tail feathers, with black spots near the ends. The long legs have short stubby toes, which are adapted for walking, not for grasping prey.

The Secretary bird feeds by walking along the ground, in search of insects, small rodents and snakes. Small items are picked up in the bill and swallowed, but large ones, such as snakes, are first killed by stamping on them. Although the bird spends most of its time on the ground, it can fly well, and often soars like a stork. In fact, it has a spectacular aerial display, resembling that of some other raptors, involving a marked undulating flight, in which the bird swings upward, then tips gently forward into a steep dive, which is followed by another upward swing, and so on. In another display, on the ground, the pair run around with raised wings, and are sometimes joined by other individuals who perform similarly. Normally, however, a pair occupying a ter-

ritory will chase away other individuals. Territories may cover anything from 7.7sq mi (20sq km) to more than 77sq mi (200sq km), depending on region.

The nest is built on a flat-topped tree, often an acacia. Two or three greenish-white eggs are laid, and the incubation and nestling periods last 45 and 65–105 days respectively. Since the bird cannot carry prey in its feet, it brings food to the nest in its bill or crop, and either delivers it to or regurgitates it for the young.

One of the most distinctive birds of prey, the **osprey** is a large fish-eating bird. Its markings are unusual in being dark brown above and white beneath, a camouflage similar to that often used on warplanes. Its feet are very strong, since they take the first shock of the water as it dives for fish; the claws are long and sharp, and the toes have horny spines on their undersides to give a good grip on slippery fish. Furthermore, the outer toe is large and can be moved to face backwards, as in the owls. The toes' grip is so good that there are reports of osprey being dragged under by large fish.

Ospreys breed throughout the world except in South America, where they occur only in winter. They are highly migratory, and withdraw completely from boreal and temperate regions in winter. The European birds migrate to Africa, leaving a small resident population in the Mediterranean, and the North American birds migrate to Central and South America, leaving a resident population in Florida and the Caribbean region.

In some areas, ospreys are primarily coastal, while in others they also occur along lakes and rivers. They eat a variety of sizeable fish: whatever species are available locally. They sometimes commute more than 6mi (10km) between nesting and feeding areas. In parts of the range, particularly in eastern North America, their numbers were greatly reduced in the years around

1960 by DDT contamination. Following restrictions on DDT use, the species has begun to recover again.

Because it eats fish, the osprey has also been much persecuted, especially in Europe. It was exterminated completely in Britain, and after an absence of 50 years, began to nest again in Scotland around 1955. Since then, under careful protection, the species has increased to about 40 pairs.

The osprey hunts by cruising above the water surface and plunging in after fish. The talons are brought forward just as the bird hits the water to grab the prey. Only fish near the surface can be caught, but the bird

▼ ► **Representative species of birds of prey.**
(1) King vulture (*Sarcorhamphus papa*), a New World vulture which inhabits dense tropical forests. (2) Osprey (*Pandion haliaetus*), with a fish, almost its sole diet. (3) Laughing falcon (*Herpetotheres cachinnans*), a South American species with a striking black face mask. (4) A female Common kestrel (*Falco tinnunculus*) hovering. (5) A male Common kestrel (*Falco tinnunculus*). (6) Andean condor (*Vultur gryphus*), in soaring flight. (7) Head of a male Andean condor (*Vultur gryphus*) showing the fleshy wattle on top. (8) A female African pygmy falcon (*Polihierax semitorquatus*). (9) Aplomado falcon (*Falco femoralis*). (10) Secretary bird (*Sagittarius serpentarius*), a distinctive African species. (11) Crested caracara (*Polyborus plancus*). (12) Barred forest falcon (*Micrastur ruficollis*) eating a Black-spotted barbet.

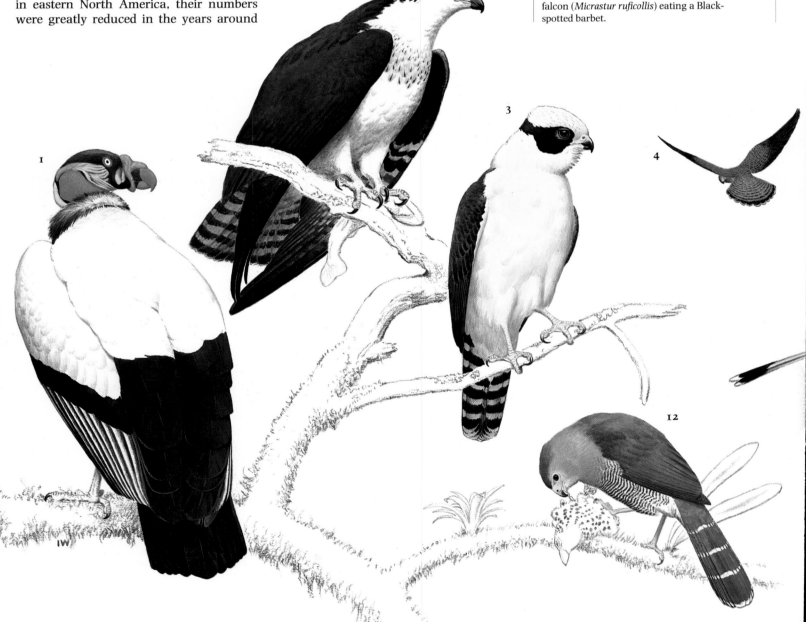

sometimes submerges completely. As it rises, with wings outspread on the surface, the bird shakes the water from its plumage, and carries the fish, head forward, to a suitable feeding perch.

The osprey has a spectacular aerial display which involves carrying a fish, and calling. Sometimes a bird may rise with rapid and pronounced wingbeats up to 1,000ft (300m) or more, then hover there for a moment with tail fanned and legs dangling, displaying the fish in its feet, before diving down on closed wings, only to rise again and repeat the performance. Such displays last for several minutes at a time, and serve to attract or retain a female.

Ospreys nest on the tops of trees or rock pinnacles, but on islands lacking mammalian predators they also nest on the ground. They build huge nests of sticks, which are normally used over long periods of years. Two to four eggs are laid, and the incubation and nestling periods span about 38 and 50 days respectively. The birds do not breed until their third or fourth year, and in extreme cases they may live for 15–20 years.

For most people, a kestrel hovering over the verge of a major road is probably the most familiar image of a bird of prey. Kestrels are **falcons** (family Falconidae), the second largest of the raptor families. Falcons are generally similar to the other great family of raptors, the Accipitridae, but differ in not building nests, in producing eggs with inside shells that appear buff against the light instead of pale green, in the sequence of molt in the primary feathers, and in some details of skeletal structure. There are four subfamilies of Falconidae: the large group of true falcons, forest falcons, the Laughing falcon, and caracaras.

The true falcons range from the tiny Philippine falcon, only 6in (15cm) long, to the spectacular gyrfalcon and Peregrine falcon, the falconer's choice *par excellence*. They can be considered as two main groups: the typical falcons of the genus *Falco* and the pygmy falcons.

The typical falcons have a wide range of types, and are found throughout the world, mainly in open or fairly open habitats. The largest of them are stocky, powerful birds of exceptionally swift flight, with pointed wings and relatively short tails. They are highly accomplished fliers, and habitually kill their prey, principally birds, in full flight, either striking them dead by a blow or seizing them with their talons and bringing them to ground. The largest species, the gyrfalcon, inhabits the Arctic tundra of North America and Eurasia and feeds largely on ptarmigan. It occurs in three main color phases, whitish, grayish and brown, depending on region.

The Peregrine falcon is one of the world's most spectacular birds. It is a perfect performer in the air, capable of feats of speed and precision flying scarcely equalled by any other bird. Maximum speed is achieved when the bird dives on prey, known as "stooping." Estimates vary from the conservative, which insist that the impression of great speed is illusory and that the bird hardly exceeds 100mph (160km/h), and the extravagant which claim that 250mph

► **Stooping to conquer.** The Peregrine falcon lives mainly on birds, which it kills by diving ("stooping") at very high speed—there are controversial claims of 250mph (400km/h). The wings are folded back to increase speed, and the prey is killed by the sharp claw on the hind toe.

▼ **Kestrel in the straw.** A Common kestrel ferries its rodent prey back to the nest in a straw rick.

(400km/h) is reached on occasion. Whatever the real figure, a stooping peregrine is a most impressive sight, and makes the species the falconer's first choice. In much of its range it was greatly reduced in numbers during the 1950s and 1960s by DDT and other organochlorine pesticides (see pp114–115), but is now recovering well.

Many raptors take quite small prey, and the hobbies, a group of small, long-winged, exceedingly fast falcons, live largely upon insects, although they can also take small birds, including swifts, in flight. They catch almost all their prey on the wing and hardly any on the ground. Two other species are

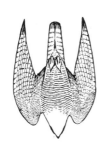

similar to hobbies, namely Eleonora's falcon, which breeds on certain Mediterranean and other islands, and the Sooty falcon, which inhabits the North African deserts. Both these species breed in late summer, so that they have young in the nest at a time when small birds, on which they prey, are migrating from Europe to Africa.

The kestrels are a large group of typical falcons, found on every continent, which hover in search of small mammals and insects on the ground. Typical representatives include the Common kestrel in Europe and Africa, and the American kestrel of the New World. There are several island forms, one of which, the Mauritius kestrel, is one of the rarest birds in the world, with fewer than five pairs left in the wild.

In their breeding habits, typical falcons are fairly uniform. Their displays, both aerial and perched, are often centered on nest-sites, and entail the male drawing the female's attention to potential sites. Thus the male kestrel has a special flight in which he glides down onto the site, with wings held up in a V, and many species have bowing displays at the site itself. They either breed on a scrape on a cliff ledge which may be resorted to year after year, or they appropriate the old stick nest of some other bird, such as a crow. Some use tree cavities. Their eggs are all very handsome, being generally buffish in ground color, thickly speckled with dark red-brown, sometimes obscuring the ground color completely. Clutches usually contain 2–3 eggs in hobbies, 3–6 in other small falcons and 3–5 in large species; the eggs are laid at 2–3-day intervals. Incubation periods range from 25–32 days in small species to 32–35 days in large ones; and nestling periods from 25–32 days in small species to 40–49 days in large ones. Vocalizations are heard mainly in the breeding season, and consist of chattering notes. Many species protest loudly when the nest is visited.

Pygmy falcons and falconets are the smallest of all birds of prey. The Philippine falconet, the smallest of all, hunts insects

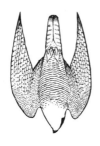

from the tops of trees in the manner of a fly-catcher; it breeds in old holes of woodpeckers. The African pygmy falcon is likewise very small, but is capable of killing small birds as well as the large insects which form the major part of its food. In South Africa it breeds in the huge communal nests of Sociable weavers, and in East Africa it uses the thorny nests of Buffalo weavers.

Forest falcons are long-tailed, long-legged birds, with a partial face ruff, a feature which has sometimes led them to be classified with harriers. They are in fact primitive falcons, which have become adapted for life in dense forests. They have the short broad wings and longish tail typical of other forest-dwelling raptors, which gives them great maneuverability in moving among the trees. They live largely on birds but are otherwise little known.

The Laughing falcon is a buzzard-sized bird, dark above and buff below, with a striking white crown set off by a black mask. It is found only in the forests of tropical South America, where it eats reptiles and other small animals. It nests in tree cavities, and produces only one young at a time, but again is very poorly known.

Caracaras are a group of large (buzzard-sized), long-legged birds that look quite unlike falcons. They inhabit open country, forest or savanna, and eat insects, and a range of food; they like carrion. Caracaras are very common in parts of Central and South America, and in general are rather sluggish birds, spending much of their time perched, or walking about on the ground; but they can run swiftly. They associate with New World vultures at carrion and sometimes force these and other caracaras to disgorge their food. Unlike the true falcons, caracaras build their own nests; they lay 2–3 eggs, and have incubation and nestling periods lasting about 32 and 42

▶ **Species of birds of prey** CONTINUED.
(13) Little eagle (*Hieraaetus morphnoides*) feeding young. (14) Gray chanting goshawk (*Melierax poliopterus*) calling on top of a termite mound. (15) Bald eagle (*Haliaeetus leucocephalus*). (16) Honey buzzard (*Pernis apivorus*) digging out a wasps' nest. (17) Red kite (*Milvus milvus*) with rabbit prey. (18) African harrier-hawk (*Polyboroides radiatus*) hunting for insects. (19) Black-breasted snake eagle (*Circaetus gallicus pectoralis*), a subspecies of the Short-toed eagle, with a snake. (20) Bearded vulture (*Gypaetus barbatus*). (21) Long-legged buzzard (*Buteo rufinus*). (22) Ornate hawk eagle (*Spizaetus ornatus*). (23) Black-mantled sparrowhawk (*Accipiter melanochlamys*) with newly captured prey. (24) Pied harrier (*Circus melanoleucus*).

19

20

21

22

18

23

17

24

days respectively. One species, the Guadaloupe caracara, has become extinct within historical times.

A snail-eating kite, carrion-devouring vultures, snake-eating eagles—these and many more belong to the family **Accipitridae**, the largest family of birds of prey. Because of these and other feeding specializations, their appearance is diverse.

Extreme specialization and versatility are both found in kites and honey buzzards. Honey buzzards eat wasp grubs; the Bat hawk eats bats caught at dusk as they emerge from caves or tree roosts; and snail kites eat aquatic snails. At the other extreme, the Black kite is one of the most noticeable and versatile raptors in warmer parts of the Old World, scavenging in hundreds in towns and villages.

Specializing mainly on fish, water-birds and carrion are the fish eagles, the most famous of which is the Bald eagle, the national emblem of the USA. This group also includes the remarkable Palm-nut vulture, which feeds mainly on the fruit of the Oil palm, with which it is always associated.

Although many birds of prey sometimes take carrion, the Old World vultures eat little else. Most are very large, with bare or down-covered heads and necks for "wallowing in putridity" as Darwin put it. The Egyptian vulture, which breeds in caves, is one of the few tool-using birds, breaking eggs by throwing stones onto them. The Bearded vulture has the curious habit of dropping bones onto rocks to gain access to the marrow. (See also pp116–117.)

Snake eagles are large birds, with large owl-like heads and yellow eyes, short toes adapted to killing snakes, which are carried in the crop and regurgitated to the single young. The unusual bateleur has very long wings and a very short tail; its name derives from the French for "juggler," a reference to its acrobatic courtship displays.

Harrier hawks and the Crane hawk are medium-sized woodland hawks. They have unique "double-jointed" legs which can bend either way at the middle joint; these are used, among other things, for reaching nestling birds and other small creatures in tree holes and crevices. Otherwise, the birds hunt by slow methodical searching of the ground for small animals.

Another group which hunts by slowly searching grassland and marshes are the harriers, a uniform group of medium-sized, slim-bodied, long-winged, long-tailed hawks. They feed mainly on small mammals and birds, and some reptiles and insects. They have owl-like faces, with ears spe-cialized to locate prey in thick vegetation. The males often maintain "harems" of females. Most nest amid tall herbs on the ground, laying 5–7 whitish eggs, but the Australian spotted harrier nests in trees.

The largest genus of raptors comprises the chanting goshawks, goshawks and sparrowhawks. They are small to medium-sized hawks, all with short rounded wings and long tails, adapted for woodland or forest; many feed largely or entirely on birds. The chanting goshawks eat various small animals caught on the ground.

Buzzard, buteonines and harpies are a large varied group feeding mainly on mammals and some birds. The largest and most powerful is the Harpy eagle, which inhabits tropical South American forests and eats monkeys, other mammals and large birds. The rare Monkey-eating eagle of the Philippines has a striking appearance, a spiky head plume giving it an oddly human face. The buteonines are particularly widespread, including the Common buzzard of Europe and the Red-tailed hawk of North America.

The true or booted eagles are distinguished from other eagles by having feathered legs. They feed mainly on live prey, but those of genus *Aquila* take some carrion and the Indian black eagle is specialized to feed on birds' eggs and nestlings. This group includes the Golden eagle.

All the Accipitridae build their own nests of sticks or similar material, usually on trees or cliffs, and lay whitish or pale-greenish eggs, often with brown marks. The small species lay 5–7 eggs and the largest species only one; incubation and nestling periods range from 32 days and 26 days respectively in small species to around 50 and 120 days respectively in large ones.

Like some other raptors, the Accipitridae are noted for their spectacular aerial displays. Some consist of little more than soaring over the nest-area, either single birds or the pair together, but others involve great flying skill. Some develop into "mock attacks," in which one bird may dive at the other, and even touch or grip feet, spinning down in cartwheeling fashion. Most species have a "sky-dance" display, which involves marked undulations, as a bird swings up on flapping wings and then down on closed wings, repeatedly. In some species the wing beats are slower and more exaggerated than normal. The harriers have a spectacular aerial food pass, in which the flying male drops food to the female, who flies up, turns over and catches it in mid air. In most other species, the food transfers usually take place in a perched position.

▲ **Aerial food pass.** In Marsh harriers, the male, when bringing food for the young, does not return to the nest. Instead, the female flies up to him, turns upside down and catches the prey dropped by the male.

▶ **Tail fanned** like the flaps of an airplane, an Augur buzzard (*Buteo rufofuscus*) swoops low. The pronounced aerofoil section of the wings is especially prominent here. The Augur buzzard is the most common buzzard of East and southern Africa.

▶ **Aerial courtship displays.** Not surprisingly, the birds of prey use their superb flying skills in courtship. BELOW LEFT "Whirling." A pair of African fish eagles grapple with each other's talons, tumbling together in cartwheels or swinging from side-to-side like falling leaves. (1) Undulating display. These undulations may be shallow or pronounced. In the Hen harrier the bird dives with wings partly closed, then regains height by flapping. (2) "Pot hooks." In this extreme form of undulating display, shown by Tawny eagles, the bird dives and swoops without wing flapping. (3) "Pendulum." In this display, shown by Verreaux's eagles, the bird describes a figure of eight over and over.

▶ **Landing the catch** OVERLEAF. An osprey brings a sizeable meal back to its mate and young nesting in mangrove vegetation in the Red Sea. Ospreys are found throughout most of Europe, Asia and North America.

Nearly every raptor species that has been studied performs some sort of migratory movement in at least part of its range. The longest journeys are made by those birds which fly regularly between eastern Siberia and southern Africa (eg Eastern red-footed falcons), or between northern North America and southern South America (eg tundra-breeding Peregrine falcons). This entails flying more than 18,650mi (30,000km) on migration each year.

Most raptors have only one mate in a year; some keep the same mate for several years. Some large eagles are generally thought to "pair for life," but as yet there is really little evidence for this. Polygyny, in which one male may have more than one female at a time, is frequent among harriers, and polyandry, in which one female may have more than one male, is frequent in the Harris hawk, a desert species of central America. Both mating systems have occasionally been recorded in other raptors too.

In most raptors there is a marked division

of labor during the breeding cycle. The male provides the food and hunts mainly away from the nest, while the female stays near the nest, and is responsible for incubating the eggs and for looking after the young. The difference between the parents persists at least until the young are about half-grown, after which the female may also begin to leave the nest area to hunt. The young themselves hatch with a full covering of down and with their eyes open, in contrast to most other nest-reared birds. In the majority of raptors the mother initially tears up small pieces of meat for the young, which they take from her bill, but before fledging they learn to tear up prey for themselves.

In vultures, the partners share parental duties more equally, as they take turns on the nest, and between times seek their own food, some of which they later regurgitate to the young.

As a group, raptors vary in the way they space themselves in their habitat, depending largely on how their food is distributed. Three main systems are found. In the first, pairs are spaced out in individual home ranges. This seems to be usual in about 75 percent of the 80 raptor genera, including some of the largest, such as *Accipiter, Buteo, Aquila* and *Falco*. Each pair defends the vicinity of the nest and a variable amount of surrounding terrain, so that home ranges may be exclusive or overlapping. Throughout suitable habitat, the nests of different pairs tend to be spaced fairly regularly, at distances from less than 650ft (200m) apart in some small raptors to more than 18.5mi (30km) apart in some large ones. Most species that space themselves in this way feed on live vertebrate prey and show considerable stability in numbers and distribution from year to year. Individuals usually hunt and roost alone.

In the second system, birds nest in loose colonies and hunt solitarily. This system is shown, among others, by the Black and Red kites and the Letter-winged kite, and by the Marsh harrier, the Hen harrier and Montagu's harrier. Groups of pairs nest close together in "neighborhoods" and range out to forage in the surrounding area. The different pairs may hunt in different directions from one another, or several may hunt the same area independently, from time to time shifting from one area to another. The breeding groups usually contain less than ten pairs, with nests spaced at 230–650ft (70–200m) apart. Larger groups have sometimes been found, including up to 30 pairs of Montagu's harriers and some 54 pairs of kites (49 Black kites and five Red

kites). In harriers, the tendency to coloniality is sometimes accentuated by polygyny, because each male may have two or
more females nesting close together, and in
both harriers and kites it is accentuated by
the frequent need to concentrate in patches
of restricted nesting habitat. Even where
nesting cover is widespread, however, the
colonial habit is still apparent. Such species
often exploit sporadic food sources, such as
local grasshopper or rodent plagues. They
are nomadic to some extent, concentrating
to breed wherever food is temporarily plentiful, so that local populations may fluctuate
substantially from year to year. Not all pairs
of such species nest in groups, however.

Outside the breeding season, kites and
harriers tend to base themselves in communal roosts, from which they spread out to
hunting areas during the day. Kites roost in
trees and harriers in reeds or long grass, in
which each bird tramples the vegetation to
form a platform. The roosts usually contain
up to 20 individuals, occasionally more, and
up to 300 harriers of several species were
counted at one place in Africa. The same
roosts may be used year after year, but by
greatly varying numbers of birds.

In the third system, pairs nest in dense
colonies and forage gregariously. This
system is shown by the small snail-eating
Everglade kite, by the insect-eating kites of
the genera *Elanoides*, *Gampsonyx*, *Elanus* and
Ictinia; by the insect-eating Lesser kestrel,
Red-footed falcon, Eastern red-footed falcon
and Eleonora's falcon, and by the large Griffon vultures. In these species, the pairs typically nest closer together—often less than
230ft (70m) apart—and in larger aggregations than do those mentioned above. They
also feed communally in scattered flocks or,
in the case of the vultures, spread out in the
air, but crowd together around carcasses.
The feeding flocks are not stable, but change
continually in size and composition, as birds
join or leave. Colonies usually contain up to
20 or 30 pairs, but those of Everglade kites
sometimes reach about 100 pairs and those
of some Griffon vultures more than 250. The
food sources of these various species are
even more sporadic and fast-changing than
those of the previous group. Food may be
plentiful at one place on one day and at
another place on the next. Such species
roost communally at all times and, when
not breeding, may gather in enormous
numbers. The insect-eating falcons in their
African winter quarters use the same roosts
year after year, which often contain
thousands of individuals of several species.
One was found to hold 50,000–100,000

birds, mainly Eastern red-footed falcons.
Such birds exploit local flushes of food, such
as termites and locusts, and move around
over long distances in response to changes
in prey availability.

Whatever their dispersion, most raptors
choose special places for their nests. Such
places may be cliffs, isolated trees, groves of
trees, or patches of forest or ground cover,
depending on the species. Many such places
are occupied over long periods of years. Particular cliffs are known to have been used
by successive pairs of Golden eagles or of
White-tailed eagles, Peregrine falcons or
gyrfalcons for periods of 70–100 years.
Among 49 British Peregrine cliffs known to
falconers between the 16th and 19th centuries, at least 42 were still in use during
1930–39. In trees, too, certain eagle nests
have been used for longer than a man's
lifetime and, added to year after year, have
often reached enormous size. One historic

▲ **Ugly ducklings** or rather Ferruginous hawk
(*Buteo regalis*) chicks, a species of western North
America.

▶ **A Booted eagle** (*Hieraaetus pennatus*) and its
young, showing the immature plumage. Booted
eagles are forest-steppe-dwelling species and
they nest on wooded mountain slopes and in
ravines.

Larger than the Male

One of the most interesting features of raptors is the marked difference in size between the sexes, with the female being larger than the male—up to twice as heavy in some species. This sexual dimorphism is evidently connected with the raptorial life-style, because the same occurs in other predatory birds, such as owls and skuas. In general, the difference in size increases with the speed and agility of the prey. At one extreme, those vultures that feed entirely on immobile carcasses show no consistent size difference between the sexes. In raptors which eat very slow moving prey, such as snails, the female is only slightly bigger than the male. The insect feeders and reptile feeders show a somewhat greater size difference, the mammal and fish feeders somewhat more, while the bird feeders have the largest difference of all. The greatest size difference is shown by the species that take the largest prey in relation to their own size. Thus the bird-feeding raptors often kill prey heavier than themselves. In such species, the size difference between the sexes is so marked that males and females eat mainly different sizes of prey. Despite this link with diet, it is not known why the female is the larger sex and not the male, but probably this is connected with the female's role in breeding.

Bald eagle nest in America spanned 86 sq ft (8sq m) on top and contained "two wagonloads" of material, while another was 10ft (3m) across and 16.5ft (5m) high. Such nests sometimes become so heavy from the continued addition of material over the years that the branch supporting them breaks off, and the birds are forced to start anew. Some osprey nests have been in continuous use for periods exceeding 40 years, and even patches of ground cover have been used by Hen harriers for several decades. In general, of course, sites on rock must be more permanent than those in trees, and sites in trees more permanent than those in herbaceous cover.

Colonial raptors also tend to nest in the same places year after year, and in southern Africa many cliffs whose names indicate that they were used by vultures in previous centuries are still used by these birds today. As in other colonial birds, the individuals defend only a small area around their nests, so that, given enough ledges, many pairs can crowd onto the same cliff, leaving other apparently suitable cliffs vacant.

Because of their special nesting requirements, raptors are among the few groups of birds whose numbers and nest success are in some regions clearly limited by numbers

of nest sites available. For example, the breeding density of cliff dwellers may be limited by the number of cliffs with suitable ledges, and their breeding success by the accessibility of these ledges to predators. Other raptors may be limited in open landscapes by shortage of trees. This is particularly true in the prairies, steppes and other grassland areas, which offer abundant food for raptors but also have huge areas without trees for nesting. Even in woodlands, nest sites may sometimes be fewer than they first appear. In a large area of mature forest in Finland, covering several hundred sq mi, less than one in a thousand trees were judged by a biologist to be suitable for nests of White-tailed eagles, while in younger forests, suitable open-crowned trees were scarcer or non-existent. It has often proved possible to increase the breeding density of birds of prey by providing nest sites artificially. Nest boxes for kestrels are an obvious example, but several species have taken readily to buildings and quarries where natural cliffs are lacking, and ospreys in North America nest freely on special platforms provided for the purpose.

Where nesting sites are surplus to needs, and where the birds are not reduced by human activities, their numbers seem to be limited by food supplies. Species with varied diets tend thereby to have fairly stable food supplies. Their breeding populations also remain stable, fluctuating in particular areas by no more than 10 percent of the mean over long periods of years. They provide extreme examples among birds of long-term stability in numbers. Examples include

HUNTING FOR FISH
—The White-bellied sea eagle

▲ **Feet first,** an eagle closes in for the kill.

▶ **Impact** BOTTOM. The force of the talons usually kills the fish outright. Here the impact has dragged the eagle's legs behind it as it begins to fly away with its catch.

▶ **The eagle's grasp** MIDDLE. The grip of one foot is sufficient to secure the prey as the eagle flies off to a safe perch to devour its catch.

▶ **Lost prey** TOP. An eagle is forced to drop its catch by harassment from two more eagles.

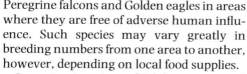

Peregrine falcons and Golden eagles in areas where they are free of adverse human influence. Such species may vary greatly in breeding numbers from one area to another, however, depending on local food supplies.

In contrast, raptors which have restricted diets, based on prey with seasonal population extremes, fluctuate in breeding density from year to year in any one area, in parallel with their prey. Examples include kestrels, Hen harriers and Rough-legged buzzards, which feed on rodents, and goshawks which in boreal regions feed on hares and grouse. The rodents and their various predators usually show intervals of 4 years between population peaks, and the hares, grouse and their predators more like 7–10 years. The goshawk is particularly instructive, because its breeding populations tend to remain stable in areas where prey-supplies are stable and fluctuate where prey supplies are unstable.

In general, small species of raptors, which feed on small and abundant prey, occur at higher densities than the larger raptors, which feed on larger, sparser prey. A small kestrel, for example, would normally have a hunting range of 0.4sq mi (1sq km) or less, a buzzard would have a range of 0.4–2sq mi (1–5sq km), whereas a large eagle would hunt over a much greater area. The African Martial eagle, which eats small antelopes and gamebirds, is extreme, as it occurs at one pair per 48–116sq mi (125–300sq km), with 18.5–25mi (30–40km) between pairs; it is thus one of the most thinly distributed birds in the world. Large colonial raptors, such as the Griffon vultures, occur in high numbers at their colonies, but when their extensive feeding areas are taken into account, their overall

densities are in fact extremely low. Feeding on other animals, it would of course be expected that raptors of whatever size would occur at low density compared with other birds feeding on small prey.

To counter the widespread population declines, many attempts have been made in recent years to increase raptor numbers, either by management of the birds themselves or of their habitat and food supplies. Management principles that have been applied for decades to game animals can be applied to the conservation of raptors, but conserving raptors is more difficult because of the greater land areas needed to sustain populations, and because their conflicts with other human activities create unsympathetic attitudes. For raptors in general, three main factors have been identified as causing declines (or limiting numbers): restriction and degradation of habitat, persecution by man and contamination by toxic chemicals.

On a world scale, habitat destruction has already accounted for bigger reductions in raptor and other wildlife populations than has any other factor; and with the continuing growth in human population and development, it is still the most serious threat in the long term. Irrespective of any other adverse influence, habitat sets the ultimate limit on the size and distribution of any wild population.

Since the carrying capacity of any area for raptors is usually set by nest-sites or food

supplies, for some species a shortage of nest-sites can be rectified by adding sites artificially, as discussed above. Raising the carrying capacity of an area through increasing the food supply is much more difficult, because it usually entails changing the land-use to promote an increase in prey. Often the best that can be achieved is to preserve existing areas of good habitat, or prevent their further degradation. In North America and Africa, the larger national parks provide some excellent raptor habitat, capable of maintaining large populations; but in more heavily peopled countries, most areas that can be preserved in this way are too small

▲ **A secure future?** A Bald eagle chick in its nest high over the coniferous forest and lakeland habitat. The existence of suitable nest-sites is a prime factor in the conservation of birds of prey.

▶ **Feeding perch.** A Bald eagle has brought a Pink salmon to what is obviously a favorite feeding place on a jutting branch.

Preying on Game

The natural feeding habits of raptors inevitably lead some species to take gamebirds and domestic stock. This forms the major conflict between raptors and men, and is the main reason why raptors have been so heavily persecuted. In fact, the impact of raptors on game or domestic animals is usually negligible, though in a few cases it can be severe.

One serious problem in parts of Europe is predation by goshawks on intensively reared pheasants. The young pheasants are hatched in incubators, and when they are six weeks old are put out in woodland in open pens, from which they are gradually released to the woodland, and encouraged to stay by the regular provision of grain or other food. Goshawks often concentrate in pheasant rearing areas, and despite regular trapping programs, may take a substantial proportion of the stock. These pheasants would otherwise be available to the hunters, who have paid for their production. In Finland alone, some 4,000–8,000 goshawks are killed each year

by game hunters, yet here these hawks seem to maintain their numbers.

Other problems concern eagles. Wherever these birds live alongside sheep, they feed on dead sheep and lambs, and also kill some live lambs. This is true of the Golden eagle in parts of Europe and North America, the White-tailed eagle in Norway and Greenland, the Wedge-tailed eagle in Australia, and the Black and Martial eagles in southern Africa. In most areas, their impact on the lamb crop is generally negligible, but in some localities it can be serious. As a result, Golden eagles were killed on a considerable scale in western Texas and southeast New Mexico after the discovery that these birds could be shot down from airplanes. Over a period of 20 years, until it was banned in 1962, 1,000–2,000 birds were shot annually in sheep-ranching areas.

In most countries birds of prey are now protected by law, but some exceptions are made to deal with troublesome species in local areas. The law is hard to enforce, however, and illicit killing is common.

to support many birds. This is especially true of the large species that require huge areas to sustain them.

Human persecution is less serious now than in the past, at least in northern countries where bounty schemes have increasingly given way to protective legislation. At the time of writing, 14 European countries afford full protection to all raptors, 16 afford partial protection (certain species, certain regions or certain seasons), while one country (Malta) gives no protection. In North America, Japan and the Soviet Union, all species are fully protected. Such legislation has met with varying success in different countries, as attitudes towards it have ranged from respect to scorn, and bird protection is anyway difficult to enforce and to monitor.

The only long-term solution against the effects of pesticides is to reduce the use of the chemicals involved, so that their concentration in the environment falls. In northern countries this has been achieved by substituting other chemicals which are less toxic or less persistent than the offending ones.

At the same time, a number of different measures have been taken to counter the effects of organochlorine pesticides, until environmental levels fall sufficiently to enable the birds to survive on their own. These mostly entail the movement of eggs and young from one area to another or from captivity to the wild.

Several species have been propagated in captivity for release to the wild. The most notable is the Peregrine falcon, which has been recently re-established in the eastern United States from captive-bred stock. Similar schemes have involved the reintroduction of Griffon vultures in France, Bearded vultures in Switzerland, and Bald eagles in New York State. Other reintroduction schemes have entailed transplanting young birds from one region to another, as in the current program to re-establish the White-tailed eagle in Scotland. Wherever a species has been eliminated by human activities from otherwise suitable habitat, reintroduction is clearly worthwhile, for the long-term security of any species depends on its maintaining a diversified population. The distribution of many large raptors has been so fragmented by human activities that there is now little hope of such species recolonizing isolated patches of habitat naturally—at least not within the foreseeable future. For these, reintroduction schemes offer the best chance of success, wherever habitat is still good.   IN

Shell-shock

Pesticides and birds of prey

Of all pesticides yet used widely, the so-called "organochlorines" have had the most harmful effects on wildlife populations, especially of predatory birds, some of which have been exterminated over areas up to half the size of the USA. Besides being toxic, these chemicals have three main properties which contribute to their devastating effects. Firstly, they are chemically extremely stable, so they persist more or less unchanged in the environment for many years. Secondly, they dissolve in fat, which means that they can accumulate in animals' bodies, and pass from prey to predator, concentrating at successive steps in a food chain. Raptors are at the top of their food chains, and are thus especially liable to accumulate large amounts. Thirdly, at sublethal levels of only a few parts per million in tissues, organochlorines can disrupt the breeding of certain birds, and reduce the number of young produced. Moreover, organochlorine pesticides can become dispersed over wide areas in the bodies of migrant animals, and in air and water currents, so can affect populations far removed from areas of usage. Some other pesticides may cause heavy mortality among wildlife locally, but because these pesticides break down more quickly they neither have lasting effects, nor do they affect organisms in areas remote from places of application.

All bird species that have been studied have been found to be susceptible to these pesticides. The most marked population declines have occurred in bird-feeding raptors, especially the Peregrine falcon, but also the sparrowhawk in Europe and the Sharp-shinned hawk and Cooper's hawk in North America. Certain fish-eaters have also declined greatly, including the osprey and the Bald eagle in parts of North America and the White-tailed eagle in northern Europe.

DDT, the first and commonest of the organochlorines, is not particularly toxic to birds, but its principal breakdown product, DDE, causes thinning of eggshells. Such shells often break during incubation, so that fewer young are produced. DDE and other breakdown products may also cause embryo deaths in intact eggs, thus further lowering the hatching success. If the birds

▲ **Fragile niche.** The Peregrine falcon was affected more severely than most birds of prey by the ravages of persistent pesticides. The peregrines are recovering but still need safe nest-sites and unspoiled habitat.

▶ **Toxic effect.** A peregrine egg, its shell thinned by the effects of DDT, has been crushed during incubation, resulting in the death of the young.

◀ **Fiercely maternal,** a sparrowhawk broods her young in the rain. In parts of the Northern Hemisphere, populations of birds of prey are slowly recovering from the damage inflicted by pesticides, but in developing countries many species are now threatened.

The more toxic organochlorines, such as aldrin and dieldrin, kill adult birds and in some cases have led to population decline. These chemicals were held responsible for the elimination of the Peregrine falcon and sparrowhawk from large parts of Britain in the period 1957–60. They were used as dressings on cereal grains to protect the grains against insect attack; some of the grains were eaten by seed-eating birds, and these birds were then in turn eaten by the raptors.

Death from organochlorine poisoning is often delayed. These chemicals are stored in body fat, and a bird may die when its fat is used to provide energy and the organochlorine is released to the other, more sensitive tissues. Thus birds may die during periods of food shortage or migration, from organochlorines accumulated in the body during the previous months.

Birds of prey which breed in areas free from pesticide use do not escape contamination if they, or their prey species, migrate to winter in areas where these chemicals are used. Peregrine falcons nesting in arctic North America have recently declined, as a result of increasing DDT usage in Latin America, where these Peregrines winter. Other migrant birds which breed in the Northern Hemisphere are also likely to decline, as a result of growing organochlorine use in tropical and subtropical countries.

In areas where organochlorine use has been curtailed, these birds have mostly begun to recover in numbers, and to recolonize areas from which they were eliminated. However, certain DDT residues—particularly DDE—are so persistent in soils that they could well remain a problem for birds of prey and other animals for several decades after use of DDT has ceased. There is as yet no sign that any bird species has developed any degree of resistance to organochlorine pesticides.

In Europe and North America, the use of organochlorines reached a peak in the 1960s, but since then it has declined, as one country after another has banned them. However, their use in the developing countries of the tropics and subtropics is increasing rapidly, under pressure from agriculturalists and from manufacturers, eager to exploit these new markets. Preliminary signs are that raptors and other wildlife are declining there as they did in the northern countries, twenty years earlier. Alternative pesticides are now available, which have less severe environmental effects, but many are more expensive than DDT.   IN

do not produce enough young to offset the normal adult mortality, the population declines, eventually becoming extinct. Different groups of birds vary in their sensitivity to DDE residues. Birds of prey are particularly vulnerable, partly because a given level of DDE produces more shell thinning than in other birds, and also because, being predators, they accumulate larger amounts than most other birds. As assessed by shell-thinning, herons and pelicans are also relatively sensitive to DDE, whereas game-birds and songbirds are relatively insensitive.

Nature's Scavengers
Old and New World vultures

Vultures vary considerably in their nesting and foraging habits. The most strongly gregarious are the large griffons: the Griffon vulture (Eurasia), Rüppell's griffon (northern Africa) and Cape vulture (southern Africa), which nest on cliffs in big colonies numbering up to 100 pairs or more, with some nests only a few yards apart. One of the largest concentrations known is around the Gol escarpment in East Africa. It contains more than 1,000 pairs of Rüppell's vultures, distributed in several colonies, and supported largely by the big game populations of the Serengeti Plain. Such birds feed entirely from large carcasses and, being dependent on migrant animals, they often have to fly great distances for food, taking more than one day over each trip. They have been followed up to 93mi (150km) from the colony.

The food searching of Griffon vultures is extremely efficient. Following the Charge of the Light Brigade in the Crimean War (1854), so many birds gathered on the battlefields that shooting squads were posted to protect the injured. Abilities to find isolated carcasses and to gather quickly in large numbers in areas where they had apparently been scarce have caused some people to suspect a sensitivity to smell or telepathic ability, while some native Africans think that vultures dream the locations of food. In fact Griffons rely on vision, but

▶ **Plague of vultures.** Vultures are always on the look-out not only for carcasses but signs that other vultures have spotted a carcass. Hence the vast flocks that can gather very quickly. Their role as scavengers, although it might seem distasteful, is beneficial in speedily removing carcasses before putrescence has set in. These are Asian white-backed vultures.

◀ **Mobbing.** Birds of prey often suffer mobbing attacks by smaller birds. This Griffon vulture is being mobbed by ravens at 12,500ft (3,800m) in the Himalayas.

▼ **Stripped to the bone.** These Rüppell's griffons in Kenya will have devoured the wildebeest within half an hour. Contrary to popular belief, they normally eat only very fresh meat.

most find food indirectly by watching the activities of neighboring birds in the air.

If a bird spots a carcass, it begins to circle lower. Its neighbors notice this, and fly towards the scene. These birds are in turn noticed by their neighbors, so that, within minutes, birds are converging from all points of the compass. If trees are available, the birds sit for a while before descending, but once the first few individuals are down, there is a rush for a place at the carcass. A small animal, such as an antelope, can be stripped to the bone in 20 minutes. The birds themselves squabble and fight while feeding, and the more dominant individuals can cram so much food in their crops that they can hardly take wing again. With their efficient food-searching, Griffons are extremely effective scavengers. Their only drawbacks are that they cannot operate at night, nor can they compete with large mammalian carnivores, which can easily drive them from a carcass. Also, their gregarious habits make them extremely vulnerable where carcasses have been poisoned by man.

Other similar species, including the African and Asian white-backed vultures, also feed entirely on carcasses, but they depend more on resident and less on migrant game, and so travel less far than the cliff-nesting Griffons. They tend to nest in smaller, more scattered colonies, and occasionally as individual pairs, but on trees rather than cliffs. They weigh less, so can take wing earlier in the day. Like the large Griffons, they also gather in large numbers at carcasses.

Another group of Old World vultures, including the Lappet-faced vulture and the European black vulture, behave in some respects like eagles. Individual pairs nest far apart and hold large ranges around their nests. They feed partly from large carcasses, but also take smaller items, including living prey; they do not fly long distances to forage, so it is rare to find more than one or two pairs at the same corpse.

Although several species of vulture may assemble at the same carcass, they do not all feed in the same way, or take the same tissues. In southern Europe, the Griffon vulture eats mainly the softer meat, the large Black vulture more often tears meat and skin off bones, the small Egyptian vulture pecks off tiny scraps of meat remaining on the bones, while the Bearded vulture takes the bones themselves. Moreover, only the Griffon depends entirely on large carcasses, the rest have other foods as well.

The various New World vultures and condors are not closely related to the Old World ones, but have developed some similar habits. Individuals usually nest well apart from one another, but they roost communally and feed in groups, especially the nonbreeders. Pairs of Turkey vultures or Black vultures occasionally breed in loose aggregations where large cliffs hold several suitable caves, and the two species often roost together. Unlike the Old World vultures, at least some New World species which live in forest use smell to help locate carcasses. The Turkey vulture has this sense unusually well developed compared with other birds, and is capable of finding covered carcasses or those on the forest floor. Other New World vultures, such as the King vulture, have no great sense of smell, but reach food in the forest by following other species to it. A sense of smell has enabled New World vultures to occupy forests and woodland, habitats which are closed to the Old World species which depend on sight alone. IN

GAME BIRDS

Order: Galliformes
Families: Phasianidae, Tetraonidae, Meleagrididae, Numididae, Megapodiidae, Cracidae.
Two-hundred and sixty-three species in 75 genera.
Distribution: worldwide except Antarctica and southern South America.

Turkeys   Guinea fowl

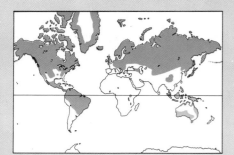

Grouse   Guans   Megapodes

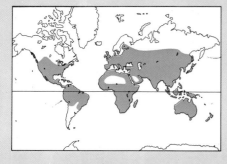

Pheasants
and Quails

Ground-dwelling **pheasants and quails** make up the largest and most widespread family in the order Galliformes, which also contains the grouse, turkeys, guinea fowl, megapodes, guans and curassows.

The family includes some remarkable birds: the Domestic fowl, man's most useful bird; the Blue peacock, a byword for beauty and mythology; the Crested argus pheasant, which has the largest feathers of any wild species in its tail; the Tibetan snowcock, which lives at a higher altitude than any other bird. From the dense rain forests of Southeast Asia to the arid deserts of Arabia or the high rocks of the Himalayas, almost every habitat has its characteristic species of pheasants or quails. They are absent only from Antarctica, some oceanic islands, the southern half of South America (where they are replaced by tinamous) and the tundras and forests of the far north (where they are replaced by grouse).

Nearly all pheasants and quails are heavy, rotund birds with short legs and rounded wings. From the tiny Blue quail to the stately Blue peacock, they are strong runners and rarely fly except to escape from danger, when they burst from cover in an explosion of rapid wingbeats. Although some quails (*Coturnix* species) are migratory, for flying most members of the family rely only on glycogen-burning sprint muscles; they cannot remain airborne for long and are therefore sedentary, staying within a few miles of their birthplace. Except for some of the tree quails of Central America and the tragopans of eastern Asia which are partly arboreal in habits, they feed exclusively on the ground. Many species, however, roost in trees at night to avoid ground predators. Most are generalized herbivores, eating seeds or shoots, but some forest species search among leaf litter for insects or fallen fruit. All are day-active.

The family can be divided into four groups: New World quails, Old World quails, partridges and pheasants. The New World quails are most typically plump, little quails, boldly marked with black, white, buff and gray; some carry firm, forward-pointing crests or "topknots." Perhaps the best known species is the Bobwhite quail which is often pursued by hunters in the USA.

Old World quails are found throughout the grasslands of Africa, Asia and Australia. The Common quail migrates from Africa to Europe and from India to Central Asia to breed. Two other species are nomadic, invading areas in large flocks following rain: the Harlequin quail in Africa and the

Blue quail in Asia, Africa and Australia.

The partridges are a diverse collection of stocky, medium-sized game birds found in a range of habitats throughout the Old World. They include the giant snowcocks which may weigh 6.6lb (3kg) and inhabit the alpine tundras of the mountains in Central Asia. In Southeast Asia, there are several poorly known species which inhabit tropical rain forests, including the splendid roulroul. Partridges are most commonly found, however, in open habitats such as semideserts, grassland and scrub. Many species adapt well to cultivation, notably the Gray or Hungarian partridge and the chukars, which are common in farmland throughout much of Europe and have been introduced to North America. In Europe, modern agricultural techniques, in particular the widespread use of pesticides and herbicides, have caused a steady decline in numbers in recent years. Africa has only two genera of partridges, the bantam-like

▲ **Iridescent plumage** of the Himalayan monal pheasant is rivaled by few birds. The metallic hues of the male pheasant contrast with the duller camouflage markings of females.

green, black and red. For a long time, European naturalists simply dismissed these birds as figments of the imagination of Chinese artists, so fantastic did they seem.

There is an interesting variation in social organization within the family. Most of the smaller quails and partridges are highly gregarious but monogamous. Some of the larger pheasants, such as peafowl, are also gregarious, but many are solitary, especially those that inhabit dense forest. These species are usually polygynous (one male mating with several females) or promiscuous, forming no pair bonds.

Among partridges and quails the basic social unit is the covey, one family party perhaps with a few other birds attached. In species which occupy open habitats (eg snowcocks, chukars or Bobwhite quail) coveys often fuse to form larger flocks. At the other extreme, in forest-dwelling partridges such as the Black wood partridge of Malaysia or some of the francolins, adults live singly or in pairs throughout the year.

Pair formation usually takes place before the covey breaks up, although males often join another covey to seek a mate. As recent experiments with Japanese quail have demonstrated, this is probably to avoid inbreeding, although the quail were found to prefer their first cousins to more distant relatives when choosing a mate.

Among the larger, polygynous pheasants, courtship involves long and spectacular rituals. An extraordinary but rarely seen sight is the display of the male Satyr tragopan from India and Nepal, which lowers a fleshy, electric-blue lappet from its throat and inflates two slender blue horns on its crown. In the Himalayan monal pheasant the iridescent males display in flight over the high cliffs and forests, calling wildly—a breathtaking sight. Perhaps the most exciting of all displays is the dance of the Great argus pheasant in the forests of Malaysia. Adult males have huge, broad, secondary wing feathers, each adorned with a series of circular, golden decorations shaded to appear three-dimensional. An adult male prepares a special dance floor on the top of a hill in the middle of the forest. From this site he plucks leaves and stems and blows away leaf litter by clapping his enormous wings. Early each morning he gives loud, wailing cries to attract females. If a female arrives, he begins to dance about her and, at the climax of his dance, throws up his wings into two enormous semicircular fans and makes hundreds of "eyes." In the gap between his wings, his real eye can be seen staring at the female.

Stone partridge and the diverse francolins of which there are more than 40 species, most of them confined to Africa. These partridge-like birds are sturdy, live in a variety of habitats, and tend to be rather noisy.

The term pheasant is usually reserved for the large, colorful, long-tailed members of the family. Of these 48 species in 16 genera, all but one are confined to Asia. The exception is the extraordinary and beautiful Congo peacock, the late discovery of which, by W. L. Chapin in 1936, was an ornithological sensation. Pheasants are forest birds; some live in the rain forests of Southeast Asia, others at various altitudes on the great mountains of Central Asia. Despite colorful male plumage and loud, raucous calls, most are shy and rarely seen. Extreme examples of this are the ruffed pheasants of western China—the Golden and Lady Amherst's (or Flower) pheasants. Males of both species are astonishingly gaudy, the Golden in red, yellow and orange, Lady Amherst's in white,

In the two species of argus pheasants, the display may end with mating, after which the female leaves to rear the brood unaided. However, in jungle fowl and Ring-necked pheasants the male forms bonds with a number of females and guards them as his "harem" until the eggs are laid. This mating system is almost unknown in other birds (though common in mammals).

With the exception of tragopans, all pheasants and quails nest on the ground, forming a single scrape, usually in dense, herbaceous vegetation. Clutch size varies from two in argus pheasants to nearly 20 in the Gray partridge (the largest clutch size of any bird). Predators often take a heavy toll of the eggs and female Ring-necked pheasants may make two or more nesting attempts each season. The female Red-legged partridge lays two clutches, one for the male to incubate, the second for herself. Apart from this species, males take little or no part in incubation. In captivity, female Golden pheasants have been found to incubate continuously without food, water, or even moving, for 22 days. In one case so still did the bird sit that a spider built its web across her back. Whether this happens in the wild, in China, has yet to be established.

The young are well developed—they leave the nest within a few hours, feed themselves from birth and can fly as young as one week old. Young Blue quail can and do breed when only two months old. Because they are so prolific, pheasants and quails can sustain heavy predation losses and man has learnt to exploit this by managing them for hunting. Many species are hunted, notably the Ring-necked pheasant.

The Red jungle fowl has an even more intimate relationship with man. Still a wild native of India and Southeast Asia, this species was domesticated at least 5,000 years ago. Since then it has been transformed into the many different forms of Domestic fowl used by man for purposes as diverse as egg production and cock fighting.

Unfortunately, the fact that pheasants and quails are good to eat has also led to excessive persecution. Not only have some species been hunted to the brink of extinction—over the brink in the case of the Indian mountain quail (although there are recent unconfirmed sightings) and the New Zealand quail, but many are vulnerable to destruction of habitat. This is because they are sedentary and, as ground feeders, are direct competitors with man's most effective ally in the destruction of natural ecosystems—the goat. The species in most serious trouble are the large, forest pheasants of the Himalayas and eastern Asia. More than one-third of pheasant species are threatened with extinction.

However, there is a glimmer of hope. Many pheasants can be bred in captivity with comparative ease. Breeding of the Cheer pheasant of India by aviculturalists, for instance, is so successful that a captive surplus population exists, and attempts have been made to return captive-bred birds of this (and other species) to the wild in areas of Pakistan in which they have become extinct. Such efforts have proved extremely difficult, but there are successes. The Masked race of the Bobwhite quail, for example, has been reintroduced successfully to Arizona. To educate the young quails about the real world it has proved necessary to scare them with simulated attacks from coyotes and men with guns. To teach them the arts of courtship and mating they were mixed with vasectomized quails of another wild subspecies.   MWR

The endless coniferous forests and tundra are home to most **grouse**. When the northern lands in winter are still and nearly empty of other birds, the grouse are there to be seen and heard. Their size and number make them important foods for many predators such as the Red fox and goshawk.

Many grouse inhabit coniferous or deciduous forest. They exploit the northern plant formations with roughly one species for each, eg the Spruce and Blue grouse in boreal forest. Others inhabit more open

▲ ▶ **Gaudy ruff or collar** of the male Golden pheasant ABOVE is spread forward, fanlike, and covers the beak during courtship. Both "collared pheasants" (the other is Lady Amherst's pheasant) are secretive inhabitants of the forests of central China. Competition for mates may flare, RIGHT, involving use of males' spurs, but confrontations rarely result in injury.

▼ **Popular game bird** in North America, the Bobwhite quail inhabits open country from Canada south to Guatemala. Males (distinguished by black-and-white head coloration from the female's buff-yellow) employ their "bob-white" call to attract a mate in spring. In winter, coveys may number up to about 30 birds.

areas, such as Red Grouse in moorland. Generally, grouse migrate short distances between a winter and a summer range within their local distribution.

In shape grouse resemble a plump chicken; in size they range from pigeon to goose; and they live mostly on the ground. They fly with a burst of wings and a long glide. All have camouflage markings but in display they startle with brilliant color, erect plumage, and arresting sounds. Many are well adapted to the winter cold and snow. Grouse have large flight muscles which also function in generation of heat, and storage of nutrients. The large crop and gizzard, and two very large ceca in the hindgut, permit the holding and digestion of large quantities of fibrous food.

The diet of most grouse is notable for its monotony and low quality. Throughout winter most species feed on one or two species of trees or shrubs. Moreover, these may contain oils that are distasteful or poisonous to other animals. The spring and summer provide a more varied diet of new growth and invertebrates. There is a steady ingestion of grit to the gizzard for the grinding of foods and perhaps supply of minerals.

In spring, usually at dawn and at dusk, males contend for mates by calling, wing fluttering, display of neck, tail and wing plumage and colors of the beaks, combs, and air sacs of the neck, and fighting. Females behave similarly but more subtly. Mating may be promiscuous, polygamous, or monogamous depending on species.

About half the species of grouse occupy a solitary territory; the others (eg Black, Sharp-tailed and Sage grouse, and Prairie chicken) form leks on traditional lekking grounds or arenas. A lek is a cluster of males gathered from often great distances and organized into a tight hierarchy of dominance. Hens visit the lek and usually mate with the central and most dominant males.

Some grouse present the puzzle of cyclic fluctuations in numbers. For example, Rock ptarmigan are abundant or scarce at 9–10-year intervals. While many believe that food supply and predators control grouse populations directly, grouse regulate their density by their behavior to each other. What drives this behavior and how it is geared to the environment are unknown. In Blue grouse it is almost certain that populations are regulated in spring by behavior between members of the same species. The nutrient quality of food may limit density by affecting spacing behavior. Another view is that interaction causes a rapid genetic change in the frequency of aggressive or more peaceful individuals in the population. Aggressive individuals take large amounts of space and cause populations to stop growing or decrease, peaceful animals tolerate crowding and allow an increase of population. Such genetic selection may enable grouse populations to adjust to change in the amount of shelter, food and predators.

In the tundra, grouse are little affected by man, while populations of forest and open country species are decreased or increased by logging, grazing or farming. Most endangered is the Prairie chicken of North America; some subspecies are near extinction. There is concern also over the magnificent Sage grouse. In parts of Europe, there appears to be a new long-term decline in numbers of Black grouse and capercaillie that may be caused by acid rain.

Many millions of grouse are killed each year for sport, food and trophies. Habitat management helps preserve and even increase populations of game birds such as Ruffed grouse in North America and the British Red grouse, a subspecies of Willow ptarmigan that lacks white plumage in winter. The plumage of ptarmigan makes the warmest and lightest clothing and bedding. The feather adornments and foot-stamping dance of the plains Indian are a derivative of the plumage and courtship display of the Prairie chicken. Tail feathers of the Black grouse adorn the traditional Scotsman's bonnet.   JFB

Spanish explorers of the 16th century introduced the **turkey** to Europe and it is thought that Mexican Indians first domesticated this valuable source of meat. Today's Domestic turkey probably originated from a Mexican race of the Common turkey.

Turkeys are large birds with strong legs, which in the male have spurs. The two members of the family differ in plumage, especially the tail, and the spurs on the males' legs. They generally walk or run, but can fly strongly for short distances. Both

▲ **Puffed-up gobbler** appears twice its actual size, already up to double that of its potential mates. Among Common turkey males at the strutting ground, most mating is by the top males of the dominant groups, established by fighting prior to the breeding season.

◄ **Burrowing into snow** ABOVE, White-tailed ptarmigans (*Lagopus leucurus*) lie low to stay out of chilling winds and avoid predators. The downy-white plumage extending from nostrils to legs, and "snowshoe" scales on the toes, are adaptations to winter survival in these northerly grouse. The two hens in summer plumage BELOW display camouflage patterning typical of all grouse.

► **Courtship display of cock Sage grouse** OVERLEAF is one of the most spectacular seen in birds. As the long, pointed tail feathers are fanned upward, huge air sacs are inflated beneath the stiff white neck and breast feathers, which are rustled. At the same time, the male utters a deep, bubbling call. Bright yellow neck patches become visible at the peak of the display, then the air sacs are suddenly emptied with a whipcrack sound audible several hundred yards away.

species have similar plumages, but the much smaller Ocellated turkey lacks the "chest tuft" of bristles found on Common turkey males and some females. Both have naked heads (red in the Common and blue in the Ocellated), bearing wattles and other ornaments used in displays. The spurs are larger and more slender in the Ocellated turkey. The characteristic eyespots on the more rounded tail of the Ocellated turkey give the species its common name.

The Common turkey is the more widespread and at the time of European colonization was found as far south as Guatemala. A wide variety of food items has been recorded in the diet of both species. The bulk of the diet is made up of seeds and berries. Acorns are known to be an important part of the diet of the Common turkey in parts of the United States and the bird has a large muscular gizzard to cope with such food items. The male has a thick swelling on the chest during the breeding season, a store of fat and oil on which it draws during its extremely energetic courtship activities.

In the early 19th century turkeys were considered serious agricultural pests and farmers often placed guards around their wheatfields to deter large groups of turkeys. Today grain is known *not* to be an important part of the diet. Small reptiles such as salamanders and lizards are also known to be taken by turkeys. Other rare food items include snakes. Many invertebrates, such as grasshoppers, make up the diet and must provide an important source of protein.

Common turkeys are polygynous (one male mating with several females). Females are thought to start breeding at one year old, whereas males usually have to wait until they are older, due to competition from older, more experienced birds. The male birds go through an elaborate display to acquire mates. Spreading their tail fans, drooping and rattling the main flight feathers, and swelling the head ornaments, they strut up and down on traditional "strutting grounds," gobbling as they do so.

After mating has taken place, the females go off by themselves and build the nest. The nests are usually not far from the strutting grounds and are no more than leaf-lined scrapes in the ground. Although the clutch size ranges from 8 to 15 eggs, one nest may have 20–30 eggs, as more than one female will often lay in a nest. The female alone incubates the eggs, and if she leaves the nest, even for a short period, will make sure the eggs are covered.

The well-developed (precocial) young are cared for by the female for their first two weeks and in the evening they are brooded. However, once the young have the basic use of their wings they spend the nights roosting in the trees. After a few weeks the brood is left to fend for itself.

The brood flock remains together until the young are around six months old, when the males will separate off to form all-male flocks. The males in such a sibling group are inseparable—even a solitary male will not try to join them. The juvenile sibling groups usually form flocks, as the older males can normally chase off the younger birds. This is a tough time for the young male, as he has to do a lot of fighting, both to determine his dominance among his siblings and to help determine his group's status within the flock. Fights can be very vicious and involve the use of wings and spurs. The contest can last for up to two hours and fights to the death have been recorded. However, once dominance has been established within a sibling group it is rarely challenged. Between groups, fights are usually won by the larger unit and, again, once dominance has been established there appears to be a fairly stable society.

Females, too, need to establish rank, but it does not appear to be anything like as overt as among the males. In general, older females are dominant to younger birds, and those females from sibling groups accustomed to winning contests also seem to win individual contests.

Towards the beginning of the breeding season the large male flocks break up, but the sibling groups remain tight. At the strutting grounds, it is males of the dominant groups that obtain most of the matings. Establishing dominance, even within a group, is vital as only the top birds mate. In one study it was shown that of 170 males present at the strutting ground, six carried out all the matings.

Very little is known of the social behavior of the Ocellated turkey. However, it is thought to be gregarious all the year round, and more readily flies, rather than runs, when disturbed.   MEB

The common name of **guinea fowl** derives from the Gulf of Guinea in West Africa, from which the common domesticated form originated. Guinea fowl are about two-thirds the

size of chickens and all species roost at night, preferably in trees. The Helmeted guinea fowl readily ventures into gardens and thrives in areas cultivated with wheat and maize, but is not a crop pest. Guinea fowl live in flocks during the drier or cooler months, but split up into monogamous pairs and smaller groups of non-breeders during the breeding season. All species occupy the same niche—that of a ground dwelling opportunistic feeder.

Guinea fowl have a virtually naked, richly pigmented head, wattles, and a distinctive adornment (often a casque or crest) on the top of the head. Variation in these features distinguishes the species. It appears that in the Crested and Helmeted guinea fowls, geographical variation in the size and shape of wattles and crown adornments, and in the extent of naked skin on the head, helps these species to regulate brain temperature in a range of different climates.

Guinea fowl probably evolved from a francolin or chicken-like ancestor. The White-breasted and Black guinea fowl are the most primitive. They have unspotted or lightly vermiculated black plumage (all other species are black, spotted white), red heads (blue or grayish-blue in other species), rudimentary wattles (well developed in most of the remaining species), spurs on the ankle or tarsus (other species unspurred) like their ancestor, and piping, musical alarm notes (other species cackle raucously). They appear to be the least gregarious of guinea fowl, associating in parties of less than 10.

The Plumed and Crested guinea fowl are much more gregarious (flock size 10–30) and much less birds of primary rain forest than the preceding two species. The Crested guinea fowl can even be found in thickets, and will venture out into open areas on the borders between forest and savanna. The distinctive feature of these two species is a feathered crest, consisting of long, straight feathers in the Plumed, and shorter, curly, downy feathers in the Crested guinea fowl. The characteristic low pitch of their cackle is perhaps due to having their windpipe (trachea) loop through a hollowed-out extension of their "wish-bone" (furcula) which may act as a resonant organ.

The Vulturine guinea fowl is the largest and most striking species. Its head adornment is a band of chestnut downy feathers running from ear to ear across the back of the head. It also has red eyes (brown in most other guinea fowls), rudimentary wattles, a well-developed hackle of long spearhead-shaped (lanceolate) feathers striped black, white and iridescent blue, and several bumps (not spurs) on the tarsus which are conspicuous in courtship displays. This sub-desert steppe dweller apparently does not need drinking water, and occurs in groups of 20–30 during the non-breeding season.

The most widespread and best known species is the Helmeted guinea fowl. There are many different forms, the variations correlating with (and presumably adapted to) differences in vegetation type, temperature and rainfall. The characteristic features, in both sexes, are a bony casque (the helmet) covered with a sheath of keratin and very well developed blue and/or red wattles. Although there is little difference of form between the sexes in this, or other, guinea fowl, there are clear sexual differences in behavior (see box). In addition, females have a characteristic two-note "buck-wheat" call, with the second note accented. Males answer this with a single-noted call; the two calls are given alternately.

The Helmeted guinea fowl is the family's
(indeed the order's!) most gregarious species. In the dry season (or winter in temperate areas) gatherings of over 2,000 birds
have been observed. These flocks are often
extremely sedentary, rarely venturing more
than 1.2mi (2km) from a central area which
possesses a key resource, such as a drinking
hole, a roost or an important foraging patch.
Flocking seems to serve to detect patchily
distributed, but locally very abundant, food
(mainly dense concentrations of underground storage organs), and also to give
protection against enemies. In the early
morning the birds move in single file from
their roost in a tree to a supply of water. The
dominant males which usually take the lead
are probably "scouts" since they spend a
much higher proportion of their time than
other flock members in alert postures. Later,
the flock may advance in line abreast
presumably in a "sweep" for food. In a third
formation, the swarm, the birds are packed
in a dense cluster. This defensive grouping
is adopted when a potential predator (such
as a jackal, baboon or snake) approaches a
flock containing very young birds. In such
cases the more vulnerable young occupy a
position in the center of the flock or on the
side furthest from the threat.

The Helmeted guinea fowl has been
domesticated and is found on farms (and
dinner tables) the world over. The isolated
Moroccan populations of this species are
severely threatened if not already extinct
due to hunting and habitat destruction. The
only other guinea fowl requiring urgent

conservation attention is the White-breasted guinea fowl, which is severely threatened by destruction of primary forest in West Africa.   TMC

The bizarre nesting habits of the robust, ground-dwelling **megapodes** set them well apart from the rest of the game birds. The eggs are laid in a variety of mounds and burrows where the heat for incubation comes from the sun, from fermenting plant matter, or even from volcanic activity. The young are well developed and independent (precocial); on hatching they burrow to the surface through the material of their "incubator," then run off into the bush. Another feature unique among birds is that the young can fly within hours.

The best studied species is the Mallee fowl of southern Australia which predominantly inhabits dry mallee scrub. The birds are strongly territorial and the males utter their calls (including a loud booming call) from anywhere in the territory during the breeding season. They probably pair for life but lead fairly solitary lives, usually roosting and feeding separately.

The mound is worked for up to 11 months of the year, but breeding is confined to spring and summer. About July, when the temperature inside the mound reaches about 86°F (30°C), the male removes the covering sand and excavates holes in the fermenting organic matter. Eggs are laid from September to January at intervals of several days. The mound is then re-covered and its temperature regulated (mostly by the male) to a constant 91.4°F (33°C) by excavating and covering the mound as necessary. Heat comes from a combination of fermentation and solar energy.

The Australian brush turkey and the three New Guinean brush turkeys of the genus *Talegalla* also build large incubation mounds of leaf litter and soil.

The maleos of the Celebes leave their rain forest homes in the breeding season and walk up to 18–19mi (30km) to sandy beaches, by preference black volcanic sand, where the females excavate holes above high water and deposit one egg in each hole. The sand covering is presumably heated by the sun. The hatchling chicks make their way back to the far-off jungle.

The widespread Common scrub fowl may in fact consist of several distinct species. It lives in montane and lowland rain forest, monsoon forest, gallery forest, dune vegetation and scrubby "coral jungles," and has managed to reach many tiny isolated islands. It builds the largest mounds of all—up to 36ft (11m) in diameter and over 16ft (5m) high—made of leaf litter and soil and, because of their size, usually encompassing

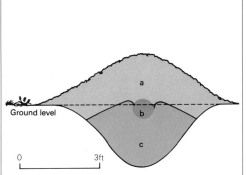

▲ **Bizarre nest-mounds of the megapodes** are unparalleled among birds. In southern Australia the Mallee fowl male works on the nest in most months of the year, digging out a hole, then scraping leaf litter into it and covering it with sandy soil (**a**); alternatively an already existing mound may be worked on. Mounds used year after year can reach over 16ft (5m) in diameter. The female lays eggs in chambers (**b**) excavated by the male. Rotting vegetation (**c**) provides heat needed for incubation—once laid and covered, the eggs themselves are ignored by both parents, as are the chicks, which hatch in 50–90 days.

▶ **Portrait of a mound bird** ABOVE, the Brush turkey of eastern Australia.

▶ **Stylish elegance** of the African Crested guinea fowl BELOW: white "bead" patterning on black plumage, and a headdress of curly black feathers top a svelte silhouette.

Mock Fights and "Dating" in the Helmeted Guinea Fowl

The break-up of the Helmeted guinea fowl flocks at the onset of their breeding season results from an increase in aggression between the males—mainly ritualized chasing. In such interactions one male approaches another side-on in a characteristic hump-backed display posture (**1**). In this display (repeated by the males in courtship), the wings are compressed into the body and elevated, to give the impression, when viewed from the side, of a much larger bird. The approach elicits pursuit by the second male (who also assumes the hump-backed display), but the chaser rarely catches up with the initiator even if the latter slows down. Such chasing is a contagious activity, with sometimes as many as eight males running in single file. Females view these ritualized chases and presumably assess potential mates by determining the strongest male, ie the one who can sustain chasing the longest.

At the same time as this increase in chasing, males and females form short-term pairs. This "dating" probably allows females to compare potential mates more rigorously. After 2–3 weeks of such "dating" stable pairs form, and usually last until the female begins to incubate the eggs. Although male and female are closely similar, the male is easily

identified, since he spends most of his time sitting and resting, in alert postures (**2**), or in aggressive encounters with males who approach his hen. At this stage of the breeding season he is more aggressive, and chasing often leads to fighting (in captivity, sometimes culminating in the death of subordinate males with no escape route). The female of a stable pair does little more than feed and preen.

Once the hen begins incubating the eggs (she does all the incubation), the male deserts temporarily, since he can be sure of the paternity of the eggs and of his hen's commitment to hatching them. He then

associates with other females or may even "rape" (forced copulation without preliminary display) solitary hens. However, when the keets (chicks) are about to hatch, he returns to his original mate and helps to rear them, especially during their first two weeks. If the male is absent at this time the brood will almost certainly fail, since the hen cannot both care for the keets and find food to recoup the energy lost during incubation.   TMC

by leaves. Most remarkable of all are those Common scrub fowls that lay their eggs *en masse* in burrows in volcanically heated soil in New Britain, the Solomons and elsewhere. The burrows are often densely concentrated—up to one nest per 215 sq ft 20 sq m on Simbo in the west Solomon Islands—and the underground hot streams and gases provide an incubation temperature of 93.2°F (34°C). Such concentrations of eggs are harvested regularly by local people, often according to strict rules. The committee at Gara village, New Britain, decrees that one man can only take 30 eggs a day and only harvest on two days, that no dogs may be used to find the nests and all eggs containing developing chicks are to be replaced. In the Celebes, rent is paid to the Government for permission to harvest at the breeding beaches of the maleo. Elsewhere, particularly on small islands in Micronesia, the gun and egg collectors are a significant threat to many island populations.   FHJC

Unlike most game birds, **guans** are chiefly tree dwellers. They are big-bodied birds with smallish heads, thin necks, short, rounded wings and long, broad tails. This Central and South American family comprises three groups, the chachalacas, guans and curassows.

Chachalacas live fairly close to human settlements and are conspicuously gregarious, living in flocks of up to 100. The nine species of chachalacas (genus *Ortalis*) are the smallest and dullest, being generally plain brown with bare patches on the throat. They are predominantly ground feeders, their plumage providing excellent camouflage, but they readily take to the trees at the first sign of danger. They prefer low brush woodlands and wooded river banks, which has enabled one species, the Plain chachalaca, to survive in the remnant forests of the lower Rio Grande in southern Texas. Whole flocks usually call together, especially at dawn or dusk, and the rhythmic, repeated "cha-cha-lac-a" reverberates throughout the forest.

one or more tree bases. The temperature is regulated at 86–95°F (30–35°C)—depending upon the time after laying the egg—during the breeding season (August to January in north Queensland). The mounds attract predators, particularly the Komodo dragon and other monitors that excavate the mounds for eggs.

A large mound may be used by three or four pairs, but only one pair works at a time. Both male and female work the mound all year round. Their large strong feet sweep the ground clear around the mound. A 2.2lb (1kg) male was once seen to shift a stone which proved to weigh 15.2lb (6.9kg)! Mounds may be used for many years. Several in the Northern Territory have been used as "archaeological sites" to determine fire frequency (as indicated by charcoal layers) in the recent past.

Several species may lay eggs in the same mound. There is evidence that the Common scrub fowl parasitizes mounds of *Talegalla* and also other scrub fowls. Where sufficient natural heat is available, scrub fowls may not build a mound at all. On small islands and beaches they lay eggs in warm sand above high tide or even in rock clefts covered

Guans are larger than the chachalacas and have a more colorful plumage, with some whitish edges to the body feathers, which range from deep green to black, often with a glossy sheen on the back and wings; most have long crown feathers which form a crest. The outer primaries are rather spine-like, strengthened and curved, and produce a peculiar drumming sound when the wings are vigorously shaken. These feathers are most developed in the two piping guans and

THE 6 FAMILIES OF GAME BIRDS

Ex Extinct.　V Vulnerable.　R Rare.　E Endangered.

Pheasants and quails
Family: Phasianidae
One-hundred and eighty-three species in 48 genera.
Total threatened species: 21.

N America, northern S America, Eurasia, Africa, Australia. Introduced to New Zealand (after extinction of native species), Hawaii and other islands. Some species widely introduced in Europe and America. Habitat: forest, woodland scrub, grassland, desert, farmland, alpine tundra; almost exclusively terrestrial. Size: length 5.5in–4ft (14–122cm) (excluding display trains) and weight 1.5oz–11lb (43g–5kg). Plumage: commonly brown, gray and heavily marked, but males often boldly patterned with blue, black, red, yellow, white or iridescent colors. Sexual dimorphism varies from almost none to extreme with males 30 percent larger than females and equipped with elaborate display structures and spurs. Voice: usually simple, brief but loud whistles, wails and raucous crows. Sociable species call often, solitary ones only at dawn or dusk in breeding season or when alarmed. Nests: chiefly simple ground scrapes, lined, if at all, with grass. Tragopans may nest in trees. Eggs: usually 2–20 whitish to dark olive, sometimes with markings; weight 0.15–4oz (4.8–112g); incubation 16–28 days; period in nest no more than a few hours or days. Diet: varied, chiefly seeds and shoots; also invertebrates, roots and fallen fruit. Chicks are mostly insectivorous.

New World quails
Thirty species in 10 genera, from Paraguay to S Canada.
Species include: **Bobwhite quail** (*Colinus virginiatus*), **tree quails** or **wood partridges**, 3 species of *Dendrortyx*.

Old World quails
Eleven species in 3 genera, from Africa, Asia, Australia (Common quail migrates to Europe).
Species include: **Blue quail** (*Coturnix chinensis*), **Common quail** (*C. coturnix*), **Harlequin quail** (*C. delegorguei*), **Japanese quail** (*C. japonica*), and the extinct **New Zealand quail** Ex (*C. novaezealandiae*).

Partridges
Ninety-four species in 19 genera, from Africa, Europe, Asia, Australia. Species include: **Black wood partridge** (*Melanoperdix nigra*), **chukar** (*Alectoris chukar*), the **francolins**, 41 species of *Francolinus*, **Gray partridge** (*Perdix perdix*), **Indian mountain quail** (*Ophrysia superciliosa*), **Red-legged partridge** (*Alectoris rufa*), **roulroul** or

Crested wood partridge (*Rollulus roulroul*), **Stone partridge** (*Ptilopachus petrosus*), **Tibetan snowcock**, (*Tetraogallus tibetanus*).

Pheasants
Forty-eight species in 16 genera, from Asia; 1 species in Africa.
Species include: **Blue peacock** or **peafowl** (*Pavo cristatus*), **Cheer pheasant** E (*Catreus wallichii*), **Congo peacock** (*Afropavo congensis*), **Crested argus pheasant** R (*Rheinardia ocellata*), **Golden pheasant** (*Chrysolophus pictus*), **Great argus pheasant** (*Argusianus argus*), **Green peacock** V (*Pavo muticus*), **Himalayan monal pheasant** (*Lophophorus impejanus*), **Lady Amherst's** or **Flower pheasant** (*Chrysolophus amherstiae*), **Red jungle fowl** (*Gallus gallus*), **Ring-necked pheasant** (*Phasianus colchicus*), **Satyr tragopan** (*Tragopan satyra*), **Western tragopan** E (*T. melanocephalus*).

Grouse
Family: Tetraonidae
Sixteen species in 7 genera.

N America, N Asia, Europe. Habitat: forest, prairie, tundra. Size: 12–36in (31–91cm) long, and 10.5oz–14lb (0.3–6.4kg); in some species sexes very different in size (male capercaillie up to twice weight of female). Plumage: males black or brown, with white markings, and combs red to yellow; females brown and black flecked with white. Ptarmigan white in winter. Wings short, rounded, tail of various shapes, often large. Voice: hoots, hisses, cackles, clucks, clicks and whistles. Most drum wings. Nests: a simple depression in the ground. Eggs: usually 5–12, whitish to light brown and darkly blotched, weight 0.7–1.9oz (19–55g); incubation 21–27 days, by the female. Diet: adults eat leaves, needles, buds, twigs, flowers, fruits and seeds; chicks largely eat invertebrates.
Species include: **Black grouse** (*Lyrurus tetrix*), **Blue grouse** (*Dendragapus obscurus*), **capercaillie** (*Tetrao urogallus*), **Hazel grouse** (*Bonasa bonasia*), **Prairie chicken** (*Tympanuchus cupido*), **Red grouse** (*Lagopus lagopus scoticus*), **Rock ptarmigan** (*Lagopus mutus*), **Ruffed grouse** (*Bonasa umbellus*), **Sage grouse** (*Centrocercus urophasianus*), **Sharp-tailed grouse** (*Tympanuchus phasianellus*), **Spruce grouse** (*Dendragapus canadensis*), **Willow ptarmigan** (*Lagopus lagopus*).

Turkeys
Family: Meleagrididae
Two species in 2 genera.
New World. Habitat: wide-ranging (woodland and mixed open forest preferred) in regions with temperate winters. Size: both species 3–4ft (90–120cm) long; weight 6.5–20lb (3–9kg), to 40lb (18kg) in some domesticated forms; males may be twice the weight of females. Plumage: generally dark, with brilliant metallic reflections of bronze and green especially in males; head and neck naked. Voice: a variety of gobbles and clucks. Nest: well concealed, on the ground; built by female. Eggs: 8–15, cream-colored, speckled with brown; incubation 28 days; young leave nest usually after one night. Diet: mainly vegetation, but also invertebrates and small vertebrates.
Species: **Common turkey** (*Meleagris gallopavo*) from E USA to Mexico. **Ocellated turkey** (*Agriocharis ocellata*), from Yucatan to Guatemala.

Guinea fowl
Family: Numididae
Six species in 4 genera.
Sub-Saharan Africa with isolated populations in Morocco; Helmeted guinea fowl introduced widely. Habitat: from subdesert steppe to tropical rain forest. Size: 15.5–22in (39–56cm) long and 2.4–3.5lb (1.1–1.6kg). Plumage: chiefly black spotted with white, two species unspotted. Males same size or slightly larger than females. Voice: usually harsh, loud cackling; two species with more musical piping notes. Nests: simple scrapes on ground, lined with leaves, grass or feathers. Eggs: usually 4–12, white to pale brown, pitted darker; weight 1.4oz (38–40g); incubation 23–28 days; young forage within 1–2 days of hatching and can fly short distances at 2–3 weeks. Diet: highly opportunistic; chiefly seeds, bulbs, tubers, roots and disused fallen grain in drier time of year; prefer insects and other invertebrates (often crop pests) in wetter months.
Species: **Black guinea fowl** (*Agelastes niger*), **Crested guinea fowl** (*Guttera pucherani*—including *G. edouardi*), **Helmeted guinea fowl** (*Numida meleagris*), **Plumed guinea fowl** (*Guttera plumifera*), **Vulturine guinea fowl** (*Acryllium vulturinum*), **White-breasted guinea fowl** (*Agelastes meleagrides*).

Megapodes
Family: Megapodiidae
Twelve species in 6 genera.
From Nicobar Islands, through Malaysia, Indonesia, Philippines,

Australia and New Guinea, to Tonga; Marianas and Palau Islands. Habitat: primary and secondary rain forests, monsoonal scrubs, beach vegetation and one (Mallee fowl) in semi-arid eucalypt woodland. Size: weight ranges between 2–17.6lb (0.9–8kg) and length 10.6–24in (27–60cm) Plumage: generally browns, grays and black, some species with colored facial skin, combs or wattles—red or yellow. Plumage differences between sexes slight. Voice: unmusical cackles and squawks. Nests: eggs laid in mounds of vegetation and holes in hot sand or volcanic areas. Eggs: white to brown with chalky covering; clutch size (5–33) known only for Mallee fowl. Diet: insects, seeds, fruits, roots, crabs, snails etc. Species include: **Australian brush turkey** (*Alectura lathami*), **Common scrub fowl** or **Jungle fowl** (*Megapodius freycinet*), **maleo** V (*Macrocephalon maleo*), **Mallee fowl** or **lowan** (*Leipoa ocellata*).

Guans and curassows
Family: Cracidae
Forty-four species in 8 genera.
Extreme south of N America, C and S America. Habitat: dense tropical forests, low riverside woods and thickets. Size: 20–38in (52–96cm) long and 16.6oz–10.6lb (470g–4.8kg). Males generally larger than females. Plumage: chiefly plain brown, deep green, blue or black with white patches. Many species crested, some with casques. Wings blunt; tail long and broad. Voice: a variety of raucous moans and calls, booming notes and whistles often repeated. Nests: usually of twigs and rotting vegetation, low down in trees or on ground. Eggs: 2–3, exceptionally 4, dull white or creamy; incubation 22–34 days, by female only; average weight 2.2oz (62g). Diet: chiefly fruits, berries, seeds; some take small animals or insects.
Species include: **Black-fronted piping guan** E (*Aburria jacutinga*), **Common piping guan** (*Aburria pipile*), **Crested guan** (*Penelope purpurascens*), **Helmeted curassow** (*Crax pauxi*), **Highland guan** or **chachalaca** (*Penelopina nigra*), **Horned curassow** (*Crax unicornis*), **Horned guan** E (*Oreophasis derbianus*), **Nocturnal curassow** (*Nothocrax urumutum*), **Plain chachalaca** (*Ortalis vetula*), **Red-billed curassow** E (*Crax blumenbachii*), **Sickle-winged guan** (*Chamaepetes goudotii*), **Wattled guan** (*Aburria aburri*), **White-winged guan** E (*Penelope albipennis*).
Total threatened species: 6.

▲ **Noisy "cha-cha-lac-a" call** and bare throat-patch give the Rufous-vented chachalaca of Venezuela its name. The Rufous-vented or Red-tailed chachalaca (*Ortalis ruficauda*) has the broad, long tail and plain brown plumage typical of the chachalacas of Central and South America, members of the guan family.

Curassows are the largest and heaviest members of the family and are poor fliers, spending most of their time at ground level. They range in plumage from deep blue to black, invariably with a purple gloss, and all have rather curly crests. The distinguishing feature, especially of the genus *Crax*, is the head or facial adornments of wattles and knobs which vary from yellow to bright crimson and blue; the Helmeted and Horned curassows have "horns" on the forehead which are used in elaborate courtship displays. The Nocturnal curassow, with its chestnut-colored plumage and red and blue bare face skin, is one of the most colorful of the whole family, yet this species is entirely nocturnal.

Like the chachalacas, the rest of the family are noisy, necessarily so, to maintain contact in the dense and often dark forests. The windpipe of some species, notably the guans, is adapted for amplifying calls which are some of the loudest and most far-reaching of all birds. Curassows utter one or two booming or whistling notes.

All members of the Cracidae are mainly vegetarian, chiefly fruit eaters but also eating leaves, buds and flowers; some also take small animals, large insects or frogs. The chachalacas and curassows, with their long legs, big feet and strong claws, scratch the litter on the forest floor in chicken-like fashion. Curassows are able to consume nuts and tough seeds by swallowing small stones which aid digestion.

Nests are either low down in a tree or on the ground under heavy cover. The usually fragile structure is quite small in relation to the adult bird. The eggs are rather large, and are smooth in some of the guans (genus *Penelope*), or rough and pitted in the chachalacas and most of the curassows. Females care for the young, which hatch with well-developed flight feathers and can leave the nest after only a few hours. The young of some species are able to fly within a few days.

Most species are relentlessly hunted for food and "sport," their tameness and inability to fly far or fast making them easy targets. The rapid destruction of tropical forest also threatens, in large areas, this little-known and strangely alluring family of birds. The White-winged guan was thought to have become extinct in 1870 but was rediscovered in 1977. Estimates of its population vary from 20 to 100 birds, all in an area scheduled for felling. The Red-billed curassow is also verging on extinction and is down to less than 100 individuals.

the Wattled and Sickle-winged guans. The spectacular drumming of their display flight through the treetops is augmented with deep raucous cackles.

Guans are the most widespread of the Cracidae. The 15 species of the genus *Penelope* are considered to be typical guans and, though tree-dwelling birds, also feed on the ground. More specialized and arboreal are the three species in the exclusively South American genus *Aburria*, which have shorter, less powerful legs and a well-developed wattle on the throat. The two species in the genus *Chamaepetes* are smaller and lack wattles. Of the remaining two species of guan, both restricted to Central America, the Highland guan is unique in that the female is larger than the male and differs in plumage. The Horned guan is the most distinctive, but also shows features of the curassows to which it is probably closely related. Its cylindrical, 2in (5cm) long horn rises from the center of its crown.

TWP

Constellation of Eyes

The dance of the peacock and its purpose

The display of the Blue (or Indian) peacock is a famous symbol of extravagant beauty. He spreads behind his proud, blue neck an enormous fan of about 200 iridescent feathers, each adorned with a glowing "eye." Since ancient times, the peacock has had a close connection with man, and has been a graceful sight around many an Indian temple or European garden. Nevertheless, until recently, few of the details of the peacock's courtship dance were known, and even less, the purpose of that splendid fan was not understood. (It is not, incidentally, a tail, but consists of enlarged tail coverts.)

Peafowl live for most of the year in small groups or family parties. In the breeding season, however, the cocks become solitary and pugnacious. Each adult male returns to a place he occupied in previous years and establishes his territorial rights, threatening intruders and calling loudly to advertise his presence. Territories are small, from 0.02 to 0.2 acres (0.05–0.5ha) and center on clearings in forest or scrub. Occasionally a junior male will challenge a senior neighbor and a long and violent battle ensues. The combatants circle each other nervously, looking for an opening, then suddenly spring up in a kaleidoscope of tails and wings to slash out with their claws and spurs. Evenly balanced fights can last for a whole day or more and are as keenly watched by other peacocks as any boxing contest! Serious injury is rare and the winner is usually the bird with most stamina, who drives his opponent away.

Within his territory the peacock has 1–4 special display sites, where the famous dance takes place. These spots are carefully chosen; a typical one is an "alcove" no more than 10ft (3m) across, enclosed by bushes, trees or walls. In one English park, a male uses the stage of an open-air theater!

The cock waits near one of these sites until he sees a group of females approach. He then goes to the site and, turning modestly away from the females, spreads his

1

2

3

great fan with a long, loud shake to bring each "eye" into place. He then begins to move his wings rhythmically up and down. As the females get nearer, he is careful to keep the unpatterned back of the fan towards them. Peahens have a reputation for being indifferent to the cocks' splendid shows, and it appears that at this stage they are drawn to the site more by chance than purpose.

As soon as a female enters the alcove, a transformation comes over the male. He backs towards her with rapidly fanning wings; she avoids him by stepping into the center of the display site. This is apparently what the cock has been waiting for. He swivels suddenly, so as to face her, ceases the movement of his wings and presses the fan forwards, almost engulfing the hen. Simultaneously, spasms of rapid shivering course through his fan causing the whole structure to rustle with a loud, silvery sound. The female normally responds by standing still for a few moments and the male then turns away and resumes his wing-fanning. Sometimes she then runs quickly round to the front of the male and, when he shivers the fan, runs excitedly behind him again. This may be repeated several times (see BELOW LEFT).

Charles Darwin recognized that the peacock's fan presents an evolutionary conundrum. Why should the females find this ornament attractive, when it is such an unnecessary encumbrance? An ingenious solution to this problem was proposed by the biologist Ronald Fisher and has been proved essentially correct.

Females choose ornamented males in order to have sons that will inherit their fathers' attractions; they merely follow the fashion. Any female with a different taste would have unattractive sons condemned by other females to evolutionary oblivion. So peahens use colorful rump feathers as a criterion of attractiveness in peacocks, and select the most adorned.

How, in practice, do females choose such a mate? The answer may lie in an extraordinary feature of the peacock's fan. The decorations on the fan are bright, bold concentric patterns with black centers—they are huge staring eyes. Peahens, like many animals, find eyes arresting, exciting, even hypnotic symbols. By suddenly exposing a peahen to this constellation of eyes, the peacock may be trying to transfix her, thus allowing him to mate. The better the performance and the brighter the eyes, the greater his chances of success. The "choice" is therefore made for her. MWR

▲ ◄ **Huge, staring "eyes"** of the peacock's fan are arresting, even hypnotic, symbols for the peahen. During courtship, the peacock, after backing toward the female (1, LEFT), turns suddenly (2), exposing to her a shivering constellation of eyes. Sometimes, just as the male swivels toward the female, he suddenly launches himself forward with a strangled hoot and attempts to catch hold of her. The female usually dashes out of the way (3). However, on occasion she hesitates or crouches, and mating ensues (4).

4

CRANES AND RAILS

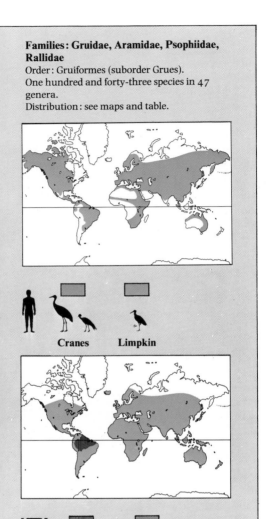

Families: Gruidae, Aramidae, Psophiidae, Rallidae
Order: Gruiformes (suborder Grues).
One hundred and forty-three species in 47 genera.
Distribution: see maps and table.

Cranes   **Limpkin**

Trumpeters   **Rails**

CRANES are birds of the superlatives. Some stand nearly 6.6ft (2m) high, making them the Earth's tallest flying birds. Some fly over the Himalayas at more than 30,000ft (9,000m) above sea level and are among the highest-flying birds. Not only are cranes among the oldest groups of birds, dating back some 60 million years, but captive cranes have lived into their 70s and 80s. Their calls are among the loudest, and cranes' beauty and grace is difficult to surpass. Unfortunately the cranes are also among the most endangered families of birds. Mankind is entirely responsible for their decline.

Generally cranes are birds of the open marshlands, grasslands and agricultural fields. Most species usually nest in secluded areas of shallow wetlands, the exception being the two species of *Anthropoides*, which often nest in grasslands or semidesert areas.

Cranes have long, powerful, straight beaks and long necks and legs. They are heavy set and have loud, shrill calls that carry for several miles. The windpipe of several species is lengthened by coiling within the breastbone and it is believed that this extended organ amplifies the calls. Cranes fly with their neck extended forward. Usually the legs are stretched straight beyond the short stubby tail during flight, but in cold weather flying cranes fold their legs, so the feet are tucked under the breast feathers. Although they are predominantly aquatic birds, their feet are not webbed, and cranes are restricted to the shallows where they breed, search for food, and rest during the night. Only the two species of crowned cranes roost in trees.

The crowned cranes are also the "living fossils" among the cranes. In the remote Eocene (54–38 million years ago) these loose-plumed birds with enormous, gaudy crests, flourished in the northern continents for millions of years before the Earth cooled and the cold-adapted cranes evolved. The Ice Age restricted the range of the crowned cranes to the savannas of central Africa, where tropical conditions were maintained during the period when northern continents

The Crane Dance

Downy chicks, still wobbly on their legs, sometimes bow and run when excited by the close approach of their parents. Groups of subadult cranes engage in "social dancing" that helps redirect aggression and develop bonds between potential pair members. The newly paired cranes engage in intensive periods of vigorous dance, particularly immediately before mating. Established pairs copulate without prerequisite dancing, indicating that dancing is important in helping to stabilize and synchronize unstable relationships, much as it does in humans.

Cranes hesitating between escape and attack dance, for example when disturbed at their nest. Then, there are amusing times when cranes seem to dance for sheer pleasure. Sometimes within a flock of preening cranes, one will start to dance, and the contagious behavior will spread to the entire group. American Indians, Australian aborigines, the Ainu of north Japan and various African tribes all mimic the crane's dance.

The dance consists of head bobbing, deep bows (1), leaps, grasping with the bill and tossing up objects (feathers, stones, tussocks) (2), running with wings flapping, and short, low ritual flights. The bows and the leaps usually alternate between pair members, one bird bowed while the other leaps (3). The "unison call" (see text) on the other hand, is given simultaneously by the male and female. If the two cranes are upright at the same time and facing each other, they at once shift into stiff threat postures—exaggerated flapping, stamping and arching (4), before again flowing into other elements of the dance.

By dancing with a captive female Whooping crane that was imprinted on humans, and by remaining with this bird from dawn to dusk through the month of April, the author stimulated her to lay an egg. This genetically valuable bird was the *sole* descendent of a pair of Whooping cranes that were alive when the worldwide population had fallen below two score. By artificial insemination, her egg was fertilized; a male crane hatched and was reared to continue the line. So even a half-human hybrid of the dance served its breeding function.   GWA

▲ **Blue cranes in Etosha National Park, Namibia.** Like the closely related Demoiselle crane, the Blue or Stanley crane is short-billed and eats a wide range of food. Unlike northern cranes, it does not migrate.

were covered by miles of ice. Two species of crowned cranes still brighten the African grasslands, and of the cold-adapted species, 13 now stalk the wetlands of the Northern Hemisphere.

Today's successful crane species are omnivorous, opportunistic feeders that have adapted within the last few thousand years to benefit from man's agricultural fields. Several *Grus* species, both crowned cranes, and both species of *Anthropoides* have short beaks with which they can effectively grasp insects, pluck ripe seeds from grass stems, and graze on fresh green vegetation in a goose-like manner. In contrast, most of the endangered species have long, powerful mandibles, used in digging for plant roots and tubers in muddy soils or for grasping aquatic animals such as small fish, amphibians and crustaceans. The aquatic feeders include the larger cranes (eg Wattled and White-naped) and the white cranes

(Whooping, Siberian, Black-necked). Both species of *Bugeranus* and half of the *Grus* species fall within this category. If a wetland is drained, these specialized cranes must move to another wet area. Land drainage has been one cause of their decline. In addition, their size and their plumage render them conspicuous and easy prey for hunters and egg collectors. The Sandhill and Common cranes breed at 3–4 years old and often rear two chicks. The rare Siberian crane does not become sexually mature until six years old and never rears more than one chick per breeding attempt.

Cranes are monogamous, and with the onset of spring or the rainy season, mated pairs retreat to secluded grassland or wetland, where they establish and vigorously defend a breeding territory that may include several thousand acres, depending on species or topography.

Mated pairs emit a loud "unison call"

duet, during which the male and female calls are distinct yet synchronized. In most species the male emits a series of long, low calls. With each male call the female produces several short, high-pitched calls. The display identifies the sex of each of the birds, a factor that assists in the development of the pair bond. However, after a stable relationship is established between two cranes, the unison call primarily functions as a threat. At dawn the crane pairs announce their territory with a unison call, and as the display is heard by neighboring pairs, the same is returned, so that for miles an extended chorus of crane calls announces occupancy of real estate.

The reproductive states of two members of a stable pair are synchronized by their bodily cycles, by the weather, length of daylight, and by elaborate displays such as nuptial dances (see box) and unison calls. Cranes begin copulating several weeks before eggs are laid. For fertility to be assured, a female crane must be inseminated two to six days before an egg is laid.

At a secluded spot within the wetland breeding territory, the pair constructs a platform nest. Crowned cranes often lay a three-egg clutch, while other cranes lay two eggs, with the exception of the Wattled crane that more frequently lays a single egg.

Male and female cranes share incubation duties. The females usually incubate during the night, while the male does so during the day. The bird that is not on the nest usually feeds at a considerable distance from it, sometimes in a "neutral area" in company with other cranes. Within the 28–36-day range, the duration of incubation depends on the species and the parents' attentiveness at the nest. Crowned cranes do not initiate incubation until the clutch is complete, and their eggs hatch simultaneously. Other cranes begin incubation as soon as the first egg is laid, and successive chicks hatch at one- or two-day intervals.

Crane chicks are well developed when they hatch (precocial) and follow their parents around the shallows and neighboring uplands until they develop flight feathers at 2–4 months of age. The larger and tropical species, such as the Wattled and Sarus cranes, have a longer pre-fledging period than do species such as the Siberian crane, in which the short arctic summer limits the period when food is available for the fast-growing chicks. Although all eggs usually hatch, many chicks die, and most of the endangered species usually only rear a single chick per breeding effort. Once fledged, the chicks remain with their parents until the onset of the next breeding season. Migratory cranes learn the migration path by accompanying their parents thousands

▶ **Black crowned cranes** OVERLEAF fly over grassland in Kenya. These loose-plumed birds with gaudy crests are "living fossils" descended from birds that flourished long ago.

▼ **Representative species of cranes, rails and related families.** (1) Purple gallinule (*Porphyrula martinica*). (2) Limpkin (*Aramus guarauna*). (3) Demoiselle crane (*Anthropoides virgo*). (4) Crested coot (*Fulica cristata*). (5) Black crowned crane (*Balearica pavonina*). (6) Red-crowned cranes (*Grus japonensis*) dancing. (7) Siberian crane (*Bugeranus leucogeranus*). Heads only of: (8) Whooping crane (*Grus americana*), (9) Sarus crane (*G. antigone*), and (10) Sandhill crane (*G. canadensis*). (11) White-winged trumpeter (*Psophia leucoptera*) (12) Water rail (*Rallus aquaticus*).

of miles south to traditional wintering grounds. Foraging behavior is also learned, while the form of displays is generally predetermined.

In North America, the Whooping cranes have recovered from 14 birds in 1941 to approximately 75 birds in the "natural range" flock, and a total, including captive birds, of about 140 cranes. The Siberian crane is now reduced to fewer than 900 individuals, Black-necked cranes to fewer than 500, and Red-crowned cranes to fewer than 1,000 birds in the wild. Fortunately, cranes are appealing birds, and recent efforts in many Asian countries have resulted in the protection of wetlands critically needed by cranes. But crane hunting continues in Canada, Afghanistan, Pakistan and the United States of America, and the pressures on the wetlands for man's use increase as human numbers soar.

Although many cranes are severely endangered, they respond well to protection and management. In an effort to ensure their survival, captive flocks of the endangered species are now being established at several zoos and specialized crane research centers. Foremost in captive breeding has been the Patuxent Wildlife Research Center in Maryland, in the USA. A captive

flock of Whooping cranes has been established at Patuxent by collecting one egg from each nest of the wild cranes containing two eggs. The eggs laid by the captive birds are now transferred from them and substituted for those in nests of Sandhill cranes in Idaho. The Whooping cranes reared by foster parents migrate south with them and learn to feed in the agricultural fields with the Sandhill cranes. The 30 or so birds constituting this new population show little interest in breeding with Sandhills, but pairing has not yet occurred between the Whoopers. GWA

The **limpkin** is the only member of the New World family Aramidae. It has anatomical features in common with the cranes and has a digestive system like that of the rails—in general appearance it is not unlike a very large rail.

In the swamps and shaded areas which are its principal home, the presence of the limpkin may be detected by the many conspicuous empty shells of large freshwater snails (*Pomacea caliginosa*) which it leaves on the muddy banks. To secure its food, the long-legged limpkin wades in shallow water, probing with its long, laterally compressed bill slightly downcurved at the tip. When it finds a snail, it carries it to the shore and sets it in the mud with the shell opening facing upwards, holding it there with its long toes tipped with long, sharp claws. With great dexterity the bird quickly removes the horny operculum that protects the snail, pulls out the mollusk and swallows it.

Limpkins walk rather slowly with a curious undulating tread that gives the impression of lameness or limping, from which the common name is derived. Although they lack webs on the feet, limpkins swim well. In flight the head and long slender neck are extended with the feet and legs projecting behind, in the manner of a crane. The wings are broad and rounded. On the ground as they move about, limpkins utter low clucking notes and then may burst into a loud "car-r-r-rao car-r-r-rao." Both parents incubate the eggs and tend the well-developed (precocial) young.

Although the limpkin also takes frogs, lizards and worms, the snail accounts for such a high proportion of its normal diet that it cannot exist without it. Where marshes have been drained, the snails have disappeared, and with them the limpkin. In the United States of America the bird is now well protected and, since the Everglades and Lake Okeechobee in Florida are too vast to drain, it is likely that the species will always survive there.   PRC

Trumpeters are non-migratory, ground-dwelling birds which live in small to sizeable flocks in the tropical rain forests of South America. The three closely related species are about the size of a domestic chicken. They may be distinguished by the color of their innermost flight feathers, inner wing-coverts and lower backs, which are gray in the Gray-winged trumpeter, white in the Pale-winged trumpeter, green in the Dark-winged trumpeter. The head in all three species appears small in relation to the body, and the large dark eyes give the head its "good-natured" expression. When it is standing, the trumpeter's very short tail is almost completely hidden by the outer webs of the secondaries. The typical hunch-

backed appearance has led to trumpeters being given the nickname, in Surinam, of "Kamee-kamee" ("camel-back"). The soft feathers on the head and long neck have an almost fur-like quality. The bill is short, stout and slightly curved.

Trumpeters have at least two different calls, a flock call and a threat call. The flock call is a booming "oh-oh-oh-oh . . . ooooo." The long drawn-out part of this call is delivered with the bill closed, which causes the sound to reverberate within its body. The threat call is a loud cackle, or trumpeting, from which the group takes its name. Trumpeters have the ability to run fast, but are rather poor fliers. At dusk they fly up rather laboriously, on deeply-rounded wings, some 20–30ft (6–9m) to roost in the forest trees, where they form noisy, quarrelsome groups.

Details of the trumpeters' breeding cycle are still imperfectly known. At the beginning of the breeding season large flocks are reported to gather in clearings in the forest where the ground is smooth and free of obstacles. Here, they perform elaborate and noisy courtship dances, which involve much strutting and leaping and sometimes even somersaulting in their excitement. After mating, a pair of trumpeters will select a nest site which may consist of a hole in a tree, or on the ground. The average clutch size is about seven, and it is the female that incubates. When the young hatch they are covered with thick, black down with elaborate pinkish streaks. They do not stay long in the nest, and are soon running about after their parents.

Trumpeters are reported to make good eating. This, combined with the fact that they are unwary birds and poor fliers, has made them easy targets for hunters who, in some parts of their former range, have hunted them to extinction.   PRC

Rails are a large but little-known family which might generously repay further efforts to tease apart the details of their lives. Most species inhabit remote areas; a few, especially the coots, are more common.

Families of Cranes, Limpkin, Trumpeters and Rails

Cranes
Family: Gruidae
Fifteen species in 4 genera.
All continents except S America and Antarctica. Habitat: shallow wetlands in breeding season, grasslands and agricultural fields in non-breeding season. Size: height 3–6ft (0.9–1.8m), wingspan 6–9ft (1.5–2.7m), weight of smallest species 6–8lb (2.7–3.6kg), largest species 20–23lb (9–10.5kg). Males usually larger. Plumage: white or various shades of gray, with bright red bare skin or elaborate plumage on head. Long, elaborate secondaries, long, overhanging tail, or ruffled, curled and raised in display. Voice: shrill, carries long distances; in 11 species sex identifiable from unison call of adult pairs. Nest: a platform in shallow water or in short grass. Eggs: 1–3, white or heavily pigmented; 4–10oz (120–270g); incubation 28–36 days. Diet: insects, small fish and other small animals, tubers, seeds and agricultural gleanings.

Species include: **Black crowned crane** (*Balearica pavonina*), **Black-necked crane** T (*Grus nigricollis*), **Common crane** (*G. grus*), **Red-crowned crane** V (*G. japonensis*), **Sandhill crane** (*G. canadensis*), **Sarus crane** (*G. antigone*), **Siberian crane** E (*Bugeranus leucogeranus*), **Stanley** or **Blue crane** (*Anthropoides paradisea*), **Wattled crane** (*Bugeranus carunculatus*), **White-naped crane** V

(*Grus vipio*), **Whooping crane** E (*Grus americana*).
Total threatened species: 6.

Limpkin
Family: Aramidae
Sole species *Aramus guarauna*.
S Georgia, Florida, Cuba, S Mexico S to Argentina, chiefly E of Andes. Habitat: swamps (wooded or open) or arid brush (as in West Indies). Size: length 23–28in (58–71cm); weight 2–2.8lb (0.9–1.3kg). Plumage: dark olive-brown with greenish iridescence on upperparts, and broadly streaked with white; sexes alike. Voice: vociferous—loud wails, screams and assorted clucks, heard mostly at night. Nest: shallow, of rushes or sticks just above waterline in marshes, or in bushes or trees. Eggs: 4–8, pale buff blotched and speckled with light brown; average 2.2in (5.6cm) long, 1.7in (4.4cm) across; incubation about 20 days. Diet: almost exclusively large snails, some insects and seeds.

Trumpeters
Family: Psophiidae
Three species of genus *Psophia*.
SE Venezuela, Guianas and Amazon basin. Habitat: on ground of tropical rain forests. Size: length 17–21in (43–53cm); Gray-winged species weighs just over 2.2lb (1kg). Plumage: chiefly black, with purple, green or bronze reflections especially

on lower neck and wing coverts; soft, velvet-like on head and neck; outer webs of tertials and secondaries (white, gray or brown) form hair-like strands over lower back; sexes alike. Voice: loud trumpeting, loud deep-pitched cries, prolonged cackles. Nests: hole in tree or crown of palm. Eggs: 6–10, white or green, weight about 2.7oz (76g). Diet: vegetable matter and insects.
Species: **Dark-winged** or **Green-winged trumpeter** (*Psophia viridis*), **Gray-winged** or **Common trumpeter** (*P. crepitans*), **Pale-** or **White-winged trumpeter** (*P. leucoptera*).

Rails
Family: Rallidae
One hundred and twenty-four species in 41 genera.
Total threatened species: 8.
Europe, Asia, Australasia, N America, S America, and many oceanic islands and archipelagos. Habitat: generally damp forest, scrub, meadow and marshland. Size: length 4–24in (10–60cm); weight 1oz (30g) (Baillon's crake) to 7lb (3.3kg) (takahe). Males same size as or 5–10 percent heavier than females. Plumage: mostly drab brown, gray and rufous, sometimes with pale spots and flashes; a few species show bright and contrasting colors; differences in color between sexes in some species, but sexes similar in most. Voice: many whistles, squeaks and grunts, in combinations

from simple to complex. Many sound "unbirdlike." Nests: in wholly aquatic species (coots) conical nest emerges from shallow water on stick or pebble (Horned coot) foundation; others within clump of grass or reeds, sometimes roofed; a few species in bushes or low trees; always wholly of vegetation. Eggs: usually 2–12, but for many species poorly documented; color usually drab stone to rich brown, often spotted with darker shades; 0.4–2.8oz (10–80g); incubation 20–30 days. Diet: medium to large invertebrates, sometimes smaller vertebrates, some seeds, fruits etc; a few species largely herbivorous.

Groups:
Long-billed rails including the **Guam rail** V (*Rallus owstoni*), **Lord Howe rail** E (*Tricholimnas sylvestris*), **New Guinea flightless rail** (*Megacrex inepta*), **Virginia rail** (*Rallus limicola*), **Water rail** (*R. aquaticus*).

Crakes and gallinules including the **Asian water cock** (*Gallicrex cinerea*), **Baillon's crake** (*Porzana pusilla*), **corncrake** (*Crex crex*), **Gray moorhen** or **Common gallinule** (*Gallinula chloropus*), **Purple gallinule** (*Porphyrula martinica*), **Purple swamp hen** or **pukeko** (*Porphyrio porphyrio*), **takahe** E (*Notornis mantelli*).

Coots including the **American coot** (*Fulica americana*), **European coot** (*F. atra*), **Giant coot** (*F. gigantea*), **Horned coot** R (*F. cornuta*).

Without exception they are birds of the ground or water level, running or swimming through a wide variety of habitats. Their distribution includes every major land mass (except Antarctica), and they are remarkable for colonizing even remote islands.

Rails are inhabitants of rather specialized, patchy habitats—such as river flood plains and forest clearings. Such habitats may be here one year and gone the next, and the life-histories of the rails are adapted to these circumstances. All rails are stout-legged and short-winged, adapted for traveling swiftly through dense, low vegetation.

Rails fall, with some degree of overlap, into three groups—the long-billed rails, the crakes and gallinules, and the coots.

The long-billed rails are characterized by a medium to long, often slightly downcurved bill. This is a generalist tool which can be pushed into mud, as the Water and Virginia rails will do when searching for worms, or used more powerfully in smashing eggshells, crushing horny grasshoppers, or even killing the occasional frog or duckling. In some of the larger rails the bill is even more of a hatchet. Larger vertebrates, even rats, may make a meal for the sturdy New Guinea flightless rail, one of few flightless birds to hold its own against man's introduced exterminators.

The social organization and behavior of most of the long-billed rails is a mystery. Most species, even the larger ones, seem to be able to breed in their first year—another adaptation to temporary habitats—and territoriality seems to be the rule. The rails are a vocal group, forced to defend their densely vegetated territories by voice, and many species seem to indulge in "duetting" in which the male and female of a pair each contribute to a coordinated song. This habit may inform potential intruders that there are indeed two adults in residence and that any incursions will be met by effective resistance.

The crakes and gallinules have shorter bills. Some species look rather like partridges, although they always have the slim body necessary for moving efficiently through dense vegetation. Their bills are not long enough to probe into mud and they depend more on surface foraging for smaller invertebrates and seeds. Some, like the endangered takahe of New Zealand, are almost entirely vegetarian. Consequently they have no great dependence on marshy and soft ground, although they may certainly be found in those places, sometimes even trotting about on lily-pads like the unrelated jacanas (Charadriiformes), and have therefore exploited a wide range of habitats. The corncrake, for instance, is a bird of coarse grasslands in the northern Palaearctic (Europe, North Africa, and northern Asia) and was formerly common all over Europe, occurring in many of the habitats where partridges are common today. Although very rarely seen, this shy bird could easily be detected by its distinctive call—sounding like a knife being scraped over the teeth of a comb. Changes in the timing of hay-mowing, and perhaps the introduction of pesticides, have eliminated this species over much of its former range, although it is still one of the more easily found crakes. However, we know almost nothing of its biology. Like many of its

◄ **Spectacular leap for food.** A Water rail shoots up 3 feet (1m) from the water surface to seize a dragonfly.

▼ **Snails are not a delicacy,** but form the major part of a limpkin's diet. This bird holds a freshwater snail in its bill before taking it to the bank, holding it on the mud with one foot and extracting the animal from its shell with its bill. Drainage of marshes removes the snails, and also the limpkins which feed on them.

group, the corncrake is suspected to be monogamous, raising usually one brood per year, and being territorial.

Some crakes and gallinules may have quite complex, even fascinating breeding systems. In the moorhen the offspring of early broods sometimes remain with the parents through the raising of later broods in the same year, and even help to feed their younger siblings. This also happens in the Purple swamp hen or pukeko of New Zealand, although this species shows more complicated social behavior—several females may lay in a single nest, each female may copulate with many of the males in the breeding group; the whole group participates in parental care and territory defense.

Unlike the other rails, the coots are truly aquatic birds, able to swim and dive well using their generously lobed toes, and rarely found far from the water. They can thus colonize deep and desolate waters, such as the high-altitude lakes of the Andes where the two largest and grandest species, the Horned and Giant coots, make their home. Because they gain their protection from open water rather than dense vegetation, they have less need of the slim profiles of their relatives, and are altogether stouter birds. They are omnivores, eating mainly plant material in winter but adding the seasonally abundant water insects to their

diet in spring and summer. The chicks are fed almost exclusively on insects for the first part of their lives, only gradually changing over to a diet of vegetation as their bodies, and intestines, grow larger and capable of coping with this relatively indigestible food.

Again unlike most rails, the coots can be gregarious, especially during winter when flocks of thousands of, for example, European coots may gather on large lakes and even the sea coast. The function of these gatherings is uncertain, but they do provide an excellent opportunity for some individuals to exploit their weaker subordinates. All coots return to the surface before eating their food haul, and this gives a chance for food stealing to occur—a bird may hardly break surface before its pondweed is snatched away by one of the pirates. During winter some individuals obtain most of their food in this way and thus avoid the costs and difficulties of deepwater diving.

All the rails have stout, well-muscled legs with three forward-facing toes and one hind toe, emerging from the leg slightly higher than the others and used as a brace during walking. The feet are important weapons in the struggle to gain a breeding territory. In the Asian water cock these male combats make spectacular sport and the birds are carefully cultivated, like champion fighting cocks. The legs and feet of newly hatched

▲ **Trotting on lily-pads** and other floating vegetation, the long-toed Black crake (*Limnocorax flavirostra*) of East Africa resembles the quite unrelated jacana of the wader family.

▶ **Coot hatchlings** BELOW bear a frontal shield that remains red in many species, but in the European coot becomes white in the adult.

▼ **Rasping call of the corncrake** was once common in coarse grasslands of Eurasia. Corncrakes of middle and northern Europe migrate to spend the winter in warmer climes of Africa or southern Asia.

Frontal Shields

A striking feature of some coots and gallinules is their frontal shield—a fleshy rearward extension of the upper bill which covers most of the forehead. In the European coot (1) it is a simple white lobe, about the size and texture of the ball of the human thumb, while in the closely related American coot (2) this is overlaid by a smaller, red callus. Easily the most complex such ornament is that possessed by the majestic Horned coot of the high Andes (3). In place of a flat shield this species, the largest of all coots, has a frilled proboscis or horn up to 2in (5cm) long!

Such forehead ornamentation is not peculiar to the family. The plantain-eaters (Musophagidae) and oropendolas (Icteridae) of the tropics have very similar shields to those of coots, while many waterfowl (Anatidae) have knobs or bulbs at the base of the bill. The puzzle is—why did they evolve?

One clue to their function is that the size of the shield in coots (and the knob in swans) is related to sex, the male's generally being larger. However there are enough exceptions to this rule to indicate that shield size is not primarily an indicator of the bird's sex.

Shields do however appear to signal status in winter flocks of coots in which food stealing is common. In food stealing incidents, the victim very rarely retaliates against the thief, but usually retreats and gives away its food as soon as the aggressor approaches. When the thief approaches a feeding individual which is facing away, and whose shield has not yet been seen, the "victim" will on occasion turn on the would-be thief and, with fierce fighting, drive it away. These are the only instances of

attempted food stealing when resistance is observed—presumably because most thieves make sure they have a good view of the victim before they attack. Shield size in winter may therefore signal differences in body size or fighting ability. Shields may signal something similar in the American coot, males of which show a rapid increase in shield size upon taking up a territory in the spring. Perhaps the shield is in effect saying "I now have a breeding territory, I have fought hard to get it, and will fight equally hard to keep it"?

JAH

rails grow faster than most other body parts, because to become mobile is of the utmost urgency in these chicks. Rail chicks are very unusual among birds in being mobile and leaving the nest soon after hatching, but being fully dependent on parents for feeding for at least the first few days of life. Young coots may obtain at least some of their food from parents for up to 60 days after hatching, although in many rails and crakes this dependency is much briefer. But in all species chicks must accompany the parents around the territory in order to solicit food—thus the importance of early mobility.

In most rails the first laid egg hatches at least one day earlier than the last, a time-lapse that introduces differences between siblings within the brood. The eldest chick may already be sufficiently strong and agile to capture its insect food at a time when the youngest of the brood is still struggling from the egg. These differences persist throughout the dependent period, and the younger chicks often starve in the competition with larger siblings for food from the parents. This feature of breeding biology, which at first sight seems to diminish the reproductive success of the parents, may have evolved as a mechanism to match the size of the brood to an unpredictable and variable food supply. In part the greater success of some chicks in obtaining food is due to the inability of the younger chicks to follow parents as they swim around the territory. But, at least as important, parents tend to have preferences for particular chicks—for most of the time each parent is accompanied only by its "favorite" chick or chicks. The way in which parents maintain this division is astonishing. If a "wrong" chick approaches an adult, it is seized by the head and shaken about before being dropped back into the water. After this treatment the chick usually retreats, indeed the longer it is shaken the longer it stays away from that parent!

The rails interact with man very little indeed. Farmers have sometimes accused certain gallinules, such as the Gray moorhen, of eating spring crops, although the evidence points to these losses being very small. Some species are killed for food, especially the coot in eastern Europe, where each hunter takes an average of three or four per year. Rails pose severe problems for man only in their conservation. They tend to live in habitats which are vulnerable. Indeed, several species have become extinct within living memory and the prospects for a number of others do not look promising.

JAH

BUSTARDS

Family: Otididae
Order: Gruiformes (suborder Otides).
Twenty-one species in 8 genera.
Distribution: Africa, S Europe, Middle East and
S Asia to Sea of Japan, Indian subcontinent,
Kampuchea, Australia and New Guinea.

Habitat: grassland, arid plains, semidesert, light
savanna.

Size: length 16in–4ft (40–120cm); wingspan
3–8ft (1–2.5m); weight 1.2–40lb (0.55–18kg).
In some species males bigger than females.
Plumage: mostly camouflage patterning on
uppersides; head and neck with distinctive

patterns combining two or more
of gray, chestnut, black, white
and buff. Males of some species
more brightly colored than
females.

Voice: larger species generally silent, but
smaller ones have distinctive, persistent,
usually unmusical calls during breeding
season.

Nest: a bare scrape on ground.

Eggs: mostly 1–2, but up to 6 in some small
species; olive, olive-brown, reddish; incubation
20–25 days. From 1.4oz in Little to 5.2oz in
Great bustard (41–146g).

Diet: generally omnivorous—shoots, flowers,
seeds, berries etc, and invertebrates (especially
beetles, grasshoppers and crickets), but also
small reptiles, amphibians, mammals, and eggs
and young of ground-nesting birds.

Species include: the **Arabian bustard** (*Ardeotis
arabs*); **Australian bustard** (*A. australis*); **Bengal
florican** (*Houbaropsis bengalensis*); **Black-bellied
bustard** (*Eupodotis melanogaster*); **Blue bustard**
(*E. caerulescens*); **Denham's bustard** (*Neotis
denhami*); **Great bustard** (*Otis tarda*); **Great
Indian bustard** E (*Ardeotis nigriceps*); **houbara**
(*Chlamydotis undulata*); **Kori bustard** (*Ardeotis
kori*); **Lesser florican** (*Sypheotides indica*); **Little
brown bustard** (*Eupodotis humilis*); **Little
bustard** (*Tetrax tetrax*); **Nubian bustard** (*Neotis
nuba*); **Red-crested bustard** (*Eupodotis
ruficrista*); **White-bellied bustard**
(*E. senegalensis*).

E Endangered.

THE name bustard (by derivation,
roughly: "the bird that walks") was
originally applied to the most northerly and
perhaps least typical member of the family,
the Great bustard. The term is however
appropriate for the whole family, for all
bustards are strictly ground dwellers. The
largest members are to the great open plains
of Africa and Eurasia what cranes are to the
world's big marshes: slow-breeding, long-
lived birds of ancient lineage, reaching considerable size and weight whilst retaining
the capacity to fly—among birds, the
ultimate expression of adaptation to their
stable habitats. Sadly, like cranes, they are
among the first to suffer once those habitats
start being exploited and disrupted by
modern man.

Africa is the major home of the bustards
and only four species do not breed there—
the Australian bustard, Great Indian
bustard, Lesser florican and Bengal florican.
Great and Little bustards have only relict
populations in North Africa; their patchy
distribution extends across the plains of
southern Europe into Russia, the Little
bustard reaching as far as the northern
Kazakh steppes, and the Great bustard ranging right through level uplands of northern
China, Mongolia and the USSR, almost to
the Sea of Japan. The houbara ranges
through semideserts of North Africa, the
Middle East, central Russia and Mongolia.
These three northern species undertake
migrations in the colder parts of their
ranges. The Arabian bustard still occurs in
the southern Arabian peninsula and in
northwest Africa, but otherwise this and the
remaining bustard species are found only in
Africa, mostly in the tropics.

Within Africa there are two clear areas
where different species have evolved: from
the Zambezi southwest to the Cape and from
the Nile to the Horn, with four species in the
former and three in the latter. The kori
occurs in both, as do the Red-crested and
White-bellied bustards, although the latter
two also have populations across the
Saharo-Sahelian savanna belt in West
Africa, and the White-bellied bustard has
another scattered population in Central
Africa. The Arabian and Nubian bustards
occur in the Saharo-Sahelian zone, extending across to the Red Sea coast. Only two
species, Denham's and the Black-bellied
bustards, are widespread in Africa; the
former has become very localized in many
areas as a result of man's activities.

The bustards are a homogeneous family,
although there are differences in structure,
color, size and behavior which cloud the

relationships between species. All are rather
long-necked and long-legged, with robust
bodies and short bills, and have lost both the
hind toe and the preen gland that most birds
possess. These losses, together with the
camouflage patterning (often exquisitely
delicate) of black on buff, rufous or brown
on the upperparts, are presumably adaptations to the dry, open landscapes they
inhabit—hind claws are associated with
birds that perch on trees or bushes and oil
from preen (uropygial) glands is used by
most birds for waterproofing. Two small species, Little and Red-crested bustards, have
relatively short legs and necks. These and
most other *Eupodotis* bustards fly with rapid
wingbeats; the larger species use slow, deep,
powerful wingbeats, but fly deceptively fast.
On the ground bustards are strong but
usually slow walkers, characteristically
nervous and alert: they move into cover at
the first sign of danger.

Bustards take their food in a slow,
meandering walk through an area of grassland or scrub. Their diet is chiefly
invertebrates, usually snapped up from the
ground or off plants, but also sometimes dug
up with the powerful bill. Small vertebrates
may also be taken, often after a short pursuit
and pounce. All species readily eat vegetable
matter, especially plant shoots, certain
flowers and fruit. Some larger species,
notably *Ardeotis*, feed on gum that oozes
from acacia trees. Concentrations of food
may cause a bird to remain in one spot for

some time. In Somalia birds have been observed leaping to snatch berries off the higher parts of a bush, and in Zimbabwe Denham's bustard has been seen to wade into water, apparently in quest of young frogs, and to defend a termites' nest, at which it was feeding, against other birds. Several species gather at bush fires to take fleeing and crippled insects. Bustards have no crop, but their powerful gizzard, long "blind gut" (cecum) and their habit of taking up quantities of grit assist the digestion of food.

No male bustard has been observed to incubate the eggs, an emancipation from parental duties that appears to have led to a variety of mating systems within the family, perhaps even within the same species. For example, it seems that Denham's bustard is monogamous in upland Malawi, whereas in South Africa males seem to mate with several females, the males keeping at least 2,300ft (700m) apart and displaying in response to each other and any passing female. Male Great bustards also operate

such a dispersed lek system, but in this species many males appear not to be territorial, moving about instead, keeping their distance from each other, and displaying at various sites (see OVERLEAF). In this and two other species which do not appear to form pair bonds, the houbara and Australian bustard, the display before copulation is very long and must often be impeded by rivals; territoriality is replaced by simple opportunism and/or a ranking system.

In southern Africa, birds in the genus *Eupodotis* with black underparts occur in quite dense grassland and savanna, give striking aerial displays, and apparently hold group territories within which one pair breeds. The newly hatched young of all species are well developed (precocial) and very soon leave the nest, but they are fed bill-to-bill by the mother initially and remain in her company for some months after hatching. Palaearctic species are notably sociable and sometimes occur in flocks; the remainder are more solitary, although some are commonly found in small groups.

◄ **Over two-thirds of bustards are African,** like this Black korhaan male in Namibia. The Black korhaan (*Eupodotis afra*) and other smaller bustards can fly strongly, but they depend more upon their strong legs and camouflage coloration to escape predators.

▼ **The Kori bustard is widespread in Africa** and is, together with the Great bustard of Eurasia, one of the largest of all flying birds.

Bustards are little known, largely because of the difficulty of studying nervous, well-camouflaged, slow-breeding birds which tend to desert their nests if once alarmed. This susceptibility to disturbance is a major cause of their decline, especially in northern parts of the family's distribution where grasslands are coming under ever more pressure from agriculture. Great bustards can tolerate a degree of disturbance—indeed they can only have colonized Europe thanks to man's felling of the forests—but the mechanization of agriculture and the reduction of croplands to monocultures by the use of herbicides and fertilizers have been disastrous for them. Farming of the steppes reduced the Russian population from 8,650 birds at the start of the 1970s to an estimated 2,980 by the end of the decade. Similarly, the Little bustard is now nearly extinct almost everywhere except the Iberian Peninsula, as a result of the disappearance of herb-rich grasslands.

It is this loss of virgin habitat that has brought all three Indian species to the brink of extinction. Both floricans are seriously endangered. The Bengal species survives only in a handful of protected areas in a widely fragmented chain along the foothills of the Himalayas (the Kampuchean population has not been seen since its discovery in 1928), while the Lesser florican appears to be restricted to tiny scattered patches of grassland ("vidis") in the far west of India, maintained as reserve grazing but in no other way protected. In the Himalayan foothills the grasslands have gone to tea estates, while in western India they are being converted to pasture; in neither case can the florican concerned survive the change.

Populations of the Great Indian bustard, though perhaps more tolerant of agriculture, have been steadily declining for decades. It now numbers less than 1,000 but, having recently been the subject of a

Courtship Displays of the Bustards

Male bustards are remarkable for their spectacular courtship displays. The Great bustard (1) inflates its neck like a balloon, cocks its tail forward onto its back, and stretches its wings back and down from shoulder to carpal. The primary feathers are kept folded so that their tips are held behind the bird's head, while the secondary feathers are lifted outwards to form huge white rosettes on either side of the body. Together with the billowing undertail coverts, this transforms a richly colored (if partly camouflaged) animal into a nearly all-white one. The posture may be held for minutes on end, and the bird is visible over great distances on spring mornings and evenings.

Male Australian (2) and Great Indian bustards cock the tail right forward and inflate the neck downwards so that it becomes a broad sack that swings around like a punchbag, scraping the ground. The kori simply inflates its neck into a puffy white ball and trails its wings. The oddest of the ground displays is that of the houbara (3), which raises its white neck-ruff right over its head, and trots around in an irregular path with very little indication that it can see where it is going.

The small black-bellied species of Africa and India give impressive display-flights or display-leaps above the grass that otherwise conceals them. The most exciting aerial display is that of the Red-crested bustard, which flies vertically up to as much as 100ft (30m) above the ground, somersaults backwards, then drops like a stone, pulling out at the last moment and gliding nonchalantly away to land. On the ground, too, this bird has a beautiful display, fully erecting its crest and using stiff, clockwork-like movements as it approaches a female.

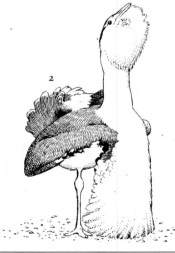

▲ **Female Little bustard** (male has black-and-white collar). Loss of grasslands has reduced the species' range in Europe to the Iberian Peninsula and part of southern France.

hunting controversy, commands a new popular interest in its survival and is currently showing signs of recovery in Rajasthan. The decline of its closest relative, the Australian bustard, is commonly attributed to continued remorseless, indiscriminate shooting from the earliest days of European settlement, but it seems certain that conversion of its habitat to farmland is the major factor in its disappearance.

The decline of the houbara is plainly the direct result of hunting. This is the one species of bustard that figures strongly in human culture, as the most prized quarry in the Arab tradition of falconry. In recent years, oil wealth and technology have vastly increased the scale and efficiency of such

hunting, so it is feared that in many parts of its range the houbara is almost completely wiped out. Unfortunately, bustard hunting by Arabs appears to be growing in other parts of Africa, notably the Saharo-Sahelian zone, and certain other species— particularly the Nubian bustard—have suffered alarming declines as a result. No other purely African bustard is known to be seriously at risk, although the restricted ranges of the Blue and Little brown bustards must be cause for sustained vigilance. Moreover, throughout Africa the pressure to grow more food is unrelenting and it cannot be long before some of these peace-loving ground dwellers emerge as new candidates for extinction.   NJC

BUTTON QUAILS AND OTHER RELATIVES

Families: Turnicidae, Pedionomidae, Mesitornithidae, Heliornithidae, Rhynochetidae, Eurypygidae, Cariamidae
Order: Gruiformes (part).
Twenty-seven species in 11 genera.
Distribution: see maps and table.

Button quails   **Seriemas**   **Sunbittern**

Plains wanderer   **Kagu**   **Finfoots**   **Mesites**

THE **button quails**, together with the Plains wanderer (see below), display one of the most complete reversals of normal sexual roles known in birds. Females are the more brightly colored sex, and are larger where the sexes differ in size; they defend territory, pugnaciously driving off other females, and initiate courtship of the males. Then, after the eggs have been laid, it is left to the male to incubate the clutch and tend the chicks. In some species, one female will mate with several males during a season.

Button quails inhabit warm, semi-arid regions of the Old World. They owe their alternative name, hemipode (half-foot), to the fact that the rear toe is missing. They are small, quail-like, essentially ground-dwelling birds, with a "crouching" posture. They are secretive and difficult to flush, even then flying only short distances. The one exception is the Lark quail of Africa, which has a strong lark-like flight, and flies some distance before alighting. Despite this general reluctance to fly in the face of disturbance, a few species are partially migratory, including the Yellow-legged button quail and the Little button quail. In regions lacking any marked seasonal variation in climate, button quails will breed opportunistically all year round and, as in the Old World quails, young can attain sexual maturity at 4–6 months old.

On the Melanesian island New Caledonia the now endangered **kagu** has become restricted, through persecution and habitat loss, to probably under 60sq mi (130sq km) in the valleys of the central mountain range. Formerly many kagu were trapped for keeping in aviaries and for decorative plumes for the millinery trade. This direct persecution has lessened (though some local people still

catch and keep them as pets), but the New Caledonian forests are still being destroyed as a consequence of nickel mining (the main island industry); wild populations of introduced mammals (pigs, cats and dogs) have spread to the remotest areas and constitute a threat to ground-nesting birds as well as being (in the case of pigs) possible competitors for food.

The kagu is a superficially heron-like bird of the forest floor, whose nearest (but not close) relative is probably the Sun bittern (see below). Both are plain-colored birds when seen at rest, but their broad wings, when opened in display, reveal striking patterns. The kagu is stocky but long-legged and stands relatively upright. It is almost flightless. The little we know of the kagu has been derived from observations of captive birds. The New Caledonian breeding season in the wild is believed to be August–January but it is April–November in captivity in, for example, Australia; the day-time activity of captive birds is at variance with suggestions from visitors to New Caledonia that the species is most active in the evening and at night—certainly the birds call a great deal at night. Most birds which lay single-egg clutches (as does the kagu) are long-lived, and captive kagus have lived for 20–30 years in warm climates.

The **Sun bittern**, like the finfoots, inhabits riversides in tropical and subtropical forests. It is not easy to locate or watch, and not particularly sociable, normally being encountered singly or in pairs along streams where the trees provide shade from the full heat of the sun. Sun bitterns seek cover within vegetation when disturbed and are easily overlooked by the would-be observer.

The Sun bittern is stout-bodied, with a

▶ **Belying its name,** the Sun bittern lives by shady riversides from Mexico to southeast Brazil. The "sun" refers to the markings displayed on the broad wings that are extended in a threat-defense posture.

▲ **Cockatoo-like crest** of the kagu is made of feathers once prized in the milliner's trade. Today the kagu is restricted to the central forests of New Caledonia and is listed as endangered.

heron-like long neck and long legs. The impression of sombre, camouflage coloration in the feeding or skulking bird is belied in flight or display, when the spread wings reveal conspicuous patches of chestnut on the primary wing feathers, and bands of the same color across the tail. Adult males are no more brightly colored than females or even juveniles, and it now seems clear that the spectacular frontal display of the Sun bittern is for threat or defense rather than courtship. In this startling transformation from a skulking to a large and threatening

bird, the patches on the broad wings stand out as big, intimidating "eyes" (supposed also to look like a rising sun). In captivity, both parents share the tasks of incubation and chick care, and the chicks stay in the nest for 3–4 weeks.

The two **seriemas** are placed, on the basis of similarities in musculature and the skull, in the same order (Gruiformes) as the cranes and rails. However, they bear a superficial resemblance to the Secretary bird (order Falconiformes) of Africa, and are its ecological counterpart on the dry pampas and scrub-savanna of South America. They are ground dwellers, with a typically upright posture. Although their wings are developed, they seldom fly, preferring to run (with head lowered) when disturbed: their long neck and legs are well adapted for living in long grass, in much the same way as in the Secretary bird and, among much closer relatives, the Old World bustards (p144). Also like bustards, seriemas live in small groups, and their displays are said to be somewhat similar. One notable feature shared by the Secretary bird and the seriemas is that their diets include small snakes (seriemas are not, however, immune to snake poison). Often seriemas feed close to cattle and horses, presumably taking invertebrates disturbed by the grazing stock.

The Black-legged seriema has a more restricted range, prefers open woodland and scrub areas and is more arboreal (nesting above ground and roosting higher up) than the better-known Red-legged (or Crested) seriema of the grasslands. The young of both are often taken alive for taming, since they make efficient "watchdogs" against approaching predators when kept with domestic fowls. Though the newly hatched young are already well covered with down, they remain in the nest (under parental care) until well grown.

The **Plains wanderer** appears in the field to be a fairly typical button quail, with its broadly similar camouflage color patterning and habits. But, unlike button quails, it retains the hind toe, it lays pear-shaped (not oval) eggs, it tends to adopt a more upright (not crouching) posture, and the carotid arteries in the neck are paired.

The Plains wanderer was formerly widespread in eastern and southeastern Australia, but declined as agriculture became more intensive. It is now scarce or rare, its range is fragmented, and it is found chiefly on unimproved grasslands and on fields left fallow in alternate years; such conditions provide the mix of grass and weed seeds needed by the birds for food. There is no evidence that they are migratory; the concentration of April–June records in the south merely reflects the quail shooting season there.

Eggs have been found in all months except March and April; probably there is breeding year-round as the opportunity arises. As in the button quails, the more brightly colored female initiates courtship, then leaves the male to incubate the clutch and raise the young. In captivity, however, females sometimes help with incubation. Once the parent-young bond has broken, the birds become well separated in ones and twos. They seldom fly, instead running off or crouching for concealment when alarmed: and they have the habit of standing on tiptoe, neck outstretched, to gain a better view through or over the vegetation.

With the progressive destruction of the Madagascan forests (only 10 percent of the island remains forested) a disproportionate number of the island's species are now endangered, including all three **mesites**. The White-breasted mesite inhabits dry forest in western Madagascar; it is now extremely rare and localized, the last reported sighting being from Ankarafantsika (fortunately now a protected area) in 1971. The Brown mesite occurs in moist evergreen forest in the east, and has always been considered

Button Quails and Related Families

[R] Rare.   [E] Endangered.

Button quails

Family: Turnicidae
Sixteen species in 2 genera.
Africa, S Spain, S Iran to E China and Australia. Open grassland, thin scrub, crop fields. Size: 4.5–8in (11–20cm) long. Plumage: buffy-brown with camouflage markings in browns, grays and cream; tail and wings short; females brighter and sometimes larger. Nests: in ground hollows lined with grass. Eggs: 3–7, oval, glossy, richly marked on pale background; incubation 12–14 days; chicks leave nest almost at once. Diet: small seeds and insects. Species include the **Lark quail** or **Quail plover** (*Ortyxelos meiffrenii*); **Little button quail** (*Turnix sylvatica*); **Yellow-legged button quail** (*T. tanki*).

Kagu [E]

Family: Rhynochetidae
Sole species *Rhynochetos jubatus*.
New Caledonia. Upland forest. Length: 24in (60cm). Plumage: drab gray, but spread wings show striking pattern of black, white and reddish; long, erectile crest. Bare parts red, bill downcurved. Nest: of sticks and leaves on ground (in captivity). Eggs:

1, light brown with dark brown blotches; incubation (probably by both parents) 35–40 days; young well developed, leave nest on hatching. Diet: snails, worms and insects from forest floor.

Sun bittern

Family: Eurypygidae
Sole species *Eurypyga helias*.
S Mexico to Bolivia and Brazil. Edges of streams and swamps in forests. Length: 18in (46cm). Plumage: camouflage patterns shown at rest, but chestnut marks on wings and tail conspicuous in display. Nest: of stems and leaves up to 20ft (6m) up in bush or tree. Eggs: 2, buff to off-white, with darker blotches; both parents incubate (27 days) and care for hatchlings. Diet: mollusks, crustaceans, aquatic insects.

Seriemas

Family: Cariamidae
Two species in 2 genera.
S America. Eggs: 2, off-white to buff with brown markings; both parents incubate (25–26 days) and tend young. Diet: omnivorous. Species: **Black-legged** or **Burmeister's seriema** (*Chunga burmeisteri*), dry open

woodland and scrub in W Paraguay, N Argentina; length 28in (70cm); black-tipped tail, negligible crest; black bill and legs; nest in bush or tree. **Red-legged** or **Crested seriema** (*Cariama cristata*), grasslands in Brazil to Uruguay and N Argentina; length 32in (82cm); white-tipped tail, large frontal crest; red bill and legs; nest of sticks on ground.

Plains wanderer

Family: Pedionomidae
Sole species *Pedionomus torquatus*.
SE and C Australia. Open grassland and stubble fields; avoids scrub areas. Length: 6–7in (15–17cm). Plumage: cryptic coloration of buff, brown and black, with collar of black spots on white; females larger and more brightly colored. Nest: a grass-lined ground hollow. Eggs: 2–5 (usually 4), gray and olive markings on yellowish; incubation 23 days; well-developed hatchlings leave nest at once. Diet: small seeds and insects.

Mesites

Family: Mesitornithidae
Three species in 2 genera.
Madagascar. Forest, marginal scrub (*Monias*). Length: 10–12in (25–30cm).

Plumage: brown to grayish above, paler below and (not Brown mesite) spotted. Bill straight or (monia) downcurved. Nests: a twig platform 3–6ft (1–2m) up in bush. Eggs: 1–3, off-white with brown spots; hatchlings leave nest at once. Diet: seeds and insects. Species: **Bensch's monia** [R] (*Monias benschi*); **Brown mesite** [R] (*Mesitornis unicolor*); **White-breasted mesite** [R] (*M. variegata*).

Finfoots

Family: Heliornithidae
Three species in 2 genera.
C and S America, Africa, SE Asia. Rivers and lakes in forest. Nests: on low branch or flood debris. Eggs: 2–4 (Masked finfoot 5–6?), reddish-brown or cream; incubation 11 days (Sun grebe). Diet: frogs, crustaceans, mollusks, aquatic insects. Species: **African finfoot** (*Podica senegalensis*), length 23in (60cm), white-spotted back, bill and legs orange-red; **Masked finfoot** (*Heliornis personata*), length 22in (56cm), back plain, face and throat black, yellow bill, green legs; **Sun grebe** (*Heliornis fulica*), length 12in (30cm), olive-brown, scarlet bill, black and yellow feet.

▲◄ **Button quails and related families.** (1)
Brown mesite (*Mesitornis unicolor*). (2) Masked
finfoot (*Heliornis personata*). (3) Crested seriema
(*Cariama cristata*). (4) Plains wanderer
(*Pedionomus torquatus*). (5) Little button quail
(*Turnix sylvatica*).

rare. Bensch's monia inhabits dry brush
woodland in southwestern Madagascar; it
may be less rare than the others, but is
nevertheless probably declining and is
designated rare by the ICBP.

Mesites are thrush-sized running birds of
the forest floor. They have functional wings
but rudimentary collar bones, and can probably fly weakly for short distances, despite
seldom doing so. While they build nests
above ground, these are invariably sited so
that the birds can climb or scramble up to
them. Breeding occurs in October–
December. The mating system of the White-
breasted and Brown mesites seems to be
"normal," but it may be otherwise in
Bensch's monia, in which the adult female
is the more brightly colored. Some parties
of Bensch's monia comprising males and
one dominant female have been reported,
but in a more recent study females have
been observed sharing parental duties, with
two of them (paired to one male) laying in
one nest.

All three species of **finfoots** are shy and
retiring, not easily observed in their tropical
riverside settings. It is thought that the rails
are their nearest relatives, though, seen on
the water, finfoots look more like grebes.
Finfoots combine characters of grebes and
coots (lobed feet) and cormorants (long
neck, stiffened tail). When taking flight they
patter across the water before becoming airborne, but their normal reaction to disturbance is to run ashore into dense
undergrowth, or to swim away with body
submerged and only head and neck visible.
At least one species, the Masked finfoot, is
partially migratory, reaching Malaya (probably from Thailand) in winter.

Sun grebe parents carry their young in
flight as well as on the water. The adult has
special folds of skin beneath each wing,
forming cavities into which the chicks fit,
muscular control probably helping to hold
the chicks firmly against the parent's body.
The naked, helpless hatchling chicks are
carried from the nest before even their eyes
have opened. It is not yet known whether
this remarkable feature applies also to the
two Old World finfoots. The African finfoot
is known also to lay a clutch of two eggs,
and so may have adopted such a strategy,
but the Masked finfoot is said to lay a clutch
of 5–6 eggs, though this is based on old
information. In the American Sun grebe,
both parents share the incubation, though
as yet only the male is confirmed as carrying
young; in the African finfoot, females have
been seen accompanying well-feathered
juveniles.   RH

BIBLIOGRAPHY

The following list of titles indicates key reference works used in the preparation of this volume and those recommended for further reading. The list is divided into two sections: general and regional books about birds and books dealing with particular families or groups.

General and Regional

Ali, S. (1977) *Field Guide to the Birds of the Eastern Himalayas*, Oxford University Press, Delhi.

Ali, S. and Ripley, S. D. (1983) *A Pictorial Guide to the Birds of the Indian Subcontinent*, Bombay Natural History Society/Oxford University Press, Delhi.

Ali, S. and Ripley, S. D. (1984) *Handbook of the Birds of India and Pakistan*, Oxford University Press, Delhi.

Baker, R. R. (1984) *Bird Navigation—the Solution of a Mystery?* Hodder and Stoughton, Sevenoaks, Kent.

Baker, R. R. (1978) *The Evolutionary Ecology of Animal Migration*, Hodder and Stoughton, Sevenoaks, Kent.

Blake, E. R. (1977) *Manual of Neotropical Birds, Vol. I. Spheniscidae to Laridae*, University of Chicago Press, Chicago.

Blakers, M., Davies, S. J. J. F. and Reilly, P. N. (1984) *The Atlas of Australian Birds*, Melbourne University Press, Melbourne.

Bock, W. J. and Farrand, J. (1980) *The Number of Species and Genera of Recent Birds: a Contribution to Comparative Systematics*, American Museum of Natural History, New York.

Bond, J. (1979) *Birds of the West Indies: a Guide to the Species of Birds that Inhabit the Greater Antilles, Lesser Antilles and Bahama Islands*, Collins, London.

Brown, L. H., Urban, E. K. and Newman, K. (1982) *The Birds of Africa*, vol I, Academic Press, London.

Brudenell-Bruce, P. G. C. (1975) *The Birds of New Providence and the Bahama Islands*, Collins, London.

Campbell, B. and Lack, E. (1985) *A New Dictionary of Birds*, T. and A. D. Poyser, Stoke-on-Trent.

Clements, J. (1981) *Birds of the World: a Checklist*, Croom Helm, London.

Cramp, S. (1978–85) *Handbook of the Birds of Europe, the Middle East and North Africa: the Birds of the Western Palearctic*, vols I–IV, Oxford University Press, Oxford.

Dementiev, G. P. *et al* (1966) *Birds of the Soviet Union*, vols I–VI, Jerusalem.

Dorst, J. (1962) *The Migration of Birds*, Heinemann, London.

Dunning, J. S. (1982) *South American Land Birds: a Photographic Aid to Identification*, Harrowood, Pennsylvania.

Eastwood, E. (1967) *Radar Ornithology*, Methuen, London.

Ehrlick, P. and A. (1982) *Extinction*, Gollancz, London.

Elkins, N. (1983) *Weather and Bird Behavior*, T. and A. D. Poyser, Stoke-on-Trent.

Falla, R. A., Sibson, R. B. and Turbott, E. G. (1979) *The New Guide to the Birds of New Zealand*, Collins, Auckland and London.

Farner, D. S., King, J. R. and Parkes, K. C. (1971–83) *Avian Biology*, vols I–VII, Academic Press, New York and London.

Farrand, J. J. (1983) *The Audubon Society Master Guide to Birding*, 3 vols, Knopf, New York.

Ferguson-Lees, J., Willis, I. and Sharrock, J. T. R. (1983) *The Shell Guide to the Birds of Britain and Ireland*, Michael Joseph, London.

Finlay, J. C. (1984) *A Bird Finding Guide to Canada,*, Hurtig, Edmon.

Flint, V. E., Boehme, R. L., Kostin, Y. V. and Kuznetzov, A. A. (1984) *A Field Guide to Birds of the USSR*, Princeton University Press, Princeton, N.J.

Gallagher, M. and Woodcock, M. W. (1980) *The Birds of Oman*, Quartet, London.

Glenister, A. G. (1971) *The Birds of the Malay Peninsula, Singapore and Penang*, Oxford University Press, Kuala Lumpur.

Godfrey, W. E. (1966) *The Birds of Canada*, National Museum of Canada, Ottawa.

Gotch, A. F. (1981) *Birds—their Latin Names Explained*, Blandford Press, Poole, Dorset.

Gruson, E. S. (1976) *A Checklist of the Birds of the World*, Collins, London.

Halliday, T. (1978) *Vanishing Birds: their Natural History and Conservation*, Sidgwick and Jackson, London.

Harris, M. (1982) *A Field Guide to the Birds of Galapagos*, revised edn, Collins, London.

Harrison, C. J. O. (1975) *A Field Guide to the Nests, Eggs and Nestlings of British and European Birds, with North Africa and the Middle East*, Collins, London.

Harrison, C. J. O. (1978) *A Field Guide to the Nests, Eggs and Nestlings of North American Birds*, Collins, London.

Harrison, C. J. O. (1982) *An Atlas of the Birds of the Western Palaearctic*, Collins, London.

Harrison, C. J. O. (ed) (1978) *Bird Families of the World*, Elsevier-Phaidon, Oxford.

Harrison, P. (1983) *Seabirds—an Identification Guide*, Croom Helm, London.

Howard, R. and Moore, A. (1980) *A Complete Checklist of the Birds of the World*, Oxford University Press, Oxford.

Irby Davis, L. (1972) *A Field Guide to the Birds of Mexico and Central America*, Texas University Press, Austin.

King, A. S. and McLelland, J. (1975) *Outlines of Avian Anatomy*, Baillière Tindall, London.

King B., Woodcock, M. and Dickinson, E. C. (1975) *A Field Guide to the Birds of South-East Asia*, Collins, London.

Krebs, J. R. and Davies, N. B. (1981) *An Introduction to Behavioral Ecology*, Blackwell Scientific Publications, Oxford.

Lack, D. (1968) *Ecological Adaptations for Breeding in Birds*, Methuen, London.

Leahy, C. (1982) *The Bird Watcher's Companion: an Encyclopedic Handbook of North American Birdlife*, Hale, London.

McFarland, D. (ed) (1981) *The Oxford Companion to Animal Behavior*, Oxford University Press, Oxford.

McLachlan, G. R. *et al* (1978) *Roberts' Birds of South Africa* (4th edn), Struik, Cape Town.

Moreau, R. E. (1972) *The Palaearctic–African Bird Migration Systems*, Academic Press, London.

Murton, R. K. and Westwood, N. J. (1977) *Avian Breeding Cycles*, Oxford University Press, Oxford.

National Geographic Society (1983) *Field Guide to the Birds of North America*, NGS, Washington.

Newman, K. (1983) *The Birds of Southern Africa*, Macmillan, Johannesburg.

O'Connor, R. J. (1984) *The Growth and Development of Birds*, Wiley, New York.

Penny, M. (1974) *The Birds of the Seychelles and the Outlying Islands*, Collins, London.

Perrins, C. M. (1976) *Bird Life: an Introduction to the World of Birds*, Elsevier-Phaidon, Oxford.

Perrins, C. M. and Birkhead, T. R. (1983) *Avian Ecology*, Blackie, London.

Peters, J. L. *et al* (1931–) *Checklist of Birds of the World*, Museum of Comparative Zoology, Cambridge, Massachusetts.

Peterson, R. T. (1980) *A Field Guide to the Birds East of the Rockies* (4th edn), Houghton Mifflin, Boston, Mass.

Peterson, P. T., Mountford, G. and Hollom, P. A. D. (1983) *A Field Guide to the Birds of Britain and Europe* (4th edn), Collins, London.

Pizzey, G. (1980) *A Field Guide to the Birds of Australia*, Collins, Sydney.

Schauensee, R. M. de (1982) *A Guide to the Birds of South America*, Academy of Natural Sciences of Philadelphia.

Schauensee, R. M. de and Phelps, W. H. (1978) *A Guide to the Birds of Venezuela*, Princeton University Press, Princeton, N.J.

Schauensee, R. M. de (1984) *The Birds of China Including the Island of Taiwan*, Oxford University Press, Oxford; Smithsonian Institution Press, Washington D.C.

Serle, W., Morel, G. J. and Hartwig, W. (1977) *A Field Guide to the Birds of West Africa*, Collins, London.

Sharrock, J. T. R. (1976) *The Atlas of Breeding Birds in Britain and Ireland*, British Trust for Ornithology, Tring, Hertfordshire.

Simms, E. (1979) *Wildlife Sounds and their Recording*, Elek, London.

Skutch, A. F. (1975) *Parent Birds and their Young*, University of Texas Press, Austin, Texas.

Slater, P. (1971, 1975) *A Field Guide to Australian Birds*, vol I, Oliver and Boyd, Edinburgh; vol II, Scottish Academic Press, Edinburgh.

Stresemann, E. (1975) *Ornithology from Aristotle to the Present*, Harvard University Press, Cambridge, Mass.

Tyne, J. van and Berger, A. J. (1976) *Fundamentals of Ornithology* (2nd edn), Wiley, New York.

Warham, J. (1983) *The Techniques of Bird Photography* (4th edn), Focal Press, Sevenoaks, Kent.

Watson, G. E. (1975) *Birds of the Antarctic and Sub-Antarctic*, American Geophysical Union, Washington, D.C.

Weaver, P. (1981) *The Bird-Watcher's Dictionary*, T. and A. D. Poyser, Stoke-on-Trent.

Wild Bird Society of Japan (1982) *A Field Guide to the Birds of Japan*, Wild Bird Society of Japan, Tokyo.

Williams, J. G. and Arlott, N. (1980) *A Field Guide to the Birds of East Africa*, Collins, London.

Wilson, E. (1967) *Birds of the Antarctic*, Blandford Press, Poole.

Families or Groups

Brown, L. and Amadon, D. (1968) *Eagles, Hawks and Falcons of the World*, 2 vols, Country Life Books, Feltham, Middlesex.

Delacour, J. (1977) *The Pheasants of the World* (2nd edn), Spur Publications, Hindhead, Surrey.

Delacour, J. and Amadon, D. (1973) *Curassows and Related Birds*, American Museum of Natural History, New York.

Hancock, J. and Kushlan, J. (1984) *The Herons Handbook*, Croom Helm, London.

Johnsgard, P. A. (1983) *Cranes of the World*, Croom Helm, London.

Johnsgard, P. A. (1978) *Ducks, Geese and Swans of the World*, University of Nebraska Press, Lincoln, Nebraska.

Johnsgard, P. A. (1983) *The Grouse of the World*, University of Nebraska Press, Lincoln, Nebraska.

Keer, J. and Duplaix-Hall, N. (eds) (1979) *Flamingos*, T. and A. D. Poyser, Stoke-on-Trent.

Newton, I. (1979) *Population Ecology of Raptors*, T. and A. D. Poyser, Stoke-on-Trent.

Ripley, S. D. (1977) *Rails of the World*, M. F. Feheley, Toronto.

Simpson, G. G. (1976) *Penguins*, Yale University Press, New Haven, Connecticut.

GLOSSARY

Adaptation features of an animal that adjust it to its environment. NATURAL SELECTION favors the survival of individuals whose adaptations adjust them better to their surroundings than other individuals with less successful adaptations.

Adaptive radiation where a group of closely related animals (eg members of a family) have evolved differences from each other so that they occupy different NICHES and have reduced competition between each other.

Adult a fully developed and mature individual, capable of breeding but not necessarily doing so until social and/or ecological conditions allow.

Air sac thin walled structure connected to the lungs of birds and involved in respiration; extensions of these can occur in hollow bones.

Albino a form in which all dark pigments are missing, leaving the animal white, usually with red eyes.

Alpine living in mountainous areas, usually above 5,000ft (1,500m).

Altricial refers to young that stay in the nest until they are more or less full grown (as opposed to PRECOCIAL). See also NIDICOLOUS.

Aquatic associated with water.

Arboreal associated with or living in trees.

Avian pertaining to birds.

Beak see BILL.

Bill the two MANDIBLES with which birds gather their food. Synonymous with beak.

Blubber fat, usually that lying just beneath the skin.

Bolus a ball (of food).

Boreal zone the area of land lying just below the north polar region and mainly covered in coniferous forest.

Broadleaved woodland woodland mainly comprising angiosperm trees (both deciduous and evergreen), such as oaks, beeches and hazels, which is characteristic of many temperate areas of Europe and North America.

Brood group of young raised simultaneously by a pair (or several) birds.

Blood-parasite a bird that has its eggs hatched and reared by another species.

Call short sounds made by birds to indicate danger, threaten intruders or keep a group of birds together. See also SONG.

Canopy a fairly continuous layer in forests produced by the intermingling of branches of trees; may be fully continuous (closed) or broken by gaps (open). The crowns of some trees project above the canopy layer and are known as emergents.

Carpal the outer joint of the wing, equivalent to the human wrist.

Casque bony extension of the upper MANDIBLE.

Cecum diverticulation or sac of the hind-gut.

Class a taxonomic level. All birds belong to the class Aves. The main levels of a taxonomic hierarchy (in descending order) are Phylum, Class, Order, Family, Genus, Species.

Cloaca terminal part of the gut into which the reproductive and urinary ducts open. There is one opening to the outside of the body. The cloacal aperture, instead of separate anus and urinogenital openings.

Clutch the eggs laid in one breeding attempt.

Colonial living together in a COLONY.

Colony a group of animals gathered together for breeding.

Comb a fleshy protuberance on the top of a bird's head.

Communal breeder species in which more than the two birds of a pair help in raising the young. See COOPERATIVE BREEDING.

Congener a member of the same genus.

Coniferous forest forest comprising largely evergreen conifers (firs, pines, spruces etc), typically in climates either too dry or too cold to support DECIDUOUS FOREST. Most frequent in northern latitudes or in mountain ranges.

Conspecific a member of the same species.

Contact call CALLS given by males in competition.

Contour feathers visible external covering of feathers, including flight feathers of tail and wings.

Convergent evolution the independent acquisition of similar characters in evolution, as opposed to the possession of similarities by virtue of descent from a common ancestor.

Cooperative breeding a breeding system in which parents of young are assisted in the care of young by other adult or subadult birds.

Coverts the smaller feathers that cover the wings and overlie the base of the large FLIGHT FEATHERS (both wings and tail).

Covey a collective name for groups of birds, usually gamebirds.

Creche a gathering of young birds, especially in penguins and flamingos; sometimes used as a verb.

Crest long feathers on the top of the heads of birds.

Crop a thin-walled extension of the foregut used to store food; often used to carry food to the nest.

Crustaceans invertebrate group which includes shrimps, crabs and many other small marine animals.

Cryptic camouflaged and difficult to see.

Deciduous forest temperate and tropical forest with moderate rainfall and marked seasons. Typically trees shed leaves during either cold or dry periods.

Desert areas of low rainfall, typically with sparse scrub or grassland vegetation or lacking vegetation altogether.

Dimorphic literally "two forms." Usually used as "sexually dimorphic" (ie the two sexes differ in color or size).

Disjunct distribution geographical distribution of a species that is marked by gaps. Commonly brought about by fragmentation of suitable habitat, especially as a result of human intervention.

Dispersal The movements of animals, often as they reach maturity, away from their previous HOME RANGE. Distinct from **dispersion**, that is the pattern in which things (perhaps animals, food supplies, nest-sites) are distributed or scattered.

Display any relatively conspicuous pattern of behavior that conveys specific information to others, usually to members of the same species; often associated with courtship but also in other activities, eg "threat display."

Display ground the place where a male (or males) tries to attract females.

DNA deoxyribonucleic acid; the key substance of chromosomes—important for inheritance.

Dominance hierarchy a "peck-order"; in most groups of birds, in any pair of birds each knows which is superior and a ranking of superiors therefore follows.

Double-brooded (also triple or multiple brooded) birds which breed twice or more each year, subsequent nests following earlier successful ones, excluding those when the first or all earlier nests fail, in which case the term **replacement nests** applies.

Echolocation the ability to find one's way about by emitting sounds and gauging the position of objects by timing the returning echo.

Erectile of an object, eg a crest, that can be raised.

Facultative optional. See also OBLIGATE.

Family either a group of closely related species, eg penguins, or a pair of birds and their offspring. See CLASS.

Feces excrement from the digestive system passed out through the CLOACA.

Fledge strictly to grow feathers. Now usually used to refer to the moment of flying at the end of the nesting period when young birds are more or less completely feathered. Hence **fledging period**, the time from hatching to fledging, and **fledgling**, a recently fledged young bird.

Flight feathers the large feathers of the wing, which can be divided into PRIMARY FEATHERS and SECONDARY FEATHERS.

Fossorial burrowing.

Frontal shield a fleshy area covering the forehead.

Frugivore eating mainly fruits.

Gallery forest a thin belt of woodland along a riverbank in otherwise more open country.

Generalist an animal whose life-style does not involve highly specialized stratagems (cf SPECIALIST), for example, feeding on a variety of foods which may require different foraging techniques.

Genus the taxonomic grouping of species. See CLASS.

Gizzard the muscular forepart of the stomach. Often an important area for the grinding up of food, in many species with the help of grit.

Gregarious the tendency to congregate into groups.

Guano bird excreta. In certain dry areas the guano of colonial sea birds may accumulate to such an extent that it is economic to gather it for fertilizer.

Gular pouch an extension of the fleshy area of the lower jaw and throat.

Habitat the type of country in which an animal lives.

Hallux the first toe. Usually this is small and points backwards, opposing the three forward-facing toes.

Harem a group of females living in the territory of, or consorting with, a single male.

Hatchling a young bird recently emerged from the egg.

Helper an individual, generally without young of its own, which contributes to the survival of the offspring of others by behaving parentally towards them. See COOPERATIVE BREEDING.

Herbivore an animal which eats vegetable material.

Holarctic realm a region of the world including North America, Greenland, Europe and Asia apart from the Southwest, Southeast and India.

Homeothermic warm-blooded, having the ability to keep body temperature constant.

Home range an area in which an animal normally lives (generally excluding rare excursions or migrations), irrespective of whether or not the area is defended from other animals.

Hybrid the offspring of a mating between birds of different species.

Hypothermy a condition in which internal body temperature falls below normal.

Incubation the act of incubating the egg or eggs, ie keeping them warm so that development is possible. Hence **incubation period**, the time taken for eggs to develop from the start of incubation to hatching.

Insectivore an animal that feeds on insects.

Introduced of a species that has been brought from lands where it occurs naturally to lands where it has not previously occurred. Some introductions are natural but some are made on purpose for biological control, farming or other economic reasons.

Irruption sudden or irregular spread of birds from their normal range. Usually a consequence of a food shortage.

Keratin the substance from which feathers are formed (and also reptile scales, human hair, fingernails etc).

Krill small shrimp-like marine CRUSTACEANS which are an important food for certain species of seabirds.

Lamellae comb-like structures which can be used for filtering organisms out of water.

Lanceolate (of feathers) referring to lance-like (pointed) shape.

Lek a display ground where two or more male birds gather to attract females. See DISPLAY.

Littoral referring to the shore-line.

Mallee scrub small scrubby eucalyptus which covers large areas of dryish country in Australia.

Mandible one of the jaws of a bird which make up the BILL (upper or lower).

Melanin a dark or black PIGMENT.

Metabolic rate the rate at which the chemical processes of the body occur.

Migration usually the behavior in which birds fly (migrate) from one part of the world to another at different times of year. There is also local migration and altitudinal migration where birds move, eg on a mountain side, from one height to another.

Molt the replacement of old feathers by new ones.

Monoculture a habitat dominated by a single species of plant, often referring to forestry plantations.

Monogamous taking only a single mate (at a time).

Monotypic the sole member of its genus, family, order etc.

Montane pertaining to mountainous country.

Montane forest forest occurring at middle altitudes on the slopes of mountains, below the alpine zone but above the lowland forest.

Morph a form, usually used to describe a color form when more than one exist.

Morphology the study of the shape and form of animals.

Natural selection the process whereby individuals with the most appropriate ADAPTATIONS are more successful than other individuals, and hence survive to produce more offspring and so increase the population.

Neotropical originating in the tropics of the New World.

Nestling a young bird in the nest, hence **nestling period**, the time from hatching to flying (see FLEDGE).

Niche specific parts of a habitat occupied by a species, defined in terms of all aspects of its life-style (eg food, competitors, predators and other resource requirements).

Nidicolous of young birds which remain in the nest until they can fly. See ALTRICIAL.

Nidifugous of young birds that leave the nest soon after hatching. See PRECOCIAL.

Nomadic wandering (as opposed to having fixed residential areas).

Obligate required, binding. See also FACULTATIVE.

Oligotrophic of a freshwater lake with low nutrient levels; such lakes are usually deep and have poor vegetation.

Omnivore an animal that eats a wide variety of foods.

Opportunistic an animal that varies its diet in relation to what is most freely available. See GENERALIST, SPECIALIST.

Order a level of taxonomic ranking. See CLASS.

Organochlorine pesticides a group of chemicals used mainly as insecticides, some of which have proved highly toxic to birds; includes DDT, aldrin, dieldrin.

Pair bond the faithfulness of a mated pair to each other.

Palaearctic a zoogeographical area roughly comprising Europe and Asia (except the Indian subcontinent and Southeast Asia).

Pampas grassy plains (of South America).

Parasitize in the ornithological sense, usually to lay eggs in the nests of another species and leave the foster parents to raise the young. See BROOD-PARASITE.

Passerine strictly "sparrow-like" but normally used as a shortened form of Passeriformes, the largest ORDER of birds.

Pecten a structure lying on the retina of the eye.

Pigment a substance that gives color to eggs and feathers.

Pod a group of individuals, especially juvenile pelicans, with a temporary cohesive group structure.

Polyandry where a female mates with several males.

Polygamy where a male mates with several females.

Polymorphic where a species occurs in two (or more) different forms (usually relating to color). See MORPH, DIMORPHIC.

Polygyny where a bird of one sex takes several mates.

Population a more or less separate (discrete) group of animals of the same species.

Prairie North American steppe grassland between 30°N and 55°N.

Precocial young birds that leave the nest after hatching, See ALTRICIAL.

Predation where animals are taken by a predator.

Predator birds that hunt and eat other vertebrates hence "anti-predator behavior" describes the evasive actions of the prey.

Preen gland a gland situated above the base of the tail. The bird wipes its bill across this while preening the feathers, so distributing the waxy product of the preen gland over the feathers. The exact function of this is not known; some groups of birds do not possess preen glands.

Primary feather one of the large feathers of the outer wing.

Primary forest forest that has remained undisturbed for a long time and has reached a mature (climax) condition; primary rain forest may take centuries to become established. See also SECONDARY GROWTH.

Promiscuous referring to species where the sexes come together for mating only and do not form lasting pair bonds.

Pyriform pear-shaped.

Quartering the act of flying back and forth over an area, searching it thoroughly.

Race a subsection of a species which is distinguishable from the rest of that species. Usually equivalent to SUBSPECIES.

Radiation see ADAPTIVE RADIATION.

Rain forest tropical and subtropical forest with abundant and year-round rainfall. Typically species rich and diverse.

Range (geographical) area over which an organism is distributed.

Raptor a bird of prey, usually one belonging to the order Falconiformes.

Ratites members of four orders of flightless birds (ostrich, rheas, emu and cassowaries, kiwis) which lack a keel on the breastbone.

Relict population a local group of a species which has been isolated from the rest for a long time.

Resident an animal that stays in one area all the year round.

Roosting sleeping.

Sahara-Sahelian zone the area of North Africa comprising the Sahara Desert and the arid Sahel zone to its south.

Savanna a term loosely used to describe open grasslands with scattered trees and bushes, usually in warm areas.

Scrape a nest without any nesting material where a shallow depression has been formed to hold the eggs.

Scrub a vegetation dominated by shrubs—woody plants usually with more than one stem. Naturally occurs most often on the arid side of forest or grassland types, but often artificially created by man as a result of forest destruction.

Secondary feather one of the large flight feathers on the inner wing.

Secondary forest an area of rain forest that has regenerated after being felled. Usually of poorer quality and lower diversity than PRIMARY FOREST and containing trees of a more uniform size.

Sedentary nonmigrating. See RESIDENT.

Sequential molt where feathers (usually the wing feathers) are molted in order, as opposed to all at once.

Sexual selection an evolutionary mechanism whereby females select for mating only males with certain characteristics, or vice versa.

Sibling group a group containing brothers and sisters.

Sibling species closely related species, thought to have only recently separated.

Single-brooded birds which only make one nesting attempt each year, although they may have a replacement clutch if the first is lost. See DOUBLE-BROODED.

Solitary by itself.

Song a series of sounds (vocalization), often composed of several or many phrases constructed of repeated elements, normally used by a male to claim a territory and attract a mate.

Specialist an animal whose life-style involves highly specialized stratagems, eg feeding with one technique on a particular food.

Species a population, or series of populations, which interbreed freely, but not with those of other species. See CLASS.

Speculum a distinctively colored group of flight feathers (eg on the wing of a duck).

Spur the sharp projection on the leg of some game birds; often more developed in males and used in fighting. Also found on the carpal joint of some other birds.

Staging ground/place an area where birds may pause to feed during migration.

Steppe open grassy plains, with few trees or bushes, of the central temperate zone of Eurasia or North America (prairies), characterized by low and sporadic rainfall and a wide annual temperature variation. In cold steppe temperatures drop well below freezing point in winter, with rainfall concentrated in the summer or evenly distributed throughout the year, while in hot steppe, winter temperatures are higher and rainfall concentrated in winter months.

Stooping dropping rapidly (usually of a bird of prey in pursuit of prey).

Strutting ground an area where male birds may display.

Subadult no longer juvenile but not yet fully adult.

Sublittoral the sea shore below the low-tide mark.

Suborder a subdivision of an order.

Subspecies a subdivision of a species. Usually not distinguishable unless the specimen is in the hand; often called races. See CLASS.

Subtropics the area just outside the tropics (ie at higher latitudes).

Taiga the belt of forests (coniferous) lying below (at lower latitudes to) the TUNDRA.

Tarsus that part of the leg of a bird which is just above the foot. Strictly the tarso-metatarsus, bones formed from the lower leg and upper foot.

Temperate zone an area of climatic zones in mid latitude, warmer than the northerly areas but cooler than the subtropical areas.

Territorial defending an area, in birds usually referring to a bird or birds which exclude others of the same species from their living area and in which they will usually nest.

Thermal an area of (warm) air which rises by convection.

Thermoregulation the regulation and maintenance of a constant internal body temperature.

Torpor a temporary physiological state, akin to short-term hibernation, in which the body temperature drops and the rate of METABOLISM is reduced. Torpor is an ADAPTATION for reducing energy expenditure in periods of extreme cold or food shortage.

Totipalmate feet feet in which three webs connect all four toes. (Most birds have only two webs between the three forward pointing toes, with the hind claws free.)

Tribe a term sometimes used to group certain species and/or genera within a family. See CLASS.

Tropics strictly, an area lying between 23.5°N and 23.5°S. Often because of local geography, birds' habitats do not match this area precisely.

Tundra the area of high latitude roughly demarcated by its being too cold for trees to grow.

Upwelling an area in the sea when, because of local topography, water from deep down in the sea is pushed to the surface. Usually upwellings are associated with rich feeding conditions for birds.

Vermiculation (on feathers) fine markings.

Wattle a fleshy protuberance, usually near the base of the BILL.

Wetlands fresh- or salt-water marshes.

Wing formula statement of relative lengths of wing feathers, especially of primary feathers. Used as a defining characteristic for many species.

Wintering ground the area where a migrant spends the nonbreeding season.

Zygodactyl having two toes directed forwards and two backwards.

INDEX

Picture Acknowledgments

Key: *t* top. *b* bottom. *c* center. *l* left. *r* right.

Abbreviations: A Ardea. AN Agence Nature. ANT Australasian Nature Transparencies. BC Bruce Coleman Ltd. J Jacana. FL Frank Lane Agency. NHPA Natural History Photographic Agency. OSF Oxford Scientific Films. PEP Planet Earth Pictures. SAL Survival Anglia Ltd.

Cover A/J. Swedberg. 1 A/F. Gohier. 2–3 BC/J. and D. Bartlett. 4–5 BC/J. Simon. 6–7 BC/J. and D. Bartlett. 8–9 BC/R. Williams. 13 BC. 14t Tony Morrison. 14b FL. 16 AN. 17 S. J. Davies. 18 AN. 19 A. 20 J. 21 BC. 24t Brian Hawkes. 24b BC. 25 A. 26–27 Brian Hawkes. 28b BC.

28–29 Nature Photographers. 30 P. A. Prince & B. E. Pearson. 31 Brian Hawkes. 33, 34–35, 35b BC. 36 P. A. Prince & B. E. Pearson. 37 Frans Lanting. 40b NHPA. 40–41 P. A. Prince & B. E. Pearson. 46–47 A. 48 Frans Lanting. 49 J. 50 Anthony Bannister. 51 Brian Hawkes. 52–53 J. 54 Frans Lanting. 55t P. A. Prince & B. E. Pearson. 55b, 56t Frans Lanting. 56–57 A. 58 Michael Fogden. 59 AN. 60–61 BC. 62 Eric and David Hosking. 63 J. 64b J. B. Davidson. 64–65 Eric and David Hosking. 65b BC. 69t Mark Boulton/ICCE. 69b BC. 70b FL. 70–71 J. 72, 73, 74 BC. 76 J. 77, 78–79 Nature Photographers. 80t Marion Morrison. 80b BC. 81, 82b J. 83–84 Brian Hawkes. 87 William Ervin, Natural

Imagery. 90–91 BC. 92b NHPA. 92–93 Leonard Lee Rue. 94b Premaphotos Wildlife. 94–95 SAL. 97 BC. 100–101 NHPA. 105 A. 106–107 BC. 108–109 OSF. 109b A. 110–111, 111t, 111c, 111b SAL. 112t BC. 112b OSF. 113, 114b BC. 114–115 SAL. 115b A. 116t SAL. 116–117 Brian Hawkes. 117t Eric and David Hosking. 118–119 A. 120–121 FL. 120t, 121t BC. 122t William Ervin, Natural Imagery. 122b Michael Fogden. 123 BC. 124–125 SAL. 129t BC. 129b Anthony Bannister. 131 A. 132–133 Graham Bateman. 135 BC. 138–139 PEP. 141 Ron Franklin. 142t Aquila. 142b FL. 143, 144 A. 145 BC. 146–147 AN. 148 Eric and David Hosking. 149 J.

Artwork

Abbreviations: CTK Chloë Talbot Kelly. IW Ian Willis. SD Simon Driver. PH Peter Harrison. SM Sean Milne. RG Robert Gillmor. NA Norman Arlott. Maps and scale drawings SD.

10 CTK. 12, 15 IW. 22 CTK. 32, 33 IW. 38t SD. 38, 42, 44 PH. 46, 51 IW. 66 SM. 75, 81 IW. 84, 87, 88 RG. 93 SD. 99, 101, 102, 104, 105b IW. 105r SD. 126 SM. 128t SD. 128, 132, 134 IW. 136 SM. 140 IW. 143 SD. 144 IW. 151 NA. Maps and scale drawings SD.